English ⌗ Heritage
Book of
Viking Age England

English ⌗ Heritage
Book of
Viking Age England

Julian D. Richards

B. T. Batsford Ltd/English Heritage
London

For Linda and Sam

© Julian D. Richards 1991

First published 1991
Reprinted 1992

Typeset in Great Britain
by Lasertext Limited,
Strctford, Manchester M32 0JT
and printed in Great Britain by
The Bath Press, Bath, Avon
Published by B.T. Batsford Ltd
4 Fitzhardinge Street,
London W1H 0AH
A CIP catalogue record for this book is
available from the British Library

ISBN 0 7134 6519 0 (cased)
0 7134 6520 4 (limp)

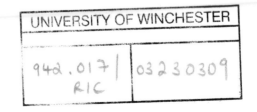

Contents

Illustrations

Colour plates

Acknowledgements

It would have been impossible to write this book before the major excavations which have been conducted over the last twenty years. My first debt must therefore be to the excavators of Viking Age England for illuminating this period. I am particularly grateful to those whose work has not yet been published, but who have nevertheless allowed me access to it, especially Martin Biddle, Martin Carver, M. Audouy and Glenn Foard, and Mike McCarthy.

Many people and organizations have generously allowed me to make use of drawings and photographs, and I wish to thank the following, who also retain the copyright:

Martin Biddle for fig. 6.

The Trustees of the British Museum for figs 5 and 74 and colour plate 2, also back cover.

L. A. S. Butler for figs 16 and 63.

Cambridge University Committee for Aerial Photography for fig. 28.

M. O. H. Carver for colour plate 1.

Chester City Council for fig. 32 and colour plate 6.

C. Michael Dixon for colour plate 11.

Durham University Department of Archaeology for figs 77 and 81.

Humberside Archaeological Unit for fig. 76.

Manchester City Council for fig. 2.

The Manx Museum and National Trust for figs 67–68 and 79 and colour plates 3–5 and 9.

The Museum of London for figs 42, 47, 75 and 83.

The Board and Trustees of the National Museums and Galleries on Merseyside for fig. 50.

Philip Rahtz for fig. 18.

Royal Commission for Historical Monuments (England) for fig. 70.

The Society of Antiquaries for colour plate 10.

Wharram Research Project for figs 60 and 69.

York Archaeological Trust for figs 7, 14, 25–6, 33–38, 43–6, 48–9, 51, 53, 57–8, 72, 84.

The Yorkshire Museum for fig. 21 and colour plate 7, also the front cover.

Additional photography was undertaken by John Bateman.

Most of the black-and-white line drawings were prepared by Dawn Flower at the English Heritage Drawing Office. Fig. 61 is by Chris Philo.

Finally, I would like to thank those friends and colleagues who gave freely of their valuable time to comment on earlier drafts of the text: Jim Lang, Richard Morris and Neil Price. Where they have saved me from errors I am especially grateful, but where mistakes remain they are, of course, my own responsibility.

J. D. Richards
York
February 1991

1

The Viking Age

This book is concerned with the development of Late Saxon England until the Norman Conquest. For three centuries, beginning shortly before 800 AD, we know from historical sources that England was subject to attacks from Scandinavia. It is no surprise that the raiders were called by many names, including 'heathens' and 'pagans' as well as 'Northmen' and 'Danes', but one of the names used to refer to them by the English was 'Vikings', and this is now used to describe not only the raiders, but also the period during which they sustained their attacks. These centuries, from the ninth to the eleventh, have become known, therefore, as the Viking Age.

The Vikings themselves can be elusive to the archaeologist. The introduction of Scandinavian art styles can be seen on jewellery and sculpture, but their actual houses and graves are often difficult to identify. Indeed, the relationship between Scandinavian settlers and the existing population must be considered to see how far the newcomers adopted native customs, perhaps rendering themselves indistinguishable from the local people and invisible to archaeologists. This story will focus, therefore, on the period rather than on the people, and will examine all the physical remains of the Viking Age.

It will be concerned particularly with England where, as a result of major excavations conducted over the last 20 years in towns such as York, Lincoln and London and in the countryside at sites such as Goltho, Raunds and Wharram Percy, we may now be closer to understanding the Viking impact. Scotland and Wales were also subject to Scandinavian influence, but are outside the scope of this book. In fact, little is known of the Vikings in Wales,

whereas Scotland has been the subject of a recent book (see Further Reading). The Isle of Man will be included, as during the Viking Age it was in regular contact with the Viking kingdoms in York and Dublin; it allows us to compare the influence of the Norse Vikings in Man with that of the Danes in England.

Two themes run through this book. Firstly, what was the Viking contribution to the development of Late Saxon England? How far did the Vikings simply modify local developments already in progress? Was there anything distinctive about Viking settlements? Were the major trading towns, such as Jorvik, already established before the Vikings arrived? What was the Viking influence on the formation of the English state?

Secondly, we shall take up the question of Viking and native interaction. What was the native response to the Vikings in the areas settled? What was it about the Viking character that meant that in some areas, such as the Danelaw, they disappeared, fusing with the local traditions, whilst in others, such as the Isle of Man, they preserved their distinctive culture? How did the Vikings adapt, both economically and in social and religious terms, to local circumstances?

The precise derivation of the term 'Viking' remains obscure. In Old Icelandic a *vik* was a bay or creek, and may have given its name to those seafaring raiders who lurked in bays and estuaries. Vik is also the name of the area around the Oslofjord, and may have been used to describe anyone from that area of southern Norway. The Old Icelandic verb *vikya*, on the other hand, meant 'to turn aside', and may have been used to describe those away from home. In the Icelandic Sagas *víkingr* came to

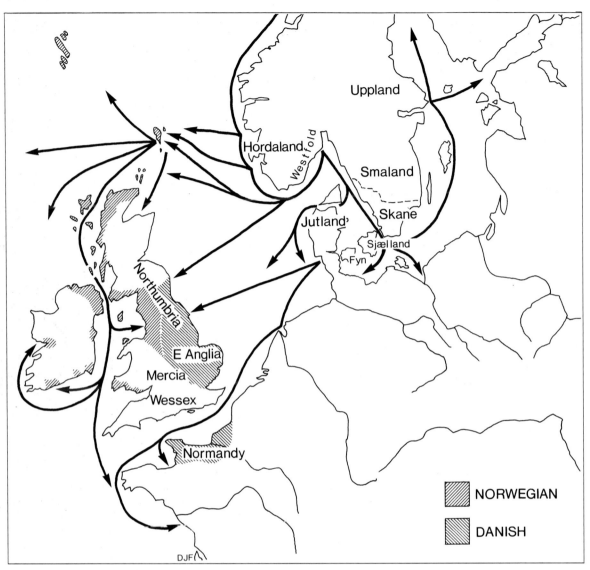

1 *North-west Europe in the Viking Age.*

be used as a noun to refer to a warrior or pirate; *víking* was used to refer to an expedition. The majority of Scandinavians, therefore, were not Vikings; only those who went 'a-viking' could really qualify for the description.

The first occurrence of *wicing* in English refers to pirates in the Mediterranean, who may not even have been Scandinavians, centuries before the Viking Age. The term does not appear to have been used to refer exclusively to raiders from Scandinavia until the tenth century, under the influence of the Viking invasions. There are five occurrences of 'wicings' in the Anglo-Saxon Chronicle, and each time the word seems to be used in connection with a small group of raiders, rather than an army. Its use appears to have died out during the Middle Ages, but it was reintroduced in the Romantic era in Scandinavia and Germany to evoke warriors with winged, and then horned, helmets. Vikings reappear in England in the novels of Walter Scott and then in the works of the Pre-Raphaelites (**2**) and it is only during the twentieth century that 'Viking' has become the standard term for Scandinavian invaders.

In general, western European historical texts

THE EXPULSION OF THE DANES FROM MANCHESTER

2 The Expulsion of the Danes from Manchester *by Ford Madox Brown (c.1880). This mural painting in Manchester Town Hall is typical of the revival of interest in Viking subjects among Pre-Raphaelite artists (The Lord Mayor's Office, Manchester City Council).*

refer to Vikings as *Dani* or Danes, and *Nordmanni* or Northmen, irrespective of their country of origin. No doubt to the English they all sounded the same, but it is in any case not clear that nationality was a meaningful distinction at the time, since the various Scandinavian states were only formed during the Viking Age. At first, the Scandinavians thought of themselves as inhabitants of particular regions, such as men of Jutland, Vestfold, Hordaland and so on. As a sense of national identity grew so did the use of national names. Ohthere, a Scandinavian visitor to Ælfred's court, distinguished between Norwegians, Swedes and Danes.

Certainly, we know that Viking armies comprised warriors of various races, just as modern mercenary armies do. The armies that attacked England in the reign of Æthelstan included men from eastern Sweden as well as from Norway and Denmark, although the English identified them by their leaders, for instance as the armies of Olafr, Sveinn, Thorkel or Knutr, and thought of them all as Danes. The loyalty of Viking warriors would have been to their leaders, rather than to any national identity. In Ireland, Danes and Norwegians fought each other, and in 838 the Britons of Devon and Cornwall formed an alliance with the Danes against the West Saxons under King Ecgbryht.

By their customs and appearance Viking settlers would initially have appeared foreign to native Anglo-Saxons. Scandinavian jewellery was unlike that of the Anglo-Saxons. Norse settlers imported the ring-headed pin from Celtic Ireland, and presumably the Irish style of cloak that went with it. They wore silver arm rings as symbols of their wealth. The men may have worn belted trousers without covering tunics, unlike the Anglo-Saxons who wore leggings and tunics. When the Vikings first appeared their hair was worn shaved, short at the back and shaggy at the front; imitation of this style was condemned by the Church. By the time of the Domesday Book Viking-descended Normans still wore their hair shaved up the nape; the English wore their hair long, and were sneered at by the Normans for effeminacy.

Some settlers must have brought their wives with them; when the Anglo-Saxons stormed Benfleet they captured goods, women and children. Viking women also followed fashions different from those of the Anglo-Saxons. They wore a tortoise brooch on each shoulder, for instance, and a trefoil brooch at the centre. Some Viking men presumably intermarried with native women. A later chronicler stated that the success of Vikings with English women was due to the fact that they bathed on Saturdays, combed their hair, and wore fine clothing.

For how long were the separate identities maintained? Certain laws of Knutr, Æthelred and Edgar demonstrate that there was a distinction between Danes and English in the second half of the tenth century. Knutr recognized or permitted differences between Danes and their customs, and the English and theirs. Because they had money to buy farms and settle, and because they remained 'foreigners', Danish families may have met with resentment and prejudice; Æthelred spoke of them as having 'sprung up in this island, sprouting like poisonous weeds among the wheat'. But were Danish settlers preserving a strong sense of their identity? The Scandinavian settlement of England was not a single event. Throughout the tenth century there would have been continued contact with Scandinavia through trade, and arrivals of new groups of Scandinavian mercenaries. In 1016 there was a fresh influx of settlers under Knutr. There is no evidence for any feeling of Danish national identity which motivated local action and caused the Danes to act as a group in areas of dispute or in support of rival claimants to the throne. Epigraphical evidence suggests that in England, at least, Scandinavian settlers quickly dropped their native language and spoke English.

Tenth- and eleventh-century observers might still speak of the Danelaw as a distinct political unit, but the definition of political boundaries was more complex than racial divisions. Political lordship and allegiance rather than Anglo-Saxon, Celtic, Danish or Norse race were the determining factors.

Scandinavia

It is possible to make some generalizations about the peoples involved in the Viking settlement in England and the Isle of Man, as their movements were inevitably determined by Scandinavian topography.

The Norwegians have always been a seafaring people. Thousands of offshore islands protect the west coast of Norway and provide a sheltered coastal sea route which gave the country its name, Norvegur or North Way. Mountains rise steeply from the fjord-indented coastline, and the population is mostly confined to narrow ledges and small plains at the head of the fjords. From the seventh century the population of Norway was expanding, first up the valleys and into the forest areas; but increasingly the Norse looked to the west. In the ninth century the country entered an expansionist phase under Haraldr Fine-Hair and his son Erik Bloodaxe.

The first Viking raiders whose presence is recorded in the British Isles were probably Norse. In 789 'there came for the first time three ships of Northmen from Hordaland and then the reeve rode to them and wished to force them to the king's residence, for he did not know what they were; and they slew him. Those were the first ships of Danish men which came to the land of the English.' Despite the confusion, it seems likely that the ships were from Norway because of the specific reference to Hordaland; the last sentence was probably added as a gloss by a later writer when the Danes were seen as the chief threat. Norse warriors must also have joined Knutr's eleventh-century army; a memorial stone was erected in Galteland, Aust Agder (Norway) by Arnsteinn in memory of his son Biorr who 'was killed in the guard when Knutr attacked England'.

Today, Denmark comprises the Jutland peninsula and the large islands of Fyn and Sjælland, plus some 500 smaller islands as well as Bornholm in the Baltic Sea. However, during the Viking Age it also included Skåne in southern Sweden. The southern frontier at the foot of the Jutland peninsula also lay further to the south, where it was defended by a series of earthworks known as the Danevirke.

The first references to Danes are as pirates raiding the Carolingian empire. Danes naturally looked to the North Sea coast, plundering Frisian territory such as the trading post at Dorestad. They continued west through the English Channel to raid France and southern England. The Danes were responsible for the main concerted raids on the British Isles in the ninth century, and many of them settled in the Danelaw. They frequently had royal backing. The Danish state was emerging under King Gorm in the early tenth century, and royal power was consolidated under his son Harald Bluetooth, who conquered Norway in the early 960s. Gorm's grandson Sveinn Forkbeard and his great-grandson Knutr both led armies against England, the latter becoming king from 1016 to 1035.

Sweden comprises a number of regions with local variations in soil, climate and relief. To the north of Skåne, the infertile and sparsely populated plateau of Småland formed a natural boundary with Denmark. Most of the people lived in the well-forested fertile zones in the central lowlands. To the north Norrland was sparsely populated, consisting of forest and bare rock. Off the east coast the island of Gotland was of particular importance, occupying a strategic position at the centre of the Baltic. Swedish Vikings looked mainly to the east, sailing down the rivers into Russia. There were few Swedish visitors in Britain but some Swedes must have served with Knutr (see **12**); a rune stone from Väsby, Uppland, for example, records that 'Alle had this stone put up in his own honour. He took Knutr's *danegeld* in England. May God help his soul.' Sweden was late in developing into a unified state and was a relative political backwater throughout most of the Viking Age.

England at the beginning of the Viking Age

By the mid-ninth century England still comprised four independent kingdoms: East Anglia, Wessex, Mercia and Northumbria. Mercia was the strongest military power, extending west to Offa's Dyke, the great earthwork constructed along its frontier with Wales, and south to the Thames. Northumbria was divided by internecine feuding between the rulers of Bernicia to the north and Deira in the south, and its northern borders were troubled by the Scots. In the south-west first Devon and then Cornwall had been absorbed by Wessex.

Between some half a million and one million people lived in England at the beginning of the Viking Age. The population structure was probably comparable to that of a Third World country today. In other words, life expectancy was worse than in England today, but better than during the Industrial Revolution. In the typical Middle to Late Saxon community represented in the cemetery at Raunds (Northamptonshire) the average life expectancy at birth was 21 years. Infant mortality was high; a sixth of all children died before reaching the age of two; a third were dead before they reached their sixth birthday. If one survived to the age of 12 one's chances of a long life were better; the average life span was now 33 years, and a few individuals reached the ripe old age of 60 or more. In fact, 12 seems to have been widely recognized as the age of maturity; the laws of Æthelstan decreed that any man over 12 years old could be killed if found guilty of theft. Poor hygiene and nutrition were probably the most common causes of death. Childbearing females were most at risk; at Raunds men were much more likely to reach their late 30s than women.

English society was rigidly hierarchical, and a small aristocracy lived off the labour of a great many peasants. At the top was the king and his ealdormen. The Danes and eleventh-century English called them jarls or earls. Then there were the thegns, or landholders, who later became knights or lords of the manor. Next there were various grades of agricultural workers, and finally a substantial slave class, possibly up to a quarter of the population.

Most of the population lived in the countryside, where the mixed-farming economy would have been familiar to Viking settlers. In the lowland zone of southern and eastern England towns were already emerging before the Viking Age. London and York acted as centres of royal and ecclesiastical administration, as well as of trade and industry. A special class of trading ports, or wics, such as Hamwic (Southampton) and Ipswich played an important role in foreign trade. Most people lived and worked in wooden buildings; stone was reserved for churches. The English were Christians, erecting stone crosses, and burying their dead in Christian graveyards.

Danish Vikings sailing westwards along the north-west coast of Europe would have been funnelled into the English Channel, from where they could attack the wealthy south coast of England and the north coast of France. For Norse Vikings sailing directly west across the

13

North Sea, the east coast of England was their natural landing point. It provided a number of sheltered inlets and suitable harbours, as well as unprotected monasteries; river estuaries gave access to the interior of the country. Many sailed round the north coast of Scotland to the Orkneys and Hebrides and continued down into the Irish Sea, from which they could raid north-west England and south-west Scotland together with Wales, Ireland and the Isle of Man.

The Isle of Man did not form part of any known kingdom at the start of the Viking Age. Historical references are scarce, but we know from archaeology that it was already inhabited by a sizeable Celtic population. This was also Christian, as shown by pre-Viking gravestones and a series of small chapels, or keeils, set amidst the graveyards. There were no proto-towns on the Isle of Man; the people followed an agricultural lifestyle little changed since the Iron Age. To the Vikings the Isle of Man occupied a nodal position in the Irish Sea which made it attractive to Norsemen sailing down the west coast of Scotland, and an ideal base for raiding in the Irish Sea. Celtic monasteries, such as Maughold, provided rich sources of plunder, and the island had good natural harbours around its coast.

The causes of Viking expansion

Historians have been much exercised in trying to explain the Viking raids, although some have suggested that they were simply an extension of normal Dark Age activity made possible and profitable by special circumstances.

Certainly the Viking expansion westwards would have been impossible without their famous longships. Ships were an essential means of transport around Scandinavia; in the eighth century the Scandinavians developed fast, light, easily manoeuvrable vessels which made long sea journeys possible. Their ships gave Vikings the advantage of surprise and a means of swift retreat. Yet whilst the ship may have made the raids possible they cannot be seen as sufficient cause by themselves.

The descendants of the Norse emigrants believed their ancestors were fleeing from the tyrannical growth of royal power in Norway. Certainly in the Isle of Man they seemed to avoid creating any excessive central authority, and may have been trying to preserve an archaic form of society. Norway was also undergoing a dramatic growth of population, with massive forest clearances in the east but limited room for expansion in the west.

No doubt a number of factors were working in combination, but to understand the basic reason that drove Vikings to cross the sea to England one has to return to internal developments in ninth-century Denmark. A number of recent excavations of Viking Age villages have revealed the emergence of magnate farms, or large privately owned estates, at about this time. Whereas land had previously been held by a family group or tribe, now it was owned and inherited by individuals. Rune-stone monuments may represent inheritance claims as much as memorials to the dead. At the top Gorm and his son Haraldr were unifying Denmark under the rule of a single king. Their power is symbolized by the distribution of royal forts of the Trelleborg type throughout the kingdom, and by the royal grave at Jelling. The Viking raids are therefore symptomatic of increased competition between the elite groups. With estates being passed to eldest sons and distributed by rulers to their followers, there would be increasingly less land to go round in Scandinavia. To maintain the system expansion was essential, and the easiest way to expand was overseas, where land, wealth and prestige could all be sought.

No doubt the lure of undefended treasure in the churches and monasteries of the west was an incentive, and Vikings may have switched between trading, raiding and settling in much the same fashion as Elizabethan privateers in the Caribbean, according to which was the most advantageous strategy.

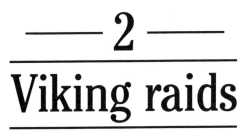

2

Viking raids

Any account of Viking raids has to be derived primarily from historical sources, which for England means the Anglo-Saxon Chronicle. Archaeological evidence is a poor witness to particular events. Political upheavals, such as those which affected York in the mid-tenth century, apparently went wholly unnoticed in Coppergate, where business was much as usual. Nevertheless, remains of fortifications, war cemeteries, memorials and hoards, together with Anglo-Saxon loot found in Scandinavia, all contribute to our knowledge of Viking activity.

Historical sources are more explicit, but they may also be less reliable. They were compiled by those on the receiving end of Viking attacks, and suffer from the usual problems of wartime propaganda. In particular, the size of the enemy forces seems to have been widely exaggerated. In ninth-century references to Viking forces in the Anglo-Saxon Chronicle a distinction can be drawn between six small fleets of between 3 and 23 ships, for which the numbers of ships appear to have been counted exactly, and four larger fleets each estimated in round figures greater than 80. The armada of 350 ships recorded for 851 looks suspiciously like a multiplication of the previous largest number (35) by ten.

It has also been pointed out that to translate the Anglo-Saxon word *here* used in the Chronicle to refer to Viking raiding forces as 'army' or 'host' may be misleading. In seventh-century laws any group larger than 35 is defined as a *here*. Given that Viking ships are likely to have had crews of some 30 men, or 50–60 at the most, then most Viking raiding parties may have been counted in hundreds, and even the larger forces may still have been under 1000. We do know that in 1142 it took 52 ships to carry a force of less than 400 mounted knights across the Channel.

The Anglo-Saxon Chronicle does allow us to distinguish several phases of Viking activity, stretching over some 300 years. It would undoubtedly be foolish to regard the Viking Age as a single phenomenon. Viking forces surely fluctuated in nature and size, as the motives for their campaigns varied.

3 *The Lindisfarne Stone (Northumbria). A late ninth- or tenth-century grave marker with a Doomsday scene of a procession of warriors waving swords and axes (English Heritage).*

Phase 1: sporadic raids and looting, 789–864

From the late eighth century onwards small groups of Viking raiders were sailing down the English Channel or round the north of Scotland into the Irish Sea, exploiting possibilities for trade or plunder as they arose (4). The earliest recorded Viking raid in England dates to 789 when three ships of Norwegians from Hordaland landed at Portland and turned on the unfortunate royal reeve from Dorchester, murdering him. It was the reeve's job to identify all foreign merchants entering the kingdom.

It was the attacks on the Northumbrian monasteries that excited most consternation; in 793 the Anglo-Saxon Chronicle recorded:

> In this year dire portents appeared over Northumbria and sorely frightened the people. They consisted of immense whirl-winds and flashes of lightning, and fiery dragons were seen flying in the air. A great famine immediately followed these signs and a little after in the same year, on 8 June, the ravages of heathen men miserably destroyed God's church on Lindisfarne, with plunder and slaughter.

Archbishop Alcuin of York reacted with indignation and horror:

> Lo, it is nearly 350 years that we and our fathers have inhabited this most lovely land, and never before has such a terror appeared in Britain as we have now suffered from a pagan race, nor was it thought that such an inroad from the sea could be made. Behold the church of St Cuthbert spattered with the blood of the priests of God, despoiled of all its ornaments.

The fact that in 792 King Offa was making arrangements for the defence of Kent against 'pagan peoples' suggests that there were other, unrecorded, raids. In 804 the monastery of Lyminge, an exposed site north of Romney Marsh, acquired a refuge within the walls of Canterbury. The Irish Annals for c.798 record an attack by the Vikings on an island called Inis Patraic, which was originally interpreted as St Patrick's Isle, off the Isle of Man, but is now seen as Inispatrick off the Dublin coast.

These early raids should be seen in the context of the Norse colonization of Shetland, Orkney and the Hebrides. Norwegian raiding groups sporadically targeted English sites, but

England was not troubled much until the second quarter of the ninth century, when the Danish attacks commenced. From 835 the Chronicle records a series of heavy raids on the south coast by Danish forces culminating in 850, when the Danish army wintered in England for the first time:

> In this year Ealdorman Ceorl with the con-tingent of the men of Devon fought against the heathen army at *Wicganbeorg*, and the English made a great slaughter there and had the victory. And for the first time, heathen men stayed through the winter on Thanet. And the same year [851] 350 ships came into the mouth of the Thames and stormed Canterbury and London and put to flight Brihtwulf, king of the Mercians, with his army, and went south across the Thames into Surrey.

Hoards

In troubled times it was prudent to keep your money buried. Finds of Viking Age hoards (5) may sometimes be related to raiding activities but care should be exercised in their interpretation. Hoards were normally buried with the intention of recovering them later; they only stayed buried, to be retrieved by archaeologists, under special circumstances such as the death of their owner. Dating their burial can also be problematic. The most recent coin is normally taken to indicate the date of deposition, but savers' hoards may contain mainly old coins.

It does seem possible to distinguish between hoards deposited by Vikings and those hidden by the English. Viking hoards may include coins, ingots, ornaments and other fragments of silver ('hack silver') which has often been nicked or pecked to test its purity. Silver from the Cuerdale Hoard (Lancashire; **colour plate 2**) had been nicked from 5 to 20 times on average. The earliest Viking hoard was found at Croydon (Surrey) in 1862. It appears to date from 872, when the Vikings wintered in London, and probably represents the accumulated loot of a member of the Viking army. The hoard comprised 250 coins, three silver ingots and part of a fourth and four pieces of hack silver, in a coarse linen bag. The coins included pennies from Wessex, Mercia and East Anglia, and Arabic and Carolingian issues. Some Viking hoards might contain no coins at all, for

4 *England, 789–864.*

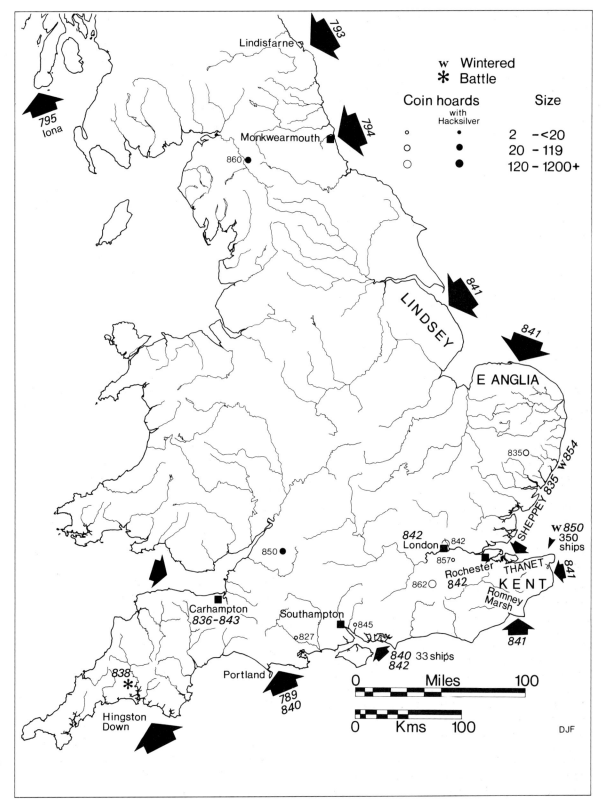

Lindisfarne

793

795
Iona

794

Monkwearmouth

860

w Wintered
* Battle

Coin hoards   Size
        with
     Hacksilver
  o   •   2   –<20
  ○   •   20 – 119
  ○   ●   120 – 1200+

841

LINDSEY

841

E ANGLIA

835 ○

SHEPPEY 835 w 854

842
London ○ 842

857 ○

862 ○

Rochester
842

THANET

w 850
350
ships

841

K E N T

Romney
Marsh

841

850 ●

Carhampton
836-843

Southampton

○ 845

○ 827

840
842 33 ships

838
*

Portland

789
840

Hingston
Down

0   Miles   100

0   Kms   100

DJF

example the 19 silver ingots from Bowes Moor (Durham), the silver neck ring and penannular brooch from Orton Scar (Cumbria), and the silver thistle brooch from Newbiggin Moor, Penrith (Cumbria).

Over 20 Viking hoards have been found on the Isle of Man, probably reflecting the use of the island as a base for Viking raiders, not all of them successful. They usually comprise silver coins, with some silver ornaments and currency rings (**colour plate 3**). The scarcity of hoards earlier than the late tenth century has suggested that the first-generation settlers were primarily concerned with their new land holdings rather than with piracy or commerce.

5 *The Goldsborough Hoard (Yorkshire) was deposited c.920. It contains 39 coins as well as ingots and jewellery including a silver thistle brooch and the hoop of a bossed penannular brooch (Trustees of the British Museum)*

From 960 onwards, however, there are many hoards containing coins from Dublin, York and the southern English mints.

English hoards, by contrast, contain only Anglo-Saxon coins, as foreign issues were excluded from circulation, and the coins do not generally show any evidence of having been tested. England had a full money economy, where coins, despite variations in weight and purity, had an agreed face value. The late-ninth-century hoard from Bolton Percy (North Yorkshire), for example, contained 1775 copper stycas buried in a small Badorf ware pot. Several hoards contain personal treasure hidden for safekeeping. Around 875 a wealthy Anglo-Saxon hid his best jewellery and some money in a leather purse in Beeston Tor Cave (Staffordshire). The hoard contained two silver disc brooches and a gold finger ring, as well as a number of plain bronze rings and some 50 Anglo-Saxon silver pennies.

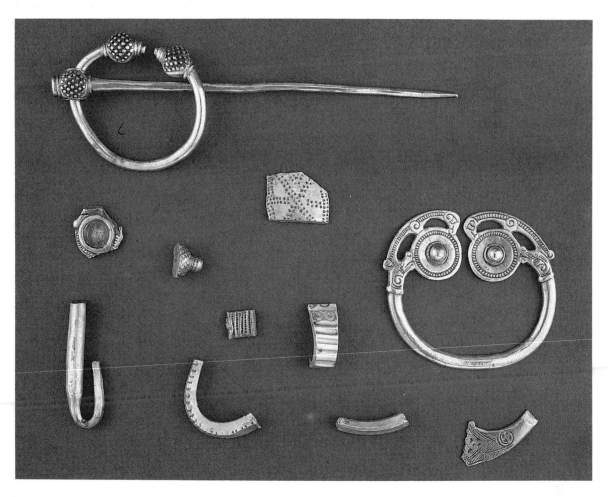

Viking armies

There is no direct archaeological evidence for the great battles which dominate the Anglo-Saxon Chronicle's account of the Viking Age, although the remains of a Viking army have apparently been excavated at Repton (Derbyshire) (6). The site was first noted in 1726, when Dr Simon Degge recorded in his journal a visit to Repton and the story told to him by a labourer, Thomas Walker, aged 88. About 40 years earlier Walker had been clearing some ground, when:

> near the surface he met with an old Stone Wall, when clearing farther he found it to be a square Enclosure of Fifteen Foot... In this he found a Stone Coffin, and with Difficulty removing the Cover, saw a Skeleton of a Humane Body Nine Foot long, and round it lay One Hundred Humane Skeletons, with their Feet pointing to the Stone Coffin...

Excavation in a mound in the vicarage garden at Repton has since confirmed the accuracy of this story. The mound, some 13 × 11 m (42 × 36 ft) in diameter, had been constructed over a massive two-roomed stone structure, possibly originally intended as a mausoleum for the Mercian royal family. The structure was aligned east–west, and was entered down a slight ramp and through a narrow doorway in the centre of the west wall. An internal doorway directly opposite led into the eastern compartment, which had been reused as a charnel house. In total, the disarticulated remains of at least 249 individuals were recovered. The central burial did not survive, but the deposit contained many objects which may originally have accompanied it, including a sword and axe, fragments of gold and silver objects and a small group of coins deposited some time after 871.

Analysis of the main burial deposit shows that 80 per cent were robust males in the age range 15–45. Although many of the bones showed signs of injury, these had healed and none had apparently died of their wounds. It has been suggested that the Repton burial deposit represents the grave of a Viking leader of the Great Army, around whom the remains of his followers were gathered.

6 *Mass grave, Repton, 873–4, within the remains of a pre-Viking building (Martin Biddle).*

Phase 2: permanent colonization, 865–896

From 865 it is possible to detect a change in the nature of Viking activity, with large armies arriving with the aim of permanent settlement in England. They were highly mobile forces, moving rapidly around the country, attacking the weakest Anglo-Saxon kingdoms in turn, and exploiting civil war in Northumbria. In 866 the Vikings captured York. In 871, after a year of battles against the Danish armies, King Æthelred died, and was succeeded by his brother Ælfred. During the next decade three partitions of land between the Danes and the English were recorded in the Anglo-Saxon Chronicle: in Yorkshire, Mercia and East Anglia:

> And that year [876] Healfdene shared out the lands of the Northumbrians, and they proceeded to plough and to support themselves.

> Then in the harvest season [877] the army went away into Mercia and shared out some of it, and gave some to Ceolwulf.

> In this year [880] the army went from Cirencester into East Anglia, and settled there and shared out the land.

7 *Late ninth-century burial, Coppergate, York: this male, wrapped in a cloak or tunic, may have been a victim of the Viking capture of York in 866, or the disastrous Anglian counter-attack in 867 (York Archaeological Trust).*

Nevertheless, the settlements did not stop the Vikings plundering the rest of England. In 878 they drove Ælfred into Somerset, where he took refuge in the marshes of Athelney. Recouping his forces he defeated the Danish leader Guthrum at Eddington, and in the Treaty of Wedmore in 886 a boundary was established between Ælfred's Wessex and Guthrum's East Anglia 'up the Thames as far as the river Lea, then up the Lea to its source, and then straight to Bedford, and then up the Ouse to Watling Street'. The area to the north and east of this line became known as the Danelaw, to distinguish that part of the country where Danish custom prevailed, in contrast to the areas of English law.

Ælfred made use of this treaty to consolidate his position in Wessex. He initiated a system of defended towns or burhs (see Chapter 4), organized a militia system whereby his peasant army was always half at home and half on active service, and according to the Chronicle built fast, high ships with 60 or more oars 'neither on the Frisian nor the Danish pattern, but as it seemed to him himself that they would be most useful'.

From the 890s there were further attacks on Wessex by fresh groups of Vikings, but Ælfred's defensive measures proved effective and in 896 the Viking army dispersed. Some settled in East Anglia and Northumbria; others sailed to Normandy. The Chronicle recorded

8 *(Right) England, 865–96.*

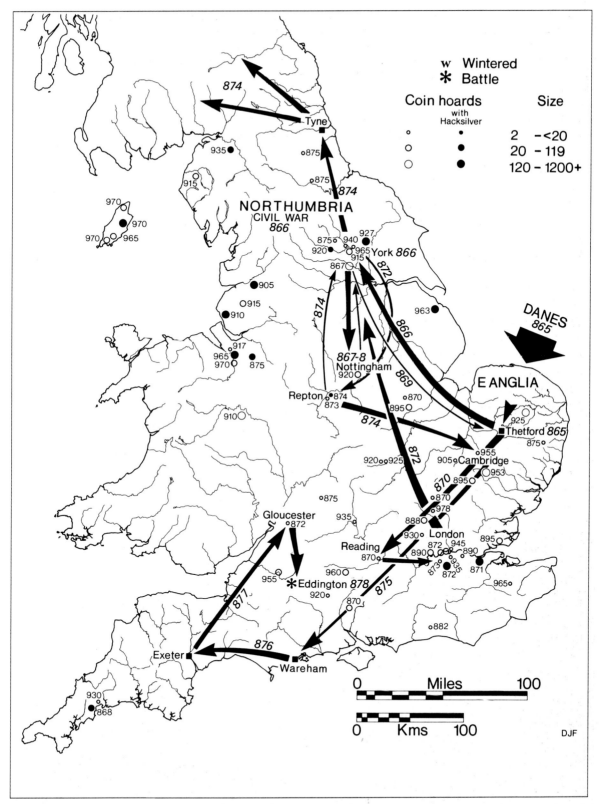

Wintered: w
Battle: *

Coin hoards
with Hacksilver

Size
2 – <20
20 – 119
120 – 1200+

874

Tyne
935
915
875
874

NORTHUMBRIA
CIVIL WAR
866

970
970 965
970
905
915
910

875 940 927
920 965 York 866
867 915
872

963

DANES
865

874
874

867-8
Nottingham
920

Repton 874
873

870
895

E ANGLIA

925
Thetford 865
875

874

917
965 875
970

910

872

920 925

905 Cambridge
955
953

870
875

895
870
978

875

935

888

Gloucester
872

930 London
872 945
890 890
Reading 873 935 871
870 872

895

965

960
955

*Eddington 878
920

877

870

875

876
Exeter

Wareham

882

0   Miles   100

0   Kms   100

DJF

that 'by the grace of God, the army had not on the whole afflicted the English people very greatly'.

The Anglo-Saxon Chronicle does not describe events in the north-west, but an Irish source, supported by references in Welsh sources, records the settlement in the Wirral (Cheshire) of a band of Vikings under the leadership of Ingimundr who had become fugitives after their expulsion from Dublin in 902. This appears to have led to internecine warfare between Danes and Norwegians, particularly after 919, when the Norse took control of York.

In southern England Ælfred's policies were continued by his daughter Æthelflaed, who married Æthelred, king of Mercia, and then by his son Edward. Gradually the Danelaw was reconquered by Ælfred's children. Their task was made easier by the fact that there were better pickings for Viking raiders elsewhere in Europe. In 920 the Northumbrians and Scots submitted to Edward, and after the Battle of Brunanburh in 937, Danish power in the north collapsed. In 954 Erik Bloodaxe, the last Viking king of York, was expelled from the city.

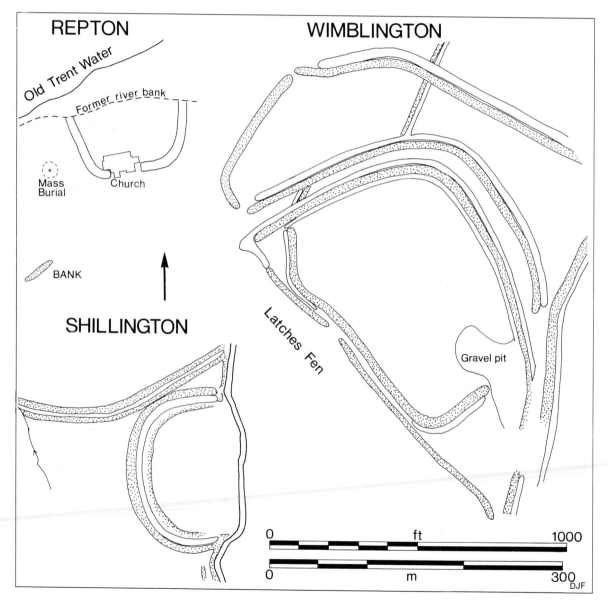

Viking fortifications

Viking armies wintering in England needed to camp in a defensible position. At first they appear to have made use of natural islands, such as the Isle of Sheppey and Thanet, but from the late ninth century there are a number of references in the Anglo-Saxon Chronicle to purpose-built fortifications. In 885 the Danes 'made fortifications round themselves' at Rochester, and in 892 they built forts at Milton Regis near Sittingbourne, and at Appledore on the edge of marshes between Rye and Ashford in Kent. In 893 there are references to forts at Benfleet and Shoebury on the Essex coast, and in 894 a fort was built by the river Lea, about 32 km (20 miles) above London, and another at Bridgnorth on the river Severn. In 917 they 'made the fortress at Tempsford, and took up quarters in it and built it, and abandoned the other fortress at Huntingdon'.

These forts were probably fairly rudimentary, comprising an earthwork bank-and-ditched enclosure, perhaps with a timber rampart. Such earthworks are notoriously difficult to recognize and to date archaeologically, and one must be cautious of sites with names such as Danes' Dyke (Humberside), which are likely to be earlier landscape features which were attributed to the Vikings in antiquity. Nevertheless, there is one excavated example and several possibilities, particularly along the Danelaw frontier (**9**). Each would have sheltered an army numbering in the hundreds, rather than the thousands.

The Chronicle references suggest that the Vikings preferred to make use of the sea or a river or marsh to protect them on one side, and at these sites one might expect to find a D-shaped enclosure, such as those erected around Scandinavian coastal trading sites at Hedeby and Birka. The fort at Gannock's Castle near Tempsford has often been described as Danish, but is now recognized to be a twelfth- or thirteenth-century site. In fact, the fort at Tempsford referred to in the Anglo-Saxon Chronicle is more likely to have been a 2-ha (5–6-acre) site adjacent to the river Ivel at Beeston, near Sandy (Bedfordshire), 5 km (3 miles) south of Tempsford.

A number of similar D-shaped sites have been identified in Bedfordshire: at Church Spanel, Shillington, where a gravel island had been artificially fortified with a bank, at Stonea Camp, Wimblington, where an enclosure was built against the fen edge, and at Bolnhurst. Willington and Etonbury (Bedfordshire), and Longstock (Hampshire) may be comparable sites with provision for protecting boats within them in dry docks and harbours. At Repton a D-shaped enclosure was constructed as a winter camp for the Viking army of 873–4. The river Trent formed one side and the rest of the site was surrounded by a bank and ditch into which the monastery church was incorporated as a gatehouse. It has been estimated that this fort would have taken five weeks to construct with 200 men. At Shoebury (Essex) a rampart enclosing a semicircular area, approximately 460 m (1495 ft) across, adjacent to the sea, may be the Viking camp of 893.

Where a suitable site was not available adjacent to water circular fortifications may have been constructed, although none as fine as the Danish Trelleborg-type forts have been found. A number of possibilities have been identified, with wide ditches and internal banks or regular circular hollows with low banks, although without excavation such sites might equally well be Roman amphitheatres or Norman ringworks. Limited excavation has demonstrated that Warham Camp (Norfolk) originated in the Iron Age, although the site may still have been remodelled in the Viking Age. At Howbury (Bedfordshire) there is an almost perfectly circular enclosure, 40 m (130 ft) in diameter, with ramparts 3 m (10 ft) high with a wide water-filled ditch on the outside. The site commands the highest spur east of Bedford, and gives a view along the Ouse valley. At Hawridge Court on the Hertfordshire–Buckinghamshire border there is a regular earthwork with a flat central area, 60 m (200 ft) in diameter, with a bank 5 m (16 ft) high and a ditch still about 1 m (4 ft) deep. Finally, at Ringmere (Norfolk) there is another circular enclosure, 32 m (104 ft) in diameter, with a double bank and ditch.

9 *Plans of Viking camps at Repton and possible unexcavated examples at Shillington and Wimblington: in each case the camp takes the form of a D-shaped bank-and-ditched enclosure, protected by water on the long side (after Dyer 1972 and Hall 1990).*

Phase 3: extortion of tribute, 980–1012

Towards the end of the tenth century the Scandinavians were no longer able to plunder Russia and turned their attention back to the west. These new armies differed from those of the previous century in that they now included Swedish Vikings as well as Danes and Norwegians, and also in that they apparently had no interest in settlement, but used their power to extort tribute, or Danegeld (10), from the native population. Edgar of Wessex had been recognized as king of all England, and even the Christianized Danish population had recognized him as their overlord. After Edgar's death in 975 there was a period of dynastic weakness. Edward, his son, was murdered in Corfe Castle, and Æthelred (the Unready) succeeded to the throne. From 980 onwards the Anglo-Saxon Chronicle records renewed raiding against England. At first the raids were probing

10 *Graph of Danegeld payments recorded in the Anglo-Saxon Chronicle. Although the accuracy of the figures is open to debate they probably do give some indication of the escalating scale of 'protection money' levied by the Viking armies.*

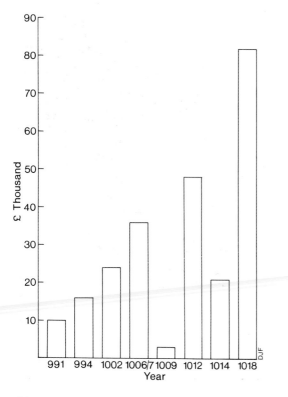

ventures by small numbers of ships' crews, but soon grew in size and effect, until the only way of dealing with the Vikings appeared to be to pay protection money to buy them off:

> 'And in that year [991] it was determined that tribute should first be paid to the Danish men because of the great terror they were causing along the coast. The first payment was 10,000 pounds.'

Over the next decade payments grew dramatically (see 10), causing widespread hostility to the Vikings and leading to demands for increasingly desperate reprisals. On St Brice's Day 1002 Æthelred ordered that all Danes living in England should be killed. His order is presumed not to refer to established settlers in the Danelaw, but amongst those slaughtered were the sister and brother-in-law of Sveinn, king of Denmark.

Nevertheless, the English lacked any consistent policy and effective means of defence against the Viking threat, and the later compilers of the Anglo-Saxon Chronicle become increasingly scathing about Æthelred:

> and when [the Danes] were in the east [in 1010], the English army was kept in the west, and when they were in the south, our army was in the north. Then all the councillors were summoned to the king, and it was then to be decided how this country should be defended. But even if anything was then decided, it did not last even a month. Finally there was no leader who would collect any army, but each fled as best he could, and in the end no shire would even help the next.

> All these disasters [in 1011] befell us through bad policy, in that they were never offered tribute in time nor fought against; but when they had done most to our injury, peace and truce were made with them; and for all this truce and tribute they journeyed none the less in bands everywhere, and harried our wretched people and plundered and killed them.

Scandinavian evidence

A number of Anglo-Saxon objects found in Scandinavian graves testify to the looting of English monastic sites. They include shrines

11 *(Right) England, 980–1012.*

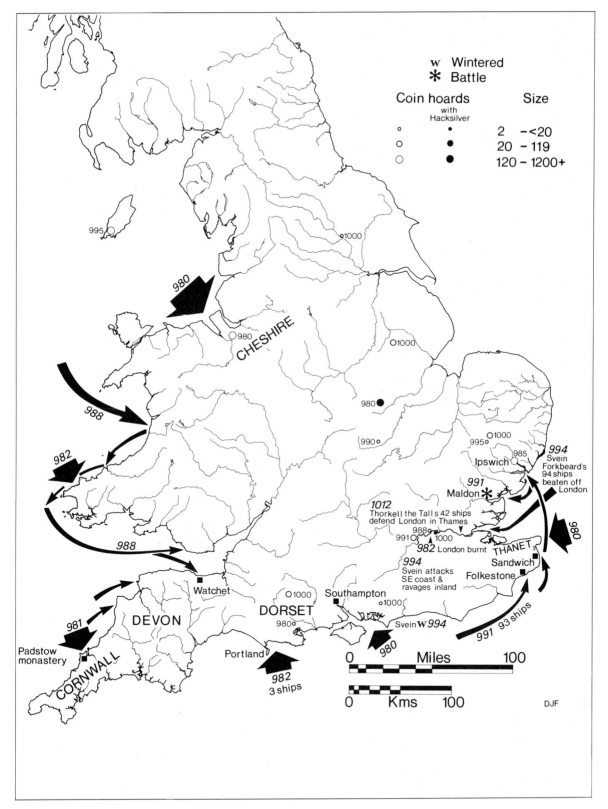

w Wintered
* Battle

Coin hoards   Size
with
Hacksilver

○   •   2   – <20
○   ●   20 – 119
○   ●   120 – 1200+

995 ○

1000 ○

980

○ 980 CHESHIRE

○ 1000

988

980 ●

982

990 ○

○ 1000
995 ○   985

994
Svein
Forkbeard's
94 ships
beaten off
London

Ipswich ○

991
Maldon ***

1012
Thorkell the Tall's 42 ships
defend London in Thames

988 ○
991 ○   ○ 1000
982 London burnt

994
Svein attacks
SE coast &
ravages inland

THANET

Sandwich ■

980

Folkestone ■

988

Watchet ■

○ 1000
Southampton ○

DORSET
○ 1000
980 ○

DEVON

Portland

Svein **w** *994*

980

991 93 ships

981

Padstow
monastery ■

CORNWALL

982
3 ships

0   Miles   100

0   Kms   100

DJF

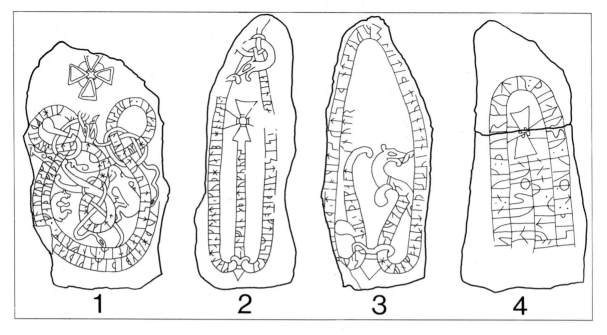

12 *Swedish rune stones from 1 Lingsberg, 2 Väsby, 3 Yttergärde and 4 Valleberga. There are some 1200 rune stones from the Uppland region of Sweden and England is one of the most common places referred to. Virtually all commemorate men killed in England and several mention the receipt of Danegeld.*

and mounts, such as the gilt copper alloy plaques stripped from book covers and placed in ninth-century Norwegian female graves at Bjørke and Alstad; and a silver hanging bowl found at Lejre, Sjælland (Denmark). There are also a number of Anglo-Saxon-style swords from Denmark, and an Anglo-Saxon gold ring found in a ninth-century context at Hon, Haug (Norway).

On the other hand, finds of ninth-century Anglo-Saxon coins are comparatively rare in Scandinavia; there are only 125 English and Frankish coins of the ninth century, distributed between some 50 finds (many of which are probably later deposits anyway), compared with some 4000 Arabic coins. There are several possible explanations. English coins may have been melted down, or perhaps conditions in Denmark allowed the hoarders to collect their treasure. Alternatively the ninth-century raiders may have settled rather than returned to Scandinavia, and used their loot as capital with which to do so.

In contrast, from 900 to 1040 more Anglo-Saxon coins are found in Swedish hoards than are known from the whole of England, demonstrating the significance of the Danegeld payments. They include c.50,000 Anglo-Saxon pennies from Gotland, c.2600–3000 from Norway, and c.15,000 in some 115 hoards from the area controlled by Denmark. English coins are also found as far afield as Finland, Russia, Poland, the Baltic Republics and Germany. These hoards contain little hacksilver, indicating that the raiders were being bought off in coin. Sometimes they appear to represent the modest profits of a common warrior, such as the 34 Æthelred pennies buried beside a large stone in Vestermarie on Bornholm; sometimes they are larger, such as the 600 coins placed in a cowhorn and buried on the beach at List on the island of Sylt.

13 *The Codex Aureus, an eighth-century copy of the four Gospels made at Canterbury and stolen by the Vikings in the ninth century. In the margins are a number of notes in Anglo-Saxon, added probably in the second quarter of the ninth century. These record how the Ealdorman Alfred and his wife Werburg bought the book back from the heathen army, paying for it in gold, and presented it to Christ Church, Canterbury.*

Phase 4: political conquest, 1013–1066

In the early eleventh century Viking activity in England entered another phase. In 1013 Sveinn of Denmark arrived with a Viking army, not for the extortion of tribute, but for conquest of the kingdom. The Chronicle recorded that 'all the nation regarded him as full king', and Æthelred fled to Normandy. The next year, however, Sveinn died, and Æthelred was able to return; but in 1016 a new Viking force arrived under Knutr. At the Battle of Ashingdown Knutr was victorious, and in the subsequent Treaty of Olney it was decreed that he should succeed to Mercia and the Danelaw, whilst Æthelred's eldest son, Edmund, should have Wessex. Edmund, however, died shortly after, leaving Knutr as king of England and of Denmark. On Knutr's death in 1035 Denmark and England became separate kingdoms again, and remained so apart from a brief interval in 1040–2 when the English invited Harthacnut, Knutr's son and successor in Denmark, to be their king. Nevertheless, the Viking Age in England can properly be said to continue until the death of the last great Viking leader, Harald Hardrada, at Stamford Bridge and the subsequent victory of William of Normandy, descendant of Viking settlers in Normandy, at Hastings. The Isle of Man, on the other hand, formed part of a Norse kingdom incorporating the Western Isles of Scotland, and continued to be under Scandinavian authority until 1266.

14 *Hogback fragment with mounted warrior, Sockburn (Durham) (Photo: York Archaeological Trust).*

15 *(Right) Map of England, 1013–66.*

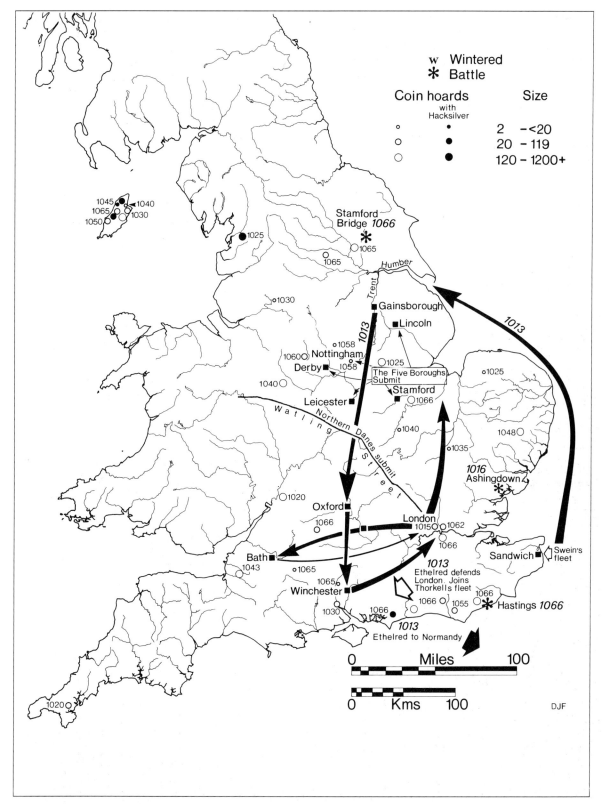

w Wintered
* Battle

Coin hoards
with
Hacksilver
Size

o   •   2 – <20
o   •   20 – 119
○   ●   120 – 1200+

1045
1040
1065
1050 1030

•1025

Stamford
Bridge *1066*
*
o1065

o1065

Humber

o1030

Trent

■ Gainsborough

■ Lincoln

1013

o1058
1060o Nottingham
Derby ■ 1058
1040 o

o1025

The Five Boroughs
Submit

■ Stamford
o1066

Leicester ■

Watling

Northern Danes submit

Street

o1040

o1035

1016
Ashingdown
*

1013

o1025

1048 o

o1020
Oxford ■
o1066

London
1015 o o1062
o1066

1013
Ethelred defends
London. Joins
Thorkell's fleet

Swein's
fleet

Sandwich ■

Bath ■
1043
o1065

1065 o
Winchester ■

o1030

o1066

o1066 o1055
*
Hastings *1066*

o1066

1013
Ethelred to Normandy

0   Miles   100

0   Kms   100

DJF

o1020

29

3

Viking colonization

Viking settlers were not pioneers carving farmsteads out of a virgin landscape. The England they found was already intensively farmed, with few open expanses where newcomers could establish their own villages. Nor was the settlement a free-for-all, with individuals seizing land as they chose. Land was allocated by Viking leaders in reward for military service, and they would expect to receive tribute irrespective of whether the land was held by their followers or by Anglo-Saxons. As with most foreign invasions, for native farmers the Viking settlement probably just meant a change in whom they paid their taxes to.

Both the impact and the scale of Viking colonization have been much debated. They can be examined from various forms of evidence, including settlement patterns and administrative systems, place-names and other linguistic evidence and the archaeological remains of the settlements themselves.

Settlement patterns and great estates

Before the Viking Age most rural land in England was organized in large estates, sometimes called 'multiple' estates because they typically grouped together several component areas, each with complementary resources, under common ownership. These estates are well known in Celtic regions such as Wales, where they have tended to survive longer, but they have also been mapped in Cumbria, Northumbria and the East Midlands. Their antiquity is uncertain, but they probably developed out of the areas over which petty lords were owed payments of food and services, possibly going back to post-Roman times. These lords also sought to divide up extensive upland grazing and hunting areas and place them under the control of their estate centres in the adjacent lowland arable areas. The great estates in the Kentish lowlands, for example, included woodland in the Weald, and may also have had coastal rights for fishing and salt production. In Middle Saxon England these estates were in the hands of kings, major lordly families and the Church. The monastery at Lindisfarne, for example, owned extensive tracts of northern England, which would be leased out to farmers, or run by estate managers. Land was rarely owned by individuals, however, being vested in communities or families. Individuals only had a life interest and could not make grants of land which would, in effect, disinherit their heirs.

From the ninth century onwards, however, there were fundamental changes in land ownership which led to the fragmentation of the great estates over much of lowland England and the rise of the private landholder. These changes might still have taken place without Viking intervention, as Anglo-Saxon kings made permanent grants of land to their followers in order to secure their loyalty. Nevertheless, they were undoubtedly hastened by the Viking settlement, and also provided a mechanism for it. The Viking colonization brought about a massive privatization of land ownership. Viking leaders gained land by conquest and also by purchase, disrupting traditional landholding patterns.

In some cases Viking settlers simply took over existing estate centres, using the established administrative structure to gain control of all the estate. In the north-west, for instance, many of the major territorial divisions bear names of Scandinavian origin, such as 'copeland' which means 'bought land' in Old Norse.

In many cases, however, Viking leaders divided estates amongst their followers in reward for military service. The large numbers of parishes in the Danelaw, particularly in Lincolnshire and the East Riding of Yorkshire, may reflect Healfdene sharing out the lands of the Northumbrians in 876. The few large parishes which were retained, such as those of Pickering and Beverley, may be those estates which remained under royal or episcopal control.

In 914, following the Battle of Corbridge, Rognald seized the lands of the Lindisfarne monks, giving some to his followers Scula and Onlafbal. In the tenth century charters record the sale of land by Scandinavians in Bedfordshire, Derbyshire and probably Lancashire. At the beginning of the eleventh century, in a classic protection-racket gambit, Æthelred was forced to grant land in Oxfordshire to a Dane called Toti in return for a pound of gold needed in order to pay Danegeld.

The Domesday Book records the end result of this process of fragmentation, with much of England under the control of large numbers of individual manors. In some areas, frequently those with less evidence for Scandinavian settlement, such as the Kentish Weald, the large estates survived, although Scandinavian settlers were not the only new landholders. There are records, for example, of English lords buying land within the Danelaw. Nevertheless, it was the Viking settlement which paved the way for the buying and selling of small parcels of land in the tenth century.

As a complementary process we might expect to see changes in settlement patterning, with the foundation of local manors and the development of villages and parishes around them. Certainly, over much of England there does appear to have been a shift away from a large number of dispersed settlements to the nucleated villages which are recorded in the Domesday Book. Evidence collected so far, however, suggests that the precise date of this change varies between different parts of the country, and there is nothing to link it directly to the Viking settlement. Indeed, in some areas it has been suggested that the Viking contribution may have caused a delay in the process of nucleation, and led to the retention of the pattern of dispersed settlement preferred in Norway. In Cumbria, for example, a combination of cultural and geographical factors meant that the parish system never completely evolved into the small-sized units typical elsewhere. Cumbria retained a dispersed pattern of small hamlets and individual family farms, rather than the nucleated villages of south and central England. Even in the south the fragmentation of holdings was irregular by the time of the Domesday Book, the size of parishes being influenced by the resources available within a given region.

Local government and land administration

Whilst Viking colonization may have had a major effect on settlement ownership and organization, there is little firm evidence that it led to fundamental changes in the administrative system of England.

The major administrative unit was the county. The boundaries of the English shire counties were drawn up in the tenth and eleventh centuries. In the East Midlands they took their names from the 'burh' towns of Derby, Nottingham, Leicester and so on, and the county may have been that area which was attached to the burh for its defence (see Chapter 4). The size of Lincolnshire and Yorkshire may therefore have been a defensive measure against renewed Viking attacks.

Within each shire settlements were grouped together in 'hundreds' and 'wapentakes', which appear to have been the administrative equivalents of the great estates. Hundreds were so called because they were originally based on a taxation unit of 100 hides, each hide being a unit of land required to support one family. Each hundred had its estate centre, or 'vill', to which the estates' inhabitants paid their rents and services. Each hundred also had an open-air meeting place where land transactions took place, cases of theft or violence were heard, and some local policing functions were organized. Secklow (Buckinghamshire) is one of twelve meeting places which have been excavated in England. It was found to consist of a mound, 25 m (81 ft) in diameter, surrounded by a roughly circular ditch some 1 m ($3\frac{1}{4}$ ft) deep, constructed in the tenth century. Such meeting places were often positioned near landmarks, such as at crossroads, on a parish boundary or near a prehistoric feature, such as a standing stone.

In the English area the hundreds survived as administrative districts into the post-Conquest period and are recorded in the Domesday Book. In Northamptonshire, for example, there were some 28 hundreds.

In North and West Yorkshire, on the other hand, the local administrative divisions are described as wapentakes, although there is no simple correlation between wapentakes and Scandinavian settlement, as hundreds were preserved in the East Riding of Yorkshire. In any case the process of government was probably the same, as the Old English *wapentake* means the brandishing of weapons at an assembly as a signal of assent.

In the multiple-estate system the central area to which outlying settlements were attached is often described by the term 'soke'; the 'soke-land' comprised those settlements which owed tribute and services to the lord. Such references were once thought to refer only to Viking leaders taking over English estates within the Danelaw and settling their followers around them; and the 'sokemen' mentioned in the Domesday Book were held to represent those free peasants who were descended from Viking settlers. In fact, the paucity of sokemen in Yorkshire has suggested to others that this is unlikely to be true, and sokes are believed to be of great antiquity; sokemen are now seen to be just as likely to be English peasants as Vikings.

The use of the 'ploughland' as a unit of assessment for taxation purposes has also been seen as a Scandinavian introduction, but since there is no evidence for its use in Scandinavia until the thirteenth century, and since the 'hide' continues in use in the Danelaw, it is just as likely to represent an eleventh-century fiscal system. Similarly, the system of counting in dozens and half-dozens has been seen as a Scandinavian introduction, with assessments in multiples of 5 and 10 in the south and west and more often in multiples of 6 and 12 in the Danelaw. Yet the evidence is far from clear cut, and in Normandy it is the decimal system which is seen as being Scandinavian in origin.

On the Isle of Man there is much clearer evidence for Scandinavian influence on the system of government, much of it surviving to the present day (16). The House of Keys, or lower house of the Manx parliament, has 24 seats, preserving its Scandinavian origin. Originally the Norse kingdom of Man and the Western Isles was regarded as consisting of

16 *The Manx Parliament, or Tynwald, still meets annually on 5 July in open session to promulgate the laws passed in the previous year. Its name is derived from the* Thing, *or Scandinavian assembly, which is also echoed in Dingwall in northern Scotland and Tingwall on Shetland (L. A. S. Butler).*

32 islands, each of which would contribute a representative. In 1156, however, the Norse lost control of half of the Western Isles, reducing the number of representatives from the Hebrides to eight, giving a total of 24. The present system of parishes on the Isle of Man is also thought to follow Norse land divisions, which in turn may be derived from earlier Celtic divisions.

Place-name evidence

Each age leaves traces of its settlement pattern in the names given to places and although the first recorded mention of most place-names is in the Domesday Book, with care it may be possible to identify those Scandinavian names given during the Viking Age.

In general, the distribution map of Scandinavian place-names (17) confirms the evidence provided by the written sources. Hardly any Scandinavian names, for example, are found south of the Danelaw, and the recorded settlements in Yorkshire, Mercia, East Anglia and the Wirral can all be seen to have left their mark. Nevertheless, there are some areas where place-names modify the picture provided by the written evidence. There are some Scandinavian names outside the Danelaw in Northamptonshire and Warwickshire, for example, and a concentration in the Lake District for which there is no documentary evidence.

Within the Danelaw there is considerable variation in the density of Scandinavian names. There are few, for example, in the north-east (Durham and Northumberland) or in Cambridgeshire and the south-east (Essex and Hertfordshire). In the East Midlands Scandinavian influence is most marked in Lincolnshire, Nottinghamshire and Leicestershire. In Cheshire, Scandinavian names are concentrated in the Wirral. Within Yorkshire, a grand total of 744 Scandinavian-influenced place-names are recorded in the Domesday Book, although Scandinavian influence is less marked in what was the West Riding. In the East Riding 48 per cent of names are of Scandinavian influence, in the North Riding 46 per cent and in the West Riding 31 per cent.

The type of Scandinavian name may help to identify the origin of the settlers, although care must be exercised as Danish terms such as -thorp may have been adopted by Norse settlers. Nevertheless, Normanby, for example, probably denotes a Norwegian settlement. Norwegian names predominate in the north-west, where a 19 km (12 mile) belt along the Lancashire coast seems to have been reclaimed from sea marshes by Norwegian farmers possibly expelled from Ireland. English names only appear on the higher ground further to the east, and in east Cheshire and Staffordshire a sprinkling of Danish names may mark the western limit of the Danish conquest of Mercia. In the north-west, Celtic names are also sometimes compounded with Norse ones, such as Aspatria (Patrick's ash).

Four main categories of Scandinavian influenced place-names have been identified. Firstly, there are those place-names which end in -by, of which some 850 examples have been recorded concentrated within the Danelaw, such as Aislaby, Balby, Brandsby, Dalby, Ferriby, Kirby and Selby. By was a Scandinavian word which appears to have been used in England to denote any kind of settlement from a single farmstead to a prosperous village. It has passed into English and is used in the term 'by-law' to mean the law of the village. The English equivalent was to use the ending -ton, as in Beeston. We can compare, for example, the place-names Osmondiston and Aismunderby, representing Osmund's tun and Asmund's by respectively. There are some 220 -by names in Lincolnshire, and some 210 in Yorkshire. In Lincolnshire they are concentrated in the Wolds and have been interpreted as farmsteads of immigrants who had sailed up the Humber estuary. In Yorkshire they are concentrated in the Vale of York. In Derbyshire, Leicestershire and Nottinghamshire there are a further 85 -by names, and 22 in Northamptonshire, 21 in Norfolk and 3 in Suffolk. Many of the -by names are compounded with a Scandinavian personal name. In Yorkshire, of the 119 -by names which comprise a personal element 109 (over 90 per cent) are Scandinavian, 7 are Old English and 3 are Old Irish.

The second place-name ending which has been interpreted as indicating a Scandinavian settlement is -thorp, as in Bishopthorpe, Danthorpe, Fridaythorpe, Newthorpe and Towthorpe. -Thorp is generally taken to indicate some form of secondary settlement, and these sites have been seen as representing subsequent exploitation of marginal land, or as outlying dependencies of estates which had their centres elsewhere, and that may have been detached from those centres by the Vikings. In Yorkshire there are some 155 place-names ending in -thorp

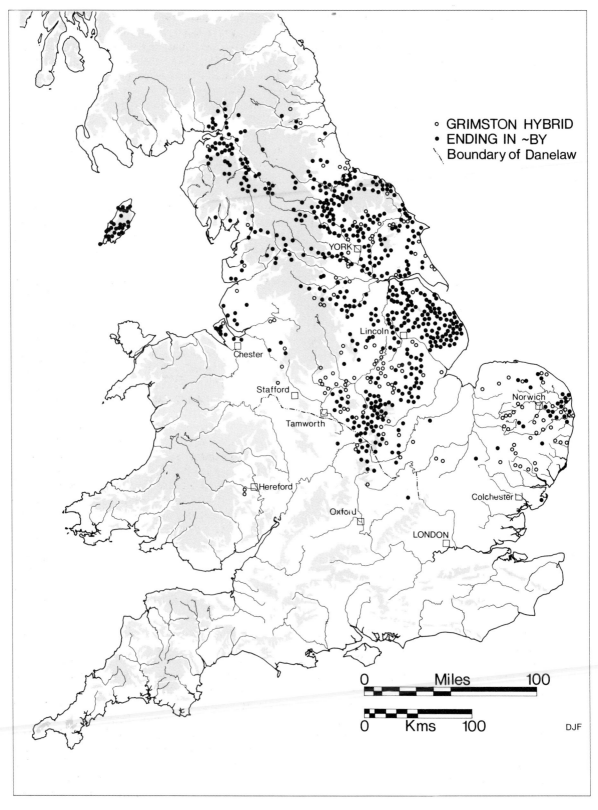

GRIMSTON HYBRID
ENDING IN ~BY
Boundary of Danelaw

YORK
Lincoln
Chester
Stafford
Tamworth
Norwich
Hereford
Colchester
Oxford
LONDON

0   Miles   100

0   Kms   100

DJF

recorded in the Domesday Book, and 109 in Derbyshire, Nottinghamshire, Lincolnshire and Leicestershire. The -thorp names are less frequently linked with Scandinavian personal names, and have therefore been regarded as being later than the -by names.

Thirdly, there is a class of place-names known as 'Grimston hybrids', which combined a Viking personal name with an Anglo-Saxon element such as -ton, as in Burneston, Catton, Saxton, Scampston, Wiggington, as well as in Grimston itself, or -hide as in Olaveside. In Lincolnshire and Yorkshire there are some 55 Grimston hybrids; in Derbyshire, Leicestershire and Nottinghamshire some 50. These names are often thought to represent English villages that were acquired by Scandinavian settlers but perhaps remained outside direct Scandinavian control.

Finally, changes in the pronunciation of Anglo-Saxon place-names to avoid un-Scandinavian sounds have also been taken as evidence for Scandinavian settlement. Thus the Anglo-Saxon Shipton becomes Skipton, and Cheswick becomes Keswick.

The high proportion of these four classes of Scandinavian-style place-names recorded in the Domesday Book has been used as one of the main arguments in support of a substantial Viking colonization of England. It is argued that even if it is accepted that the Anglo-Saxon Chronicle's account of the size of Viking armies is exaggerated, there must have been a substantial secondary migration of colonists in order to account for the large number of Scandinavian place-names.

However, there are two difficulties with this argument. The first problem is a linguistic one. We cannot be certain that individual Scandinavian place-names were coined by Viking Age settlers. Few place-names are recorded before the Domesday Book of 1086, some 200 years after the Scandinavian settlement, and as distant from them as we are from Napoleon. In the intervening years the English may have adopted many Scandinavian words into common usage, and may have taken up Scandinavian naming habits themselves. Given that it is now accepted that there were Scandinavian elements in the fourth- and fifth-century Anglo-Saxon invaders, it might also be possible that

some aspects of the Scandinavian languages could have been adopted earlier. Even if we could be sure that the Scandinavian names belong to the Viking Age rather than earlier or later, we still cannot be certain that they were coined by Scandinavians. Indeed, the people responsible for naming a settlement will not usually be those living in it but those from neighbouring sites who need to refer to it or tax it. Thus the name Ingleby might suggest a village of Angles named by Danes, whilst the name Danby might be a settlement of Danes referred to by Anglo-Saxons!

The second problem concerns the age of those settlements that received Scandinavian names. If they are evidence for a massive Scandinavian migration, then they should be new sites on virgin ground; but many may simply have been new names for existing places, just old estates under new management. Excavation at Whitby and Osbournby, for example, has revealed evidence for pre-Scandinavian settlement at both these sites. It is now widely accepted that much of England was already intensively farmed at the beginning of the Viking Age. If so, then the high proportion of Scandinavian place-names must represent a renaming of existing settlements.

A high proportion of Scandinavian style place-names involve the endings -by, -thorp or -ton compounded with a personal name, and in Yorkshire and the East Midlands 40–60 per cent of names ending in -by have a personal name as their first element. This can be explained by the fact that it was during the Viking settlement that much land passed into small-scale private ownership. Previously land had been held in the multiple estates, frequently under group ownership. In the Viking Age these large estates were broken up and their component elements handed out to individuals. Scandinavian place-names, therefore, mark not so much an extension of settlement as its reorganization under new lords and their density reflects areas of break-up of older, great estates into individual ownership rather than areas of migration. The Yorkshire Wolds, for example, were a very fertile area which had been farmed intensively from the late Iron Age. The large number of settlements bearing Scandinavian names are not new sites, but dependencies of estates based around the Wolds which were taken over by Scandinavians. We can therefore see which estates were preserved

17 *Map of Scandinavian Grimston hybrid and* -by *place-names (after Hill 1981 and Roesdahl* et al. *1981).*

and which were broken up. The area around Bardney Abbey (Lincolnshire), for example, has no Scandinavian place-names, in contrast to the area around Whitby where there are many.

There is no need to postulate, therefore, a mass Viking folk-migration in order to explain the distribution of Scandinavian place-names. Names are given to places when it becomes necessary to refer to them unambiguously. The Anglo-Saxon Chronicle records three partitions of land between the Vikings and the English, in Northumbria, Mercia and East Anglia (see Chapter 2). In each case the Viking leaders rewarded their followers with allocations of land. Both the new farmers and those expecting tribute from them would have been keen to legitimize their claims to this land, and what better way than by naming it after themselves? As the habit of buying and selling land developed in the tenth century it remained important to identify the owners, be they Anglo-Saxons or Scandinavians.

Linguistic changes

It has also been suggested that other linguistic evidence provides clear proof that the Scandinavian settlements were on the scale of mass folk-migrations. Scandinavian pronouns, verbs and other everyday words such as those for 'husband', 'knife' and 'window', were adopted into the English language. Some have contested that such changes could not have occurred unless the Vikings were in a majority, but other linguists have persuasively argued that it is misleading to draw conclusions about numbers on the basis of linguistic changes. They suggest that the influence of one language upon another depends on their relative status and the need to borrow words to describe new things. It is unlikely that ninth-century Northumbrians would have been able to understand Danes and Norwegians easily. Communication would rely on a few individuals who knew both languages. Nevertheless, the similarity between Danish and English would mean that it was easy for the English to adopt Scandinavian words. In particular, the introduction of a large number of Scandinavian words associated with farming indicates that there was an influential Danish-speaking farming population. Most evidence suggests that Scandinavians adopted English fairly rapidly, adding a few of their own words. Vernacular inscriptions from north and east England show a clear continuity in the use of English from the eighth to the eleventh centuries. There is no evidence for Scandinavians continuing to use either their runic script or their own language in England. This is in contrast to the Isle of Man, where Norse seems to have had a greater impact on the native language and where Scandinavian runic inscriptions are plentiful (see Chapter 11).

There are two schools of thought about the Norse settlement on Man. The first believes that it must represent a complete takeover and massive immigration at all levels of society; the second prefers to see the Norse as a relatively small group who supplanted the elite strata in Manx society. Under the first view Gaelic must have died out and Man would be wholly Norse-speaking for a time, until Gaelic was reintroduced c.1300; under the second view the majority of the population must have become bilingual Norse and Gaelic speakers. Either way, Norse becomes the language for public notices and is used for all inscriptions, unlike England where Anglo-Saxon is retained. Nevertheless it has been suggested that the Norse is not very good Norse; the language has lost its formal precision, perhaps because the speakers were bilingual.

Personal names

The number of individuals bearing Scandinavian personal names has also been used as a measure of the density of Scandinavian settlement. We have already seen the number of Scandinavian personal names compounded with settlement names in Yorkshire and Lincolnshire. In the Domesday Book 40 per cent of names in Derbyshire are Scandinavian, and 50 per cent in Nottinghamshire and Cheshire. Of course, name-giving habits change with fashion and are particularly prone to influence from the elite, as the number of English children christened Charles, Edward or Andrew testifies. Scandinavian names may have increased in popularity during the Viking Age, but they do not necessarily denote Scandinavians. Members of the same family mentioned in the Domesday Book have both Scandinavian and English names. We also tend to forget that documentary sources are restricted to the elite group. Most of those individuals mentioned in the Domesday Book are referred to as manor holders.

We can also look at coins for the names of the moneyers, or those responsible for coin production. The proportion of Scandinavian names increases from zero under Ælfred to 3 per cent under Edward the Elder, 5 per cent under Æthelstan and to 15 per cent under Eadred and his successors. Regionally there is considerable variation. In York c.75 per cent of names are Scandinavian by the reign of Æthelred, in Lincoln c.50 per cent, Chester c.25 per cent and London c.7 per cent. Yet even if all these individuals were born in Scandinavia they hardly represent a cross-section of tenth-century England. Name-giving habits may well have been profoundly affected by the Viking settlement, but Scandinavian names may still have been confined to the landowning and mercantile classes.

Intermarriage may have been widespread. The Manx crosses associate Celtic and Scandinavian names within families; of 44 personal names 22 are Norse and 11 Irish, suggesting a mixed population. Of course, we cannot assume that all those with Norse names were Norse in origin; Manx kings took Scandinavian names as a political ploy.

In summary, we cannot use the evidence of settlement organization, place-names or language to argue for a substantial Viking migration. What the place-names do show is that, whatever the size of the invasion, its political implications should not be underestimated. A major consequence of the Viking raids was the fragmentation of the great estates. The Vikings stimulated a new market in the buying and selling of property. Land was taken into private ownership, and often named for the first time.

Archaeological evidence

Few Viking Age rural settlements have been excavated, and even fewer can be positively identified as the homes of Scandinavian settlers (see **19**). The first problem is that most of the successful farmsteads must have grown into medieval villages and now lie buried under their modern successors. The second is that the typical rural excavation yields few finds, making cultural identification difficult. The Anglo-Saxon migrations can be recognized archaeologically from new settlements and building types which appear over southern and eastern England. Yet we cannot assume that new peoples will inevitably introduce new forms of settlement, and, especially if their way of life was identical to that of the existing population, there is no reason why their farms

should be distinguishable from those of the native inhabitants. Therefore we must examine all the settlement evidence for the period, ranging from palaces and manorial centres to isolated upland farmsteads.

The site at Cheddar (Somerset) probably functioned as a royal estate centre from the second half of the ninth century, and may well have been used by Ælfred. A double-storey long hall was erected within a palisaded enclosure with a possible gatehouse. Around 930 it was replaced by a more substantial timber hall (West Hall I) and a stone chapel (**18**). The relative cleanliness of the site suggests that it may only have been occupied periodically during royal visitations, and housed just a skeleton caretaker staff in the interim. Documentary sources suggest that the royal court was held there in 968 under Edgar. The hall was rebuilt a third time in the late tenth century (West Hall II) and a raised dais was added, probably during the reign of Æthelred.

At North Elmham (Norfolk) excavations have revealed details of life within an episcopal palace complex. A Middle Saxon cathedral community abandoned the site in the early ninth century, possibly as a result of Viking raids, but at some time after 917 the site was cleared and levelled for a new minster and ancillary buildings. A new church was erected over the earlier ruins, and a large timber hall, possibly for the use of the bishop, was erected

18 *An artist's reconstruction of Cheddar, c.1000 (P. A. Rahtz).*

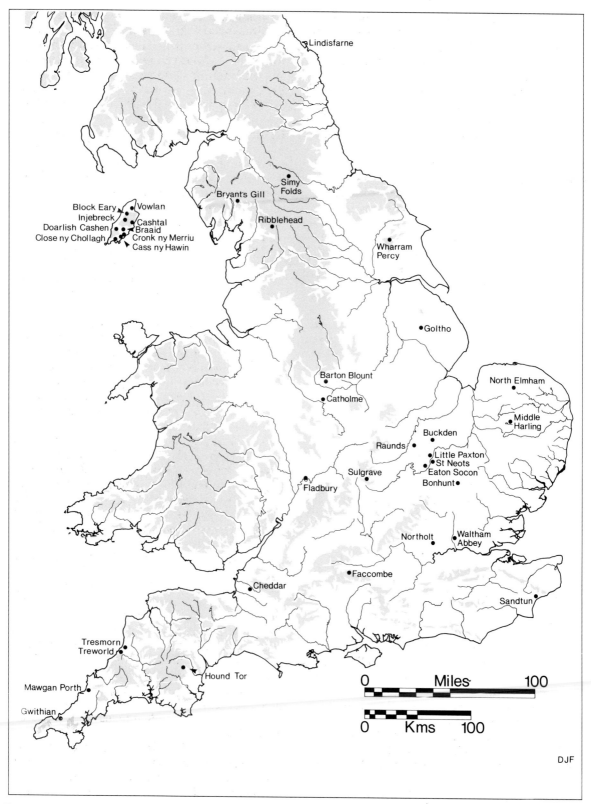

Lindisfarne

Simy Folds

Bryant's Gill

Ribblehead

Wharram Percy

Block Eary
Injebreck
Doarlish Cashen
Close ny Chollagh

Vowlan
Cashtal
Braaid
Cronk ny Merriu
Cass ny Hawin

Goltho

Barton Blount

Catholme

North Elmham

Middle Harling

Buckden

Raunds

Little Paxton
St Neots
Eaton Socon
Bonhunt

Sulgrave

Fladbury

Northolt

Waltham Abbey

Faccombe

Cheddar

Sandtun

Tresmorn
Treworld

Hound Tor

Mawgan Porth

Gwithian

0   Miles   100

0   Kms   100

DJF

nearby. In the eleventh century a new palace was built elsewhere, and the site was given over to secular use. It was colonized by farmers, with peasant dwellings, sheds and animal pens set in fenced enclosures.

Other excavations have illuminated the decline of the great estates and the evolution of the manor during the Viking Age. The extensive landscape project at Raunds (Northamptonshire) has demonstrated the fragmentation of a multiple estate into several component manors over several centuries. At Furnells Manor a Middle Saxon settlement in a ditched enclosure was replaced by a large timber hall, the proto-manor house, in the early tenth century. A small stone church was built adjacent to the enclosure. At about the same time, the first regular tenements of peasant farmers were being laid out at Furnells and West Cotton, marked by ditched enclosures. As none of the ditches could have offered more than minimal protection their main purpose must have been for laying out the land. Indeed, the evidence at West Cotton shows that equal plots, c.20 m (66 ft) wide, were created.

A similar process may have been taking place in another area of Scandinavian settlement, at Wharram Percy (North Yorkshire). The South Manor site at Wharram was occupied from the early eighth century. The date of the laying out of the peasant tofts and crofts is still problematic, but probably took place during the Viking Age, in the tenth century. The lack of Late Saxon pottery from the fields between the villages, compared with the abundance of Middle Saxon sherds, suggests that the villages were also becoming nucleated at that time. In some cases a mother settlement might be replaced by a number of daughter sites. At Chalton (Hampshire), for example, the Church Down site was abandoned by the ninth century, but the nearby villages of Chalton (Manor Farm), Idsworth and probably Blendworth were occupied from about this time.

Many pre-Conquest manorial residences were set within fortified enclosures. In some cases existing fortifications were utilized. At Portchester (Hampshire) several substantial timber houses were erected within the walls of the former Roman fort in the late eighth or ninth centuries. Finds of east Mediterranean glass and coins of Burgred of Mercia testify to the relative wealth of the site. In 904 it was acquired by the king as a royal burh, but it never became a town and appears to have continued to function as a manor site. In the late tenth century a substantial aisled hall and three subsidiary buildings were constructed, served by impressive timber-lined wells. Massive dumps of food waste may represent the remains of great feasts. In the early eleventh century the owner erected a free-standing flint and masonry tower, some 6 m (20 ft) square, on a plot of land between the hall and the subsidiary domestic buildings. This may have been a bell-tower or chapel, as it became a focus for burials.

At Sulgrave (Northamptonshire) and Goltho (Lincolnshire) new earthen ringworks were thrown up around the timber halls. At Sulgrave a separate stone building set to one side of the hall may have been a gatehouse, or possibly the tower of a church as at Portchester.

At Goltho an early ninth-century village was superseded by a fortified earthwork enclosure in which a fine bow-sided hall like that at Cheddar, a bower, a kitchen and weaving sheds formed three sides of a rectangular enclosure (20). The kitchen would have provided food for feasts when followers were entertained in the hall. The fortifications comprised a 6 m- (20 ft-) wide rampart topped by a timber palisade, surrounded by a ditch 5.4 m (18 ft) wide and 2–2.4 m (6–8 ft) deep. They are as substantial as those protecting the burhs at Cricklade and Tamworth, and must have been constructed for serious defence, perhaps against the threat of Viking raids. The manorial complex may have been founded by a member of the Saxon aristocracy, although the finding of a Viking Age bridle bit with Scandinavian parallels could be used to argue that it was a late ninth-century Viking foundation. During the late tenth and early eleventh centuries the site underwent considerable expansion. The hall was replaced by an aisled version without internal partitions which would be more suitable for use on official occasions and for estate functions, and the bower was enlarged and partitioned, with a latrine attached to it at one end. After the Norman Conquest it developed into a motte-and-bailey castle.

Not all rural sites developed into manorial complexes. Catholme (Staffordshire) was already in decline before the Viking Age and was abandoned in the early tenth century.

19 *Map of excavated Viking Age settlements.*

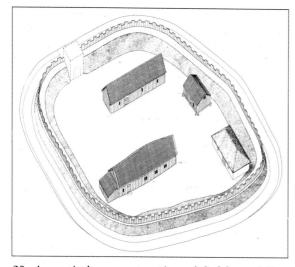

20 *An artist's reconstruction of Goltho, c.850, looking north (Guy Beresford).*

During its latest phase the settlement comprised groups of buildings linked by fences defining paddocks or small yards. Within the central enclosure a bow-sided hall was the most substantial building. Tenth- and eleventh-century buildings set within ditched or fenced enclosures have also been identified at St Neots and Little Paxton (Cambridgeshire). These appear to represent individual farm units with ancillary buildings, wells, homefields and droveways leading to a village centre. Other sites, whilst not large enough to be described as villages, comprise more than single farmsteads. At Springfield (Essex) nearly a dozen rectangular houses of the ninth to eleventh centuries have been excavated. The suggestion of a rectangular tower may mark this as another proto-manorial site; although the 15 rubbish pits contained few rich finds there was evidence for pottery and quernstones from Germany.

Within the upland zone of the north and west of England there was a vigorous upturn in the rural economy during the Viking Age (see Chapter 6). In Cumbria there was a major settlement expansion into the under-utilized wastelands of the central Lakeland massif and other marginal areas. This is unlikely to have been common ground which could be easily colonized. On a multiple estate even the most barren land would still have been put to some use, and would have belonged to someone, even if it was not inhabited. Nevertheless there

was apparently a considerable Scandinavian takeover in the tenth century, probably following the historically recorded expulsion of the Hiberno-Norse Vikings from Ireland in 902. Nine out of ten place-names in the central Lake District show Scandinavian influence, although Gaelic elements suggest that settlers from the Hebrides, Faroes and Iceland as well as Dublin and Man may also have been involved. Cumbria was exposed to seaborne attack along a considerable coastline, and the topography made defence difficult. It has been suggested that the English aristocracies survived, but deprived of much of their land and now in competition with the colonists. There was an immigrant hierarchy of mixed British, Gaelic or Scandinavian extract at the apex of society, with little sign that it was distinctively Viking.

In Northumbria the place-names associated with the upland clearances are as much Anglo-Saxon as Scandinavian. In some areas of Durham and Cleveland it has been suggested that significant numbers of Danish immigrants filled the crucial middle and lower ranks of land ownership and were able to consolidate their position by exercising patronage in favour of their fellow countrymen. By the early tenth century, however, all the evidence suggests a community moving towards cultural and ethnic integration.

Extensive survey work within the uplands has led to the identification of increasing numbers of abandoned farms, but such sites are notoriously difficult to date, and even when excavated rarely yield any material which allows us to say that they are the farmsteads of Viking settlers. One such settlement has been excavated at Ribblehead (North Yorkshire), set on bare limestone pavement at an altitude of 340 m (1125 ft) above sea level (**21**). The farmstead comprised three buildings set in an enclosed farmyard with an associated field system of over 1.2 ha (3 acres). The main building was a longhouse; the others comprised a bakery with a grindstone and limestone oven and a poorly-built smithy with a central sandstone slab for a hearth, and remains of iron scale and cinders. The few artefacts recovered suggest a mixture of agricultural and simple craft activities. They included an iron cow bell, a horse bit, a spear-head, two iron knives and a stone spindlewhorl. Local materials were used for most needs and the site was largely self-sufficient, although four Northumbrian stycas suggest some contact with urban markets and date the site to the late ninth century.

A similar range of artefacts has been recovered at Bryant's Gill (Cumbria), where a farmstead has been located at the centre of a 20-ha (50-acre) field system at 290 m (940 ft) above sea level in the north-west fells of Kentmere. The finds from in and around the longhouse include charcoal and iron slag, stone spindlewhorls and over 20 honestones (see **50**).

At Simy Folds (Durham) three sites have been examined. Each consists of the stone foundations of a single long narrow building with one or two subrectangular buildings at right angles to it, arranged to enclose a yard. The site lies within an extensive field system of prehistoric origin. The pollen evidence suggests the cultivation of cereals during the Viking Age, as well as the keeping of livestock including sheep, cattle and pigs. The finds once more include a stone spindlewhorl and a honestone, and a quernstone. The quantities of iron slag suggest that iron-working was being undertaken on a large scale, presumably based on the local iron ore.

21 *An artist's reconstruction of Ribblehead (Yorkshire Museum).*

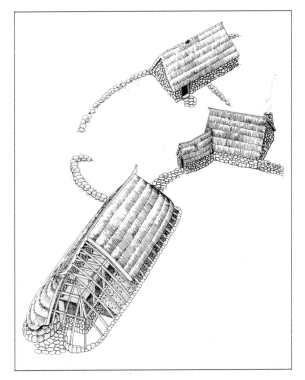

The island of Lindisfarne (Northumberland) may have been abandoned by its monks in the mid or late ninth century, but occupation apparently continued. At Green Shiel a large farmstead comprising a group of buildings linked by enclosing walls and yards has been investigated. The site was first noticed in the middle of the last century when stone from the walls was robbed in the course of construction of a wagonway. Two ninth-century Northumbrian stycas were found during this work; subsequently a spear and a penny of Æthelred of Wessex have also been recovered. At least three longhouses and a number of ancillary structures have been identified.

Similar ninth- and tenth-century farmsteads have also been recognized in the south-west, at Gwithian, Tresmorn and Treworld (Cornwall) and at Hound Tor and Hutholes (Devon). The latter sites may have been the equivalent of Norse shielings, occupied by herdsmen who grazed their stock on the open moorland pastures during the summer months.

At Mawgan Porth (Cornwall) excavations have revealed a coastal hamlet of three or more farmsteads with groups of longhouses and ancillary buildings terraced into the hillside, and its own cemetery set uphill and to the west. Each farmstead may have represented a single extended family. The most completely excavated farmstead consisted of four major buildings set around a central courtyard. The largest building could have housed some four or five people (see **39**). The settlement was probably occupied from the mid-ninth to the mid-eleventh centuries, but this settlement form continued in use into the Middle Ages. The inhabitants were pastoralists, shellfish gatherers and fishermen. They were originally thought to be Scandinavians, but we cannot be certain. They had virtually no iron tools and used stone, bone and pottery extensively. A coin of Æthelred II (*c*.990–5) shows that they maintained some contact with Wessex.

On the Isle of Man linguistic and place-name evidence suggest intensive Viking occupation, although the actual settlements have been elusive. The long sandy beaches of the glacial lowland of the north offered ideal landing places. The fertility of the plain made it an obvious settlement area, and although few settlement sites have been excavated, the cross slabs and burials confirm that Norse settlement was heaviest here. The problem with identifying

Viking settlements on the island is that the excavated sites yield few finds, and since the Norse way of life may have continued into the fifteenth century the sites are difficult to date to the Viking Age. Archaeologists have had to rely on morphological dating from the form of buildings, and have tended to interpret long-house sites as Viking habitations. As we have seen, however, they are a standard upland building form, and have been found as far afield as Cornwall and Yorkshire, and may not necessarily be associated with Vikings.

At Doarlish Cashen, for example, a small Norse-style farmstead was excavated on marginal land at about 210 m (682 ft) above sea level; its dating rests on the fact that it is a longhouse with wall benches. The only finds were a spindlewhorl and one potsherd; it could have been occupied anywhere between the ninth and thirteenth centuries. The farm had its own corn-drying kiln, and even though the climate may have been slightly better, the use of this upland area for arable farming suggests that the land must have been densely settled during the Viking Age, whether by Norse or natives. The dating of the three buildings excavated at the Braaid (**colour plate 4**) is also difficult due to the paucity of finds, and it has rested upon the form of the buildings (see Chapter 5).

The Isle of Man is notable for the series of 21 promontory forts which defend the prime landing places. Most were established during the Iron Age, but at least twelve appear to have been reoccupied during the Viking Age. It is unclear whether these should be interpreted as defended homesteads or as part of a coastal defence system dating to the Norse kingdom; alternatively they may have been used as temporary bases for relatively small groups of Vikings on long sea journeys. Although they are provided with natural cliff defences against the sea, they generally have substantial earthen ramparts protecting their landward side. Viking-style longhouses have been excavated within the ramparts at Cronk ny Merriu (**colour plate 5**), Close ny Chollagh and Cass ny Hawin. At Vowlan a series of six superimposed timber Norse-style houses was found on a small undefended promontory. This may have been a wintering base used successively during the transition between raiding and permanent settlement.

In summary, there is little evidence for a mass peasant migration of new settlers, clearing land. Rather, Viking settlers presided over the fragmentation of great estates, establishing manorial centres and accelerating the market in the buying and selling of land. Many settlements were named during the Viking Age, and concentrations of place-names do indicate the adoption of Scandinavian terms into local speech in many areas. Taken together with the great variety of Scandinavian personal names in use by the eleventh century they indicate an influential Scandinavian community in some areas of the country, although it is impossible to put a precise figure on the number of settlers. Archaeologically the Scandinavians were absorbed within the local population and local settlement forms.

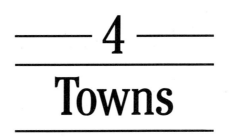

4

Towns

The Viking Age witnessed an explosion in the development of towns. At the start of the period there may have been less than a dozen places, all trading sites, which we would regard as urban centres. By 1066 there were more than 100 places with some claim to be regarded as towns (**22**). Nevertheless, they still contained only a fraction of the population, perhaps some 10 per cent. They included a great diversity of forms, from those that were little more than fortified royal estate centres such as Stafford, to massive cosmopolitan emporia such as York. Nonetheless, most had a Domesday population of more than 1000, with the larger towns such as Lincoln and Norwich having over 5000 townsfolk.

How far was the growth of trading and market sites a result of Viking stimulus, and how far was the development of fortified towns a reaction to the Viking threat? Did the Scandinavian settlers establish any towns of their own? Would towns have developed anyway, if there had been no Scandinavian influence? Was there anything particularly Scandinavian about the character of the towns or their defences? Excavations within many English towns and cities over the last two decades may mean that we are now closer to answering these questions.

Wics

In Middle Saxon England most trade was conducted at large *wics* or camps, such as Hamwic (Southampton) and Eoforwic (York), on the south and east coasts. These sites apparently developed under royal patronage, so that the traders could be protected and controlled, and royal taxes levied. At Hamwic there is evidence for a 45-ha (110-acre) site of *c*.700–850, enclosed by a bank and ditch (probably to define the trading zone as much as for defence), with properties laid out on a regular street system. Hamwic had trading contacts with northern France and the Rhineland; many of its inhabitants made their living from processing imports and exports, and by manufacturing goods from imported raw materials.

In London trade was actually transacted on the waterfront, probably from boats pulled up on the shore. Initially there was no need for storage or warehouse facilities, and trading sites may have left few archaeological traces. The location of such markets along the Thames is indicated by *wic* place-names, such as Chiswick, Greenwich, Woolwich and Twickenham.

Some trading sites may have been no more than periodic beach markets, such as Meols near the mouth of the Dee estuary. The name is derived from the Old Norse word for sandbank, *melr*, and it has been suggested that a pre-Viking beach market may have been taken over by Norse traders. Finds include some 20 Anglo-Saxon pennies of the late tenth and eleventh centuries and a variety of metalwork, including Hiberno-Norse-style copper alloy ringed pins, and a mount with Viking-style animal ornament.

At most *wic* sites, however, the threat of attack in the Viking Age led the traders to seek protection within walled towns, and may also have disrupted trade. At almost every site occupation declines or ceases during the ninth century. At Hamwic it has been argued that the coin finds indicate that it was already in decline before the Viking raids, although others have concluded that it was increased Viking activity which disrupted its trading networks. The site at Hamwic seems to have gradually

5 BOROUGHS
BURGHAL HIDAGE

York

Chester

LINCOLN

DERBY NOTTINGHAM

Stafford

Tamworth

STAMFORD

LEICESTER

Norwich

Thetford

Warwick

Northampton

Worcester

Bedford

Ipswich

Hereford

Buckingham

Winchcombe
Gloucester

Oxford

Cricklade

Wallingford

Malmesbury

Sashes

London

Southwark

Bristol

Bath

Chisbury

Rochester

Axbridge

Eashing

Canterbury

Pilton

Watchet

Langford

Wilton

Winchester

Eorpeburnan

Lyng

Shaftesbury

Southampton

Burpham

Hastings

Porchester

Lewes

Bridport

Christchurch

Lydford

Exeter

Chichester

Halwell

Wareham

0   Miles   100

0   Kms   100

DJF

been depopulated from *c*.850; there was occasional pit digging up to 900, but no new buildings can be identified.

At Fishergate, York, where an area of Anglo-Saxon Eoforwic has been excavated, a single coin of the 860s is the latest find, compared with some 40 of the eighth and early ninth centuries; the site was then abandoned until the eleventh or twelfth centuries.

In London, the extensive Saxon settlement of Lundenwic was located in the Strand area. The coin finds from this area are mainly of the eighth and early ninth centuries; the latest are a hoard of *c*.840 from the Middle Temple and a second of *c*.870 from the Thames found during repairs to the south side of Waterloo Bridge. Both hoards have been linked with documented Viking raids on London. The latest pottery from the Strand area has been dated to the ninth century. By the late ninth century there is little evidence for trade, and virtually no imported pottery.

At Hamwic, Eoforwic and Lundenwic the

22 *(Left) Map of Viking Age towns.*

23 *Plan of Viking Age London. The majority of find spots indicated are pot sherds of the late ninth to early eleventh centuries (after Vince 1990).*

Viking raids seem to have disrupted trade, but protection was sought within a defended area, and new sites were established after some delay. In Southampton *c*.900 the focus of occupation shifted to higher more defensible ground some 0.5 km (1640 ft) to the south-west of Hamwic, where it was possible to control both sides of the estuary. Ditches outlined an area of Viking Age occupation with regularly laid out streets within the medieval walled town. The new site had different trading contacts, and a reduced role in long-distance international trade; tenth-century pottery from Normandy is one of the few identifiable Viking Age imports.

In London occupation within the walled area of the Roman city does not appear to start before the late ninth century, perhaps reflecting its re-establishment as a fortified burh by Ælfred in 886 (**23**). The names used to refer to London also show a change from Lundenwic in the early ninth century to Lundenburh in the later ninth century, with a short period of overlap in the 850s. All coin finds are now from the City area, indicating that the exposed Strand site between the river Fleet and Westminster was abandoned and the old Roman fortress reoccupied. There is little evidence for tenth-century occupation outside the City walls. The Roman walls must still have survived as foundations at least; the ditch may have

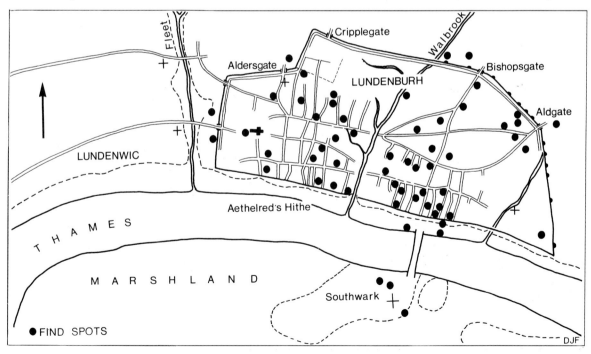

been recut, and the gates reused. A pit-free zone either side of the wall may indicate the position of a rampart. The Anglo-Saxon Chronicle records that London successfully held out against the Vikings in the 990s.

Fragments of over 40 buildings have been excavated within the walled city. A regular street plan determined by the position of the Roman gates was established, with gravelled surfaces. Timber halls were erected along the street frontages, and set back from the street, mostly along the back and sides of properties, there were sunken workshops and storage buildings (see Chapter 5). Along the tenement boundaries there were numerous latrine pits, some over 1 m ($3\frac{1}{4}$ ft) in diameter and several metres deep. Layers of cess alternate with tips of garden soil, domestic refuse and floor sweepings. By the eleventh century such pits were often provided with plank and wattle linings, suggesting that their contents were regularly cleared out.

London only began to prosper again as a port in the late tenth century, with the erection of wharfs of clay, timber and rubble against which vessels could be moored. Access to boats would have been by means of cobbled or planked walkways laid out over the embankment down onto the foreshore, as seen at the Thames Exchange site, or by jetties now represented by pile clusters, as seen at Billingsgate. London's international trade was only revived in the eleventh century, but then expanded rapidly; by 1050 there was probably an almost continuous artificial bank running in front of the wall in the eastern half of the city. By the mid-eleventh century there was a considerable settlement within the walled city and further settlements in Southwark and Whitehall, although there may still have been some areas which were unoccupied.

A similar picture is emerging from York (24). By the eleventh century York was described as a populous city to which merchants came from all quarters, especially from the Danish people (colour plate 7). In the ninth century, however, there is evidence for a hiatus in trade after the decline of Eoforwic. The exposed trading site beyond the confluence of the rivers Ouse and Foss appears to have been abandoned in favour of a more easily defended area between the two rivers and closer to the Roman legionary fortress. The walls of the Roman fort survived sufficiently for York to withstand attack in the ninth century. Although breached in several places, much of the fortress wall stood more than 3 m (10 ft) high, and the insertion of the so-called Anglian tower into a gap in the walls at some date before the Viking Age refurbishment of the ramparts has been taken as evidence for continued maintenance of the defences. Around 900 York's Viking rulers apparently renovated the defences so as to enclose an area bounded by the Roman walls to the north and west and by the rivers Ouse and Foss to the south and east, thereby enclosing the riverside area to the east of the Roman fortress. An earthen bank surmounted by a palisade was constructed along the north-east and north-west sides of the fortress, and was probably extended down to the rivers in the same manner as Viking Age defences at Chester (colour plate 6) and elsewhere. There may also have been a defended bridgehead east of the river Foss; although no trace of a Viking Age defensive line has been found beneath the medieval city walls in the Walmgate area, there was occupation and industrial activity in this area. Even excluding this settlement east of the Foss, the total enclosed area of Viking York was some 36 ha (87 acres), making it larger than the major Scandinavian towns at Hedeby and Birka.

Within the walled area, however, there is little evidence for Viking Age structures, and in most areas thirteenth-century levels immediately overlie Late Roman ones, although this could be because conditions here were not right for the preservation of Viking Age organic deposits, or because they were swept away c.1200 prior to the major medieval building programme. Scandinavian chance finds have been reported throughout the area, including manufacturing debris. There is no evidence for the imposition of a regular street layout during the Viking Age, although the Roman defences continued to influence the topography. It has been suggested that the Viking royal palace may have been sited near the south-east gate of the legionary fortress in King's Square, although no archaeological traces have been excavated. Similarly, no trace was found of the Viking Age cathedral underneath York Minster although a graveyard with Viking grave markers suggests that the church was nearby, possibly to the south-west. The former legionary barrack blocks housed Viking Age activity, including antler and bone working and

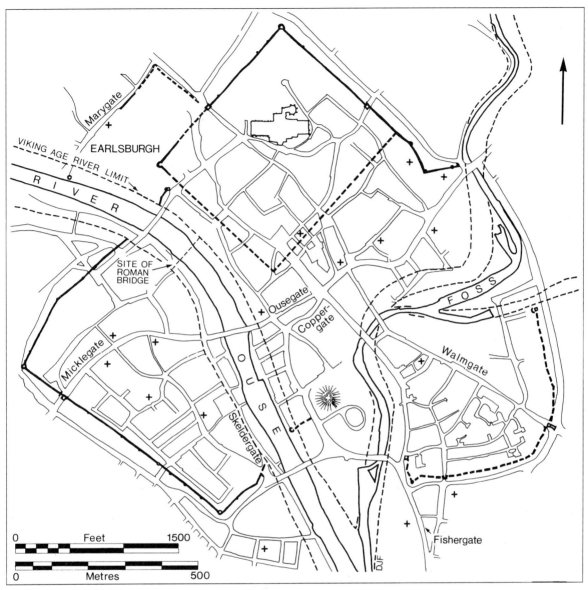

24 *Plan of Viking Age York (after Hall 1988 and OS 1988).*

ferrous and non-ferrous metalworking, with the walls of the former barracks used to demarcate the new tenements. This activity may have been under the control of the church, or may simply have been taking place adjacent to it. In the area between the Roman fortress and Marygate, where there was a defended Roman enclosure, the name Earlsburgh suggests that the later pre-conquest Anglo-Scandinavian earls must have had their residence nearby. Between 1030 and 1055 Earl Siward built or rebuilt a church or private chapel here, which he dedicated to St Olaf.

South-west of the river Ouse the area of the former Roman *colonia* or civilian settlement was also occupied during the Viking Age. There is no archaeological evidence for the defences south-west of the Ouse, but it is assumed that they were on the line of the surviving medieval walls. There appears to have been an important Anglo-Saxon ecclesiastical complex in the Bishophill area, and the street names point to continued Viking Age activity over most of the walled area. A new bridge was built across the Ouse to the east of the Roman one, and

Micklegate (literally 'Great Street') diverges from its Roman course as it heads for the new crossing. Timber buildings and rubbish pits have been found along Micklegate on the Queen's Hotel site and on Skeldergate. This new Viking thoroughfare across the Ouse focused on the Coppergate, Ousegate and Pavement area, where the most striking evidence for Viking Age York has been found within the new enclosure. In this area the city has risen on its own refuse, and rich evidence for its people and their lifestyle has been preserved in several metres of Viking Age deposits.

Evidence for intensive occupation, including timber buildings housing leather workers, has been excavated within the basement of Lloyd's Bank, Pavement, and cellared buildings once thought to be plank-lined tanning pits have been excavated at High Ousegate, but the largest sample of Viking York has been excavated at Coppergate, on sharply sloping ground leading down to the river Foss.

Post-Roman activity, including glass working, commences in the mid-ninth century, but it is not clear whether it starts before the Viking takeover as a result of people seeking the protection of the walled town or as a consequence of the Viking takeover in 866 or settlement in 876. If the walled town did not include this area until after its Viking refurbishment then the latter explanation may be more likely. The new timber Ouse bridge was presumably erected in the late ninth or early tenth century, and at some time between the late ninth century and c.930–5 the Coppergate street was established, with a series of long narrow tenements defined by wattle fence alignments running back from the street down towards the Foss. These property boundaries remained in force throughout the Viking Age and influenced all subsequent developments over the next thousand years. The plots were of equal width, perhaps implying that they stemmed from a deliberate act of town planning designed to stimulate the development of a Viking Age industrial estate.

On the four tenements within the Coppergate excavations post-and-wattle buildings were erected on the street frontage, with their gable ends facing the street (25). Their backyard areas were riddled with pits; those lined with barrels were probably wells; those with wattle lining may have been used for storage, whilst others served as latrines and cesspits (26).

Within the buildings there is evidence that iron working and other crafts were carried out on a commercial scale. Two of the tenements were used for metalworking, including copper and lead alloys, silver and gold, as well as iron. In fact, the tremendous diversity of craft activities suggests that the buildings were rented out to craftsmen rather than each being permanently occupied by one individual.

Around 975 the four buildings were simultaneously demolished and replaced by a series of plank-built sunken buildings (see 34). On three tenements the buildings were arranged in two ranks, suggesting that the reorganization was perhaps prompted by the increased intensity of occupation and the need to store manufactured and traded goods. The buildings were occupied by jewellers and woodworkers, but industrial metalworking ceased and may have been forced to move to the fringes of the densely settled area. Finally, early in the eleventh century, a large warehouse or boat shed was erected at the rear of the site, closer to the river.

The general picture which has emerged from the Coppergate excavations is of a fairly squalid urban environment which contrasts with that of Roman York. The town has been described as a large compost heap composed of rotting wooden buildings with earth floors covered by decaying vegetation and surrounded by streets and yards filled by pits and middens of organic waste. Organic refuse was being dumped at a greater rate than it was being cleared away; during the tenth century the ground level rose by an average of 25 mm (1 in.) per year. Nevertheless, whilst no doubt the exterior of the properties was foul and disgusting, their insides may have been tolerably cleanly maintained. Excavations of three late tenth-century tenements from Saddler Street, Durham, have suggested a relatively clean environment, with dumps of sand used to seal middens and pits.

25 (Above) *Four adjacent tenements, Coppergate, York. During the late tenth century there was a series of plank-walled sunken buildings along the street frontage, of which two can clearly be seen. The brick-lined well shaft is a much later intrusion (York Archaeological Trust).*

26 (Below) *Wattle-lined cesspit, Coppergate, York (York Archaeological Trust).*

The deposits from Durham are very similar to those from York, although there is nothing particularly Scandinavian about them. Indeed, one must also question whether there is anything distinctively Viking about York, apart from a new taste for Scandinavian-style ornament. Certainly there is no evidence to show that the inhabitants of Coppergate were Scandinavian in origin. As has been shown, Scandinavian traders were not responsible for establishing York and other towns as major trading sites. On the contrary, the international contacts of existing sites were disrupted, and only recovered after an interval. Where there were no existing trading sites, as on the Isle of Man as well as in Wales and Brittany, Viking activity did not lead to their formation.

Mercian burhs

Although the first Anglo-Saxon towns may have originated as trading sites, a much larger group of towns was established as defended forts or burhs, probably as a direct response to the Viking threat. The earliest English examples were established in Mercia c.780–90 by King Offa, possibly following Carolingian prototypes. The Mercian burhs should be seen as a systematic defence against Viking seaborne attack. All were associated with defensive bridges; they were placed on main rivers throughout Mercia, so that the burh and bridge blocked access upstream to warships (27). They also functioned as civil and ecclesiastical administrative centres and became important markets, although the markets may have grown up outside the walls without deliberate planning. There appear to have been two classes of site. Some were established on existing fortified Roman sites, where the walls and bridge probably survived; others developed from fortified manorial centres. The Vikings often chose them as military bases in the late ninth century, but the sites were already fortified by this date. A single spinal street normally links the burh, bridge and market areas, although the Mercian burhs may have lacked the regular planned street systems which have been observed in the burhs of Wessex. Initially, the interiors may have remained fairly open, with intensive occupation only dating from the later tenth century. For their defence they would have relied upon a peasant militia derived from the countryside rather than from within the town.

Traces of early defences at Hereford, and perhaps Tamworth, demonstrate the role of Mercia in the evolution of the Anglo-Saxon town. The town of Hereford commands a strategic crossing point on the river Wye; its name means literally 'the ford of the army'. The town lies on the north bank of the river, where a gravel and clay rampart of the mid-ninth century appears to have enclosed a rectangular area of 13.6 ha (33 acres), incorporating the minster church in its south-east quarter. In the early tenth century, possibly at the instigation of Queen Æthelflaed in 914, the walls were extended eastwards to enclose suburban growth across a 21-ha (50-acre) area, and improved with timber revetments at front and rear. Finally, c.930 the front timber facing was replaced by a stone wall, 2 m (6½ ft) thick, and 2 m high, with a slighter wall at the rear, and a fighting platform 4 m (13 ft) wide.

The Anglo-Saxon Chronicle records that in 913 Æthelflaed 'went with all the Mercians to Tamworth and built the borough there in the early summer'. This has been identified as a 20-ha (50-acre) site of similar plan to Hereford, with a V-shaped ditch and a rampart of turf and stone separated from the ditch by a wide berm. There is also evidence for a metalled intervallum road behind the rampart, and a bridge to carry the rampart walk over the gateway. As at Hereford, there are archaeological traces of an earlier defence of slighter construction, although this might just be the boundary of a Mercian royal palace, as there is nothing to link it to the burh street system.

We are told that Stafford was also fortified in 913, although excavations have failed to reveal the burh defences. In fact, Stafford has been described as a thinly disguised expansion of a rural manor. In the tenth century there was no regular street grid and no evidence for planned tenements. The central enclave appears to have contained only the minster church and three centralized crafts: butchery, bread making and pottery manufacture. The burh may have functioned as a collecting station for the agricultural wealth of the neighbourhood. Stafford ware pottery was exported to other Mercian centres (see 54), but there was no evidence of any other commerce.

Gloucester may also have been founded as a Mercian burh, although it is not listed as such.

27 *Plans of Mercian burhs at Gloucester, Chester, Tamworth and Hereford.*

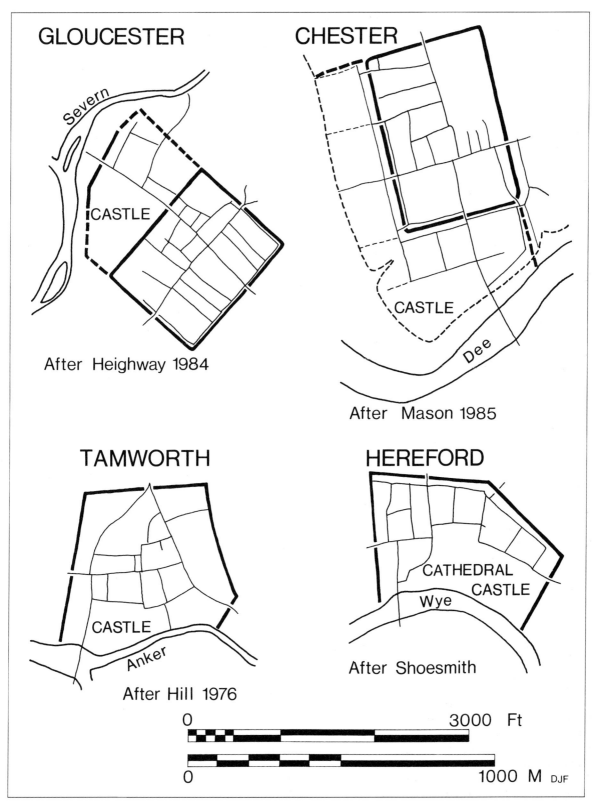

GLOUCESTER

Severn

CASTLE

After Heighway 1984

CHESTER

CASTLE

Dee

After Mason 1985

TAMWORTH

CASTLE

Anker

After Hill 1976

HEREFORD

CATHEDRAL

CASTLE

Wye

After Shoesmith

0   3000 Ft

0   1000 M DJF

From the sixth to the ninth centuries the shell of the Roman town sheltered a much-reduced population, probably working a number of rural holdings both within and outside the walls. The rapid build-up of deposits in the old forum area in the ninth century suggests that animals were stabled here. The people of Gloucester used no pottery, and wooden and leather containers were ubiquitous. They imported little from elsewhere, and the settlement at this stage should probably be seen as a series of small estates rather than an urban development. In 877 the remnants of the Danish army were able to camp within the town. In the tenth century, however, Gloucester suddenly acquired an administrative and military status. A substantial Saxon timber palace was built on the site of the Roman cemetery at Kingsholm, and the Mercian Council assembled here in 896. At about the same time St Oswald's Minster was founded, and in 914 the inhabitants of Gloucester fended off a Viking attack. Aspects of the street plan may demonstrate an element of planning, with a possible tenth-century surface in the intramural St Aldate Street. The Roman walls were refurbished on the east, south and along part of the north but apparently not to the west, where the city had crossed the Roman boundary and extended down to the river.

A similar picture of tenth-century revival is emerging from Chester (**colour plate 6**). The Anglo-Saxon Chronicle records that in 894 the Danes 'marched without a halt by day and night, until they arrived at a deserted Roman site in Wirral, called Chester. The [English] levies were unable to overtake them before they got inside the fort, but they besieged it some two days.' The Roman defences must have been largely intact if they could withstand a siege, and in 907 the north and east walls were refurbished with timber by Æthelflaed and probably extended to the river Dee. An intramural gravel road was probably laid at the same time. Within the Roman fortress there were substantial upstanding Roman remains, which were re-utilized as the scale of occupation increased in the tenth century. At Princess Street a sunken building was built within the ruined walls of a Roman barrack block. At Abbey Green Roman buildings were stripped of reusable materials in the tenth and eleventh centuries and new buildings erected alongside. Tenth-century Chester became home to a multi-ethnic trading community, with a substantial Hiberno-Norse element, living by the river Dee to the south of the old legionary fortress. At Lower Bridge Street at least five cellared buildings were erected in the tenth century, and the area was resurfaced with sandstone chippings. Under Æthelstan Chester became the most important centre for coin production in England; 24 moneyers worked in the town from 924–39. The finds from Chester show a wide range of trading contacts, with jewellery in Irish, Viking and Anglo-Saxon styles.

The burhs of Wessex

In Wessex the Vikings also provided a major stimulus to the development of towns. It is thought that Ælfred, as a means of defence against Viking raiding parties, established a network of burhs such that no part of his kingdom was more than 32 km (20 miles) from a burh (see **22**). When Edward the Elder reconquered England in 911–19 he extended the network and fortified a number of new sites.

The Burghal Hidage, a document of c.914–18, lists those burhs defending the coasts and frontiers of Wessex south of the Thames in the later years of the reign of Edward the Elder. It catalogues 30 burhs within Wessex, and a further three outside the kingdom. London is omitted, as it was technically part of Mercia; Kent is also excluded. The Hidage gives a tax assessment for each burh based upon the extent of its perimeter defences. There are two groups: those generally with a large hidage which were planned as permanent settlements and market centres, and whose streets still display traces of the original planned layout; and a second class of temporary forts which were comparatively small (less than 6.5 ha (16 acres)) and were not regularly planned. Only the first category became towns; the second group generally no longer existed by Domesday, and were probably dismantled during the reign of Æthelstan. Most of the burghal forts withered after performing their defensive role although their market function was often transferred to another site, such as from Eashing to Guildford.

Outside Wessex mention should also be made of several Viking Age towns in Kent which were not included in the Burghal Hidage, but appear to have performed similar functions to the Wessex burhs. These include the Roman walled towns at Canterbury and Rochester and the wics at Sandwich and Fordwich, as well as the sea ports of Dover, Romney and Hythe.

Where Iron Age or Roman fortifications survived, burhs were often established within the earlier defences. At Pilton and Halwell Iron Age earthworks were probably refortified; at South Cadbury the hillfort was reoccupied. In Bath, Chichester, Exeter, Portchester, Southampton and Winchester the burhs made use of surviving Roman stone walls and gates. At Bath and Winchester there is evidence that the outer ditch may have been recut during the Viking Age.

Natural defences were also utilized. A large number of burhs were established on promontory or peninsular sites, frequently controlling access from the sea. These sites include Axbridge, Langport, Lyng and Watchet in Somerset, Bredy (probably Bridport), Shaftesbury and Twynham (or Christchurch) in Dorset, Burpham and Eashing (Surrey), Malmesbury and Wilton (Wiltshire), Lewes (East Sussex), Lydford (Devon) and *Eorpeburnan* (probably Newenden) in Kent. At Sashes (Berkshire) a fort was established on an island in the Thames. Many of these burhs were small in extent or low in relief, but made use of natural defences such as marshland, streams or steep slopes and therefore had an irregular plan. The main access was usually from one direction only, and this was where the man-made defences were constructed. Lydford was sited on a wedge-shaped promotory; it was flanked by a gorge on two sides and a narrow valley on the third; the exposed side was defended by a bank c.12 m (40 ft) wide and a ditch 200 m (650 ft) in length, with a central gate.

Elsewhere new towns were created on open sites and provided with rectangular perimeter defences modelled on Roman forts (28). This group comprises Cricklade (Wiltshire), Oxford, Wallingford (Oxfordshire) and Wareham (Dorset). These burhs were often established on river sites, either controlling a river crossing as at Wallingford, or where the river ceased to be navigable as at Cricklade.

Burhs were also sited where there was already a concentration of settlement, such as around an estate centre or minster church (see Chapter 9), as at Cricklade, Malmesbury, Shaftesbury, Wareham or Wilton. These were already proto-urban sites, providing a focus for a non-agricultural population and acting as administrative, fiscal, religious and ceremonial centres, frequently with the association of a royal palace and minster church.

28 *Aerial view of Wallingford: the rectangular outline of the burh can still be clearly seen (Copyright reserved: Cambridge University Committee for Aerial Photography).*

The Saxon defences follow a common pattern (29). The ramparts were of dump construction, initially of clay or clay and turves, with varying amounts of wooden reinforcement. They were scarped at the front and sloped at the rear; a height of 2–3 m (6–10 ft) and a width of 9–12 m (30–40 ft) were normal; presumably they were crowned with timber palisades. This first defensive phase is usually assumed to be Ælfredian, although the archaeological evidence usually only proves that they are post-Roman, and they could have been constructed before Ælfred's reign.

At many burhs there is a second rampart phase, in which a stone wall was added to the bank to replace the timber palisade in the late tenth or early eleventh centuries. In some cases only a single wall has been observed, to the rear of the crest, but this may represent the rearward revetment of a fighting platform whose front wall provided a new stone facing to the rampart. South Cadbury (Somerset) is the only burh where the bank and wall are contemporary. An eleventh-century rampart was erected over the earlier Iron Age hillfort bank and faced with a mortared masonry wall. A substantial stone gatehouse was built at the south-west entrance; a bridge carried the wall

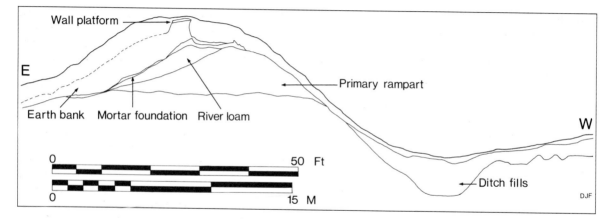

29 *Section of burh rampart, Wareham: a stone wall was added to the clay rampart during the late tenth or early eleventh centuries, probably replacing an earlier timber palisade.*

walk over the entrance. South Cadbury appears to have been founded as an emergency measure in the early eleventh century and designed to put at least one English mint in a place of safety.

Beyond the rampart it is likely that most burhs were also defended by a sequence of ditches, following the Roman fashion. These have been observed at Wareham, Cricklade, Lydford, Oxford and Twynham. At Cricklade an elaborate triple ditch system comprised two smaller ditches and a wide outer ditch outside the rampart, separated from it by a 6-m (20-ft) wide berm. This may have been the standard pattern, although excavations have rarely uncovered such an extensive area.

Finally, it appears that the defences of some burhs were razed in the eleventh century. At Cricklade, Lydford, South Cadbury and Wareham the walls were systematically destroyed and the ditches filled in, probably at the command of Knutr in order to consolidate his position after he became a king in 1016.

Within the walls evidence for deliberate and regular town planning has been recovered from those burhs which were established as permanent settlements. Land ownership was as much an issue in the towns as it was in the countryside; rectilinear street systems and property boundaries testify to the laying out of individual tenements under private ownership. Land was parcelled out, initially in large blocks, each representing small estates. As towns became more successful these plots were subdivided, each division retaining a valuable bit of street front, the tenements developing into long narrow strips. At first, however, many burhs may have contained many open spaces; areas of Chichester, Cricklade, Twynham, Wallingford and Wareham retained a rural character well into the tenth century.

At Winchester the rectilinear street plan was laid out in the 880s or early 890s. It has been calculated that there were some 8.6 km ($5\frac{1}{2}$ miles) of streets in Winchester, requiring some 8000 tonnes of flint cobbles to surface them. The High Street provided a major east–west thoroughfare; a back street running parallel to it on either side provided access to the rear of the properties. There were also regularly spaced north–south streets at right angles to the High Street and an intramural wall street. This last feature is not found in Roman towns, but was integral with the laying out of the burhs. In Winchester and Lydford individual tenements were marked by ditches; in Durham, Oxford and York wattle fences seem to have been the norm. It has been demonstrated that the systematic division of land associated with the laying out of the burhs was frequently conducted on the basis of a 4-pole unit (where 1 pole = 5 m or $16\frac{1}{2}$ ft), and these units have been observed at Chichester, Colchester, Cricklade, London, Wareham, Wallingford as well as Winchester.

The fortified burhs provided not only a haven for trade and industry but also a market for its products, and for materials and produce imported from the hinterland. Corn driers at Wallingford demonstrate that it functioned as an agricultural centre, perhaps a market town. Lydford may have been set up as a market centre for tin coming from Dartmoor. Axbridge,

Langport and Watchet each developed as small defended markets for adjacent royal estates. Winchester, unlike the earlier Hamwic, was part of a ranked hierarchy of markets, although it was the only major burh in Hampshire; others may have been deliberately supressed to remove competition. Streams running through the town provided useful resources for industry. By the end of the tenth century a number of specialized activities had developed in different sectors, reflected in street names like Tanner Street, Fleshmonger Street and Shieldwright Street. The south-east quarter appears to have been a royal and ecclesiastical centre; a stone-built tower set in an enclosure on Brook Street may have been a residential compound of an elite group, its architecture reflecting their classical aspirations.

The same spatial concentration of specialist crafts has been observed in York. In some cases the siting of industries may have been governed by the need for natural resources, such as water for tanning, but others may reflect an act of deliberate planning and organization. Markets were generally held outside the walls. At Cricklade there is some evidence for a market-place outside the west gate; in York the Scandinavian name Bootham may represent the position of market booths outside the city walls.

The Five Boroughs

There is some evidence for a well-defined group of towns in the East Midlands within the area of the Danelaw settled by the Viking Great Army. They are listed in the Anglo-Saxon Chronicle entry for 942 as comprising Derby, Leicester, Lincoln, Nottingham and Stamford (see **22**), although there is also a reference to Seven Boroughs, perhaps including Manchester and Doncaster or Torksey.

It was once believed that the Five Boroughs were specially fortified towns, established as an act of Danish policy after the partitions of 876–7, and used by Ælfred as a model for the Wessex burhs. However, they may not have become Danish strongholds until 910–20, which would mean that they were modelled upon the Wessex burhs, rather than vice versa.

The sites have a number of features in common, including their position on navigable rivers or important prehistoric or Roman land routes. Derby (Little Chester), Leicester and Lincoln had each been Roman fortifications. In Leicester the Viking Age defences probably utilized the Roman walls and ditches. In Lincoln the Roman walls continued to define a defended area, although there is no evidence for Viking Age modification. Certainly many Roman buildings were still standing in the ninth century and some were demolished when the Viking Age town was built.

By comparison with the burhs of Wessex the Five Boroughs were of a small-to-medium size. Derby may have been 29 ha (65 acres); Lincoln 38 ha (85 acres), if the Roman town was extended down to the river. Nottingham was 13.75 ha (31 acres), and at Stamford the northern burh covered only 6 ha (13 acres) and the southern one 3.75 ha (8½ acres).

All have traces of Middle Saxon occupation, probably as estate centres. In Derby (or Northworthy, as it was known before the Vikings changed its name) St Alkmund's Church was probably a Saxon minster associated with a royal or ecclesiastical estate centre. In Leicester, a Saxon minster church at Jewry Wall seems to have incorporated upstanding Roman masonry. In Lincoln there is evidence for activity in widely spread parts of the city from the fifth to the ninth centuries. The church of St Paul-in-the-Bail represents the continued existence of a religious centre in the heart of the Roman fortress.

At Nottingham and Stamford there is some evidence for Middle Saxon enclosures which pre-date the Viking takeover. The Viking army is described as wintering in a fortress at Nottingham in 868. In 918 Nottingham was captured by Edward, and two years later he built a second burh on the south bank of the river Trent opposite the Viking burh, connecting the two with a bridge. The northern burh was defended by a major ditch some 6 m (19½ ft) wide by 3.5 m (11 ft) deep. This had been recut at least once during the Viking Age, and the flattened U profile changed to a V, although it is not known exactly when.

At Stamford there is evidence of three concentric ditches below the bailey of the Norman castle, the innermost with a timber palisade. They enclosed an area of 1.1 ha (2½ acres), which is only about twice the size of the Viking fort at Repton, but could represent a Saxon estate centre similar to that at Goltho (see Chapter 3 above), a Viking temporary raiding base, or a Viking or Edwardian burh. The latter is more likely to be represented by a second defended enclosure recognized north of the

Welland. The Anglo-Saxon Chronicle records the submission of the Vikings in the northern burh in 918 and the construction of a second burh on the south bank, where another small enclosure has been found, as at Nottingham.

Whilst the Five Boroughs may have been occupied in the Middle Saxon period, none were urban sites before the Viking Age, although it has been suggested that the urban element was created by Edward the Elder in the early tenth century within the captured Viking fortresses.

So far there has been little success in finding Viking Age archaeological remains within Derby, although a cesspit and a rubble platform have been excavated within the Roman fort at Little Chester on the opposite bank of the Derwent, which may have been the Viking base. In Leicester the Southgate Street pottery kiln of the late tenth century suggests the town was a manufacturing and commercial centre, but no other evidence has so far been found.

The best evidence for urban activity within the Five Boroughs comes from Lincoln, where there was riverside activity and land reclamation in the tenth century and evidence for the establishment of a new street system on the Flaxengate and Michaelgate sites some time after the Viking takeover in 874. This lacks the regularity of the Wessex burhs, but still represents a planned development. The Flaxengate site must have been under common ownership, as extensive levelling dumps must represent coordinated building programmes. The earliest buildings were laid out with their long axes parallel to the street, perhaps suggesting that there was less pressure for space in Lincoln than elsewhere. Late ninth- and tenth-century buildings have also been excavated at Hungate and Michaelgate. However, sustained growth within Lincoln largely postdates the initial Viking settlement. The Flaxengate area may have received an initial boost in the late ninth century, but its real boom as an industrial centre belongs almost a century later, to the period c.960–1070, and especially c.960–1010 with the growth of the Lincoln mint. It was then that glass and copper-alloy working assumed industrial proportions, with specialized workshops, and that the Flaxengate development was extended into Grantham Street.

In Nottingham a number of Viking Age structures have been encountered at Drury Hill, Fishergate and Woolpack Lane, and pottery was being manufactured at Halifax Place. It has been argued, however, that urbanization did not take place until c.925–50, and industrialization not until c.1000.

In Stamford timber buildings have been found fronting onto the High Street, with wooden fences dividing one property from the next. Iron smelting and pottery production were important industries during the Viking Age, although both were dependent upon the rural hinterland for their raw materials. A grain-drying kiln found within the fortified enclosure beneath the medieval castle also suggests close links with the countryside. Within Stamford industrial activity was fairly loosely zoned, as at Thetford, and in contrast to Ipswich and Norwich where the potters were concentrated in one place.

Thus, although Scandinavians may have been responsible for establishing the Five Boroughs as fortified sites which, like the Wessex burhs, would develop into trading and industrial centres, it is unclear how far they were responsible for the development of town life within them.

There are possible Viking foundations at a number of other sites, including Thetford and Northampton. Thetford may have been a Middle Saxon royal or ecclesiastical estate centre, but was used as a wintering place for the Danish army in 869–70; this appears to have provided the main impetus for its development. It is connected by river to the Wash and the North Sea, and this favoured its growth as a trading town. The first defences were constructed on the south bank of the Little Ouse. Initially the interior was not fully occupied, but settlement expanded rapidly until it extended beyond the line of the defences in the late tenth century, eventually occupying an irregular area of some 60 ha (148 acres) south of the river and a further area of 15 ha (37 acres) to the north. The establishment of a bridgehead to control the river crossing is reminiscent of both Nottingham and Stamford.

The interior of the town was divided up into a number of properties demarcated by long boundary ditches, although the street frontages were not built up. Both sunken and surface buildings were erected within the properties, wells were sunk, and rubbish pits were dug along the boundaries. The dividing up or amalgamation of properties was common but the town retained an open plan and was never fully built up. It was originally suggested that industrial activity was zoned within the town, but later work has been less conclusive, with only the pottery kilns definitely concentrated in the north-west. Thetford gained a mint but never became an international trading port, and never imported pottery from the Continent. The town had declined by the Norman Conquest; the settlement south of the river was deserted in favour of the smaller settlement to the north.

In Northampton Middle Saxon occupation was restricted to an area of some 20 ha (49 acres) around St Peter's Church where a minster and palace may have acted as the centre of a royal estate. At St Peter's Street a timber hall was superseded by a massive stone hall of Carolingian style c.820–75. This palace may have been the centre of a royal estate which was broken up during the Danish settlement. It is possible that the stone hall was abandoned, and demolished, as a direct result of Danish occupation.

There is nothing in Northampton to imply urban status before the late ninth century. There was a dramatic intensification of activity, however, during the period of Danish occupation, between the late ninth century and the arrival of Edward the Elder in 917. An area of some 24 ha (59 acres) was enclosed by a wide ditch. Within this area there is no evidence for the deliberate laying out of a street plan, but a number of buildings were erected in a fairly loose settlement pattern comparable to that at Thetford. In the tenth century the town became the base for a large number of craftworkers, including those working in iron, copper and silver, bone and antler, and textiles. Although the site may have initially been chosen by the Danes as a military base, it rapidly developed into a town.

The Viking contribution to urbanism
Having examined the towns of Viking Age England, what was the Viking contribution to urbanism? The ninth and tenth centuries were times of urban expansion in England, even outside the areas of Viking influence. In the Isle of Man, which was devoid of towns, the Vikings founded no urban centres. In Ireland they imported an English form of town. In York

the Vikings may have contributed to the growth of the urban community, but are unlikely to have created it. Only in the case of Derby was the English name for the town changed to a Scandinavian one. Nonetheless, the Vikings did provide an indirect stimulus to urban growth both in the defended sites which they set up and, perhaps more importantly, in those maintained against them.

The transition from wics to burhs reflects a fundamental change in the economic system. In the eighth century one means by which Anglo-Saxon kings maintained royal power was by restricting the activities of foreign traders and levying tolls on controlled exchange in wics. As power was consolidated amongst a few kingdoms there was a growing need for systems of administration and control. The role of kings in the development of towns was partly passive; royal minsters and estate administrative centres provided nuclei for settlements, markets and craftsmen. But the kings of Mercia and Wessex were also active in promoting the growth of towns. The burhs were instigated as a system of national defence, but they also had an economic role as market centres. Their ramparts excluded enemies, but also provided a means of regulating comings and goings. Royal attempts to control trade and channel it through these foundations were facilitated by the proliferation of a stable royal-controlled coinage. The First Law Code of Edward the Elder decreed that 'no one shall buy or sell except in a market town with the witness of the port-reeve and of other men of credit'. Æthelstan's Second Code stated that 'no one shall buy goods worth more than 20 pence, outside a town; but he shall buy within the town, in the presence of the port-reeve or some other trustworthy man'.

As towns developed, specialization increased, and the size of the non-agricultural population which had to be supported by the rural hinterland grew. The seizure of the countryside by Scandinavian settlers may have caused some of the rural dispossessed to seek new opportunities in towns. It may not be coincidence that the fastest-growing ninth-century towns were in those areas most affected by Scandinavian land-taking.

5
Buildings

Successive invasions of England have often led to sweeping changes in the appearance of settlements as the immigrants imported their preferred style of dwellings. For the Viking Age, however, it is difficult to identify any specifically Scandinavian-style buildings in England. There are no true longhouses with cattle byres at one end and dwelling space at the other, for example, such as have been excavated in Denmark. In York, the Viking town houses seem no different from what we would expect of the Anglo-Saxons; indeed it is impossible to say that the Coppergate buildings were home to Scandinavian rather than English craftworkers. There was also little regional variation, with differences being mainly determined by the availability of raw materials such as wood and stone rather than cultural factors. Nevertheless, it may be possible to detect some Scandinavian influence if we examine the forms of excavated buildings.

Timber buildings

Over most of lowland England timber was used for most secular buildings from the end of the Roman period until after the Norman Conquest. Stone was used for the construction of some important churches from the seventh century onwards, and by Ælfred's time some royal residences were built of stone; but although it might be used for ancillary features such as porches, it rarely had a structural role in either urban or rural housing. Indeed, the Anglo-Saxon verb used to refer to construction work in early documents is normally *timbran*.

Timber buildings may be classified into two main categories, according to whether they are ground-level or sunken structures. Ground-level buildings are found in both town and country, but unlike the Early Anglo-Saxon period, when it was common to find sunken workshops in most rural settlements, by the Viking Age the sunken buildings are found almost exclusively in towns, where they are often in equal numbers to the surface buildings. In London, for example, of traces of over 50 buildings of the ninth–twelfth centuries, 60 per cent were ground-level structures, and 40 per cent were sunken.

Ground-level buildings

A basic style of single-storey town house and workshop has now been identified in many Viking Age towns. In London the ground-level buildings are usually found with their gable ends fronting onto the streets, such as at Bow Lane, Botolph Lane and Milk Street. They are generally 4–5 m (13–16 ft) wide, following the width of the tenement plots, with a greater variation in length, ranging from 6.5–10 m (21–33 ft) (**30**). Most contained only one room; they had doors in the side and gable walls. At Coppergate, York, and Flaxengate, Lincoln the houses again occupied the street frontage plots. At Lincoln, there was some evidence for internal partitioning with a cross passage joining opposing doors in the middle of the long sides, following the rural fashion.

More substantial timber halls have been excavated at the high-status sites such as Cheddar, Faccombe, Goltho, North Elmham, Portchester and Raunds. The use of internal aisle posts to partition the interior of the larger halls into three aisles has been recognized at many of these sites. A substantial eleventh-century hall, 15×7.5 m (49×24 ft) has recently been excavated at Waltham Abbey (Essex). The hall has been described as Viking, although there

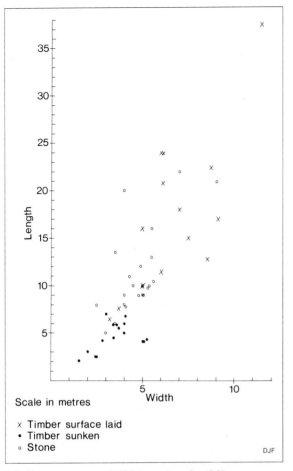

Scale in metres

x Timber surface laid
• Timber sunken
○ Stone

DJF

30 *Scattergram of Viking Age building dimensions.*

is nothing specifically Scandinavian about it. The position of the aisle posts was marked by clay foundations, but there was no trace of timber wall posts apart from continuous foundation trenches. It has been suggested that the hall had turf walls, but there is little evidence to support this interpretation. At Sulgrave, the eleventh-century timber-framed hall was erected on stone footings. It was divided into five bays, with a cobbled porch at one end and a central hearth. The service end, from which the meal was brought, was screened off; at the other end there was a two-storeyed chamber block. A detached timber building near the porch has been interpreted as the kitchen.

Bow-sided halls

A particular class of rectangular timber halls with bowed walls is often linked with Viking

influence. In fact they are part of a long building tradition which has a wide distribution, although they are associated particularly with Viking Age Denmark, and are also found in most of the areas settled by Scandinavians or under their direct influence. They are frequently identified as the houses of the rural aristocracy, and the building style may have been popular with a particular class of secular landowners which happened to be dominated by Scandinavians, rather than being specifically Viking.

Various theories have been propounded to explain their bow-sided plan. They are certainly not derived from upturned ships, as was once suggested; nor can they have been designed to provide protection against the wind, although the bow-sided structure does give some extra stability.

In England bow-sided halls have been found at Buckden (Cambridgeshire), Catholme, Cheddar, Goltho and Sulgrave, and there are smaller buildings which also have bowed sides at Chester, Durham, Nottingham and Thetford. A bow-sided building at St Neots with a planked floor over timber joists resting on sill beams has been interpreted as a granary, although it may simply be a medium-sized quality residence.

The ninth-century bow-sided halls at Cheddar and Goltho are both of similar plan and dimensions, 24 m (78 ft) long by 6 m ($19\frac{1}{2}$ ft) wide at the centre. In each case the wall posts were set in trenches, with evidence for stave walls at Goltho. At Cheddar the presence of double wall posts with the inner one sloping inwards has led to the suggestion that there was an upper storey whose floor was supported by the inner posts. At Goltho there was evidence that the hall was divided into three rooms, with a raised dais at one end and a cobbled hearth in the centre of the dais. Each hall had three doorways: at Goltho there was one at the east end of the hall, and one either side of the antechamber; at Cheddar there was also a pair of opposed doorways at one end of the hall, but the third appears to have provided access to the upper storey.

Sunken buildings

Sunken buildings are easy to recognize archaeologically as rectangular cuts into the ground surface. In London traces of 17 sunken buildings have now been excavated dating from the late ninth to the late eleventh centuries, and ranging between 2.8 and 5.6 m (9 and 18 ft) wide and 4.2 and 13.4 m (13 and 44 ft) long. There is also considerable variation in depth, between 0.41 and 2.3 m (16 and 90 ins.), and it is possible

31 *Plan of sunken building, Milk Street, London (after Vince 1990).*

to distinguish between two types of sunken buildings.

The first group, exemplified by the building excavated at Milk Street (**31**), have a floor *c*.0.5–1 m (1½–3 ft) below the ground level, and may be described as sunken-floored buildings. At Milk Street the upcast earth was piled against the outside wall and grassed over, providing a

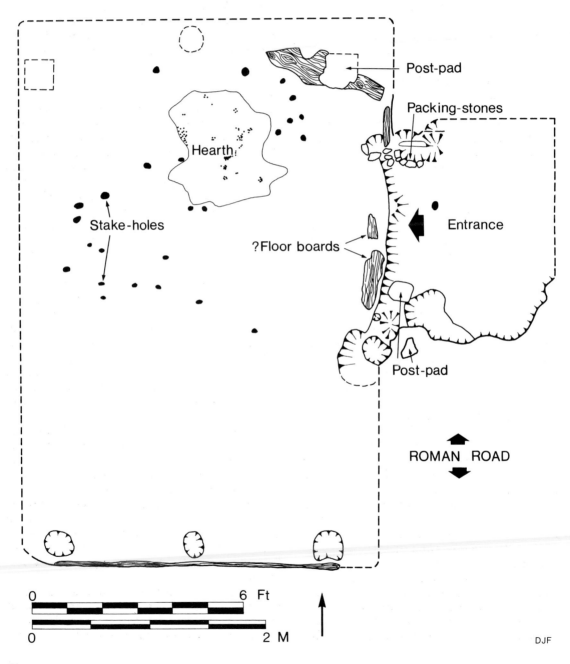

Post-pad

Packing-stones

Hearth

Stake-holes

?Floor boards

Entrance

Post-pad

ROMAN ROAD

0   6 Ft

0   2 M

DJF

wall up to 1 m ($3\frac{1}{4}$ ft) wide, and much like the stone and turf walls at sites such as Hound Tor and Hutholes in appearance. Another example is known from Lower Bridge Street, Chester, where Building 4 had a sunken floor only 0.84 m (34 ins.) below the ground surface, and must have been a single-storeyed semi-sunken building. Such sunken-floored buildings are known from the late ninth century onwards.

The second category of sunken building has a floor at c.1–2.5 m (3–9 ft) below the contemporary ground surface, and is more accurately described as a cellared building. These structures are often also distinguished by double linings of horizontal planks affixed to either side of the wall posts, and may have joisted floors. In York this new style of sunken building was introduced across the Coppergate site within a decade of 970, replacing the post-and-wattle structures. In London too, their introduction has been dated to the late tenth and early eleventh centuries. These deep-cellared buildings are invariably found away from the street frontages in London. No evidence of a hearth has been found in the cellars, which presumably must have been used for storage below a ground-level dwelling and workshop. At Wallingford and Oxford cellared buildings were laid out along the major street frontages by the early eleventh century. At Lower Bridge Street, Chester, three almost identical examples have been excavated. Each had a length–breadth ratio of 5:4 and was some 1.7–1.8 m (5–6 ft) deep, with the lower metre cut into solid bedrock. Post-holes indicated the position of timber walls around the cellars. The floors were planked across at ground level, with access to the cellar down a flight of steps from the outside (**32**). At Thetford there were traces of struts sloping in that could have supported the upper floor. At York there was no clear evidence for an upper storey but the comparative evidence from London and Chester begins to suggest that it was likely.

Sunken buildings are almost exclusively an urban phenomenon in the Viking Age and must have been built in response to particular needs. The sunken-floored type can be seen as developing out of a native tradition introduced into England by the Anglo-Saxons. They appear to have been mainly used as urban workshops, although there are a few rural examples such as the ninth-century sunken-floored bread oven at Fladbury (Hereford and Worcester). The

cellared buildings appear to be a response to developments within urban communities arising in the second half of the tenth century, probably the need to store goods in transit or stock-in-trade. The cellars would have provided cool and secure repositories for foodstuffs and other supplies, and appear to be associated with the tenth-century revival of trade and growth of trading towns (see Chapter 6). Cellared buildings also appear in Scandinavian towns such as Aarhus in Denmark in the tenth century, but it is not clear if they represent a specific Viking introduction to England or are simply part of a general north-west European development.

Foundations

Timber-framing, by which buildings are constructed around a timber frame held together by carpentered joints, was not widely used in England until after the Norman Conquest. The structural stability of Viking Age buildings therefore generally depended upon their foundation methods. The most common technique was to use earth-fast foundations. In some cases, as for the peasant houses at North Elmham and Barton Blount, the wall posts might still be set directly in the ground. In towns too, such as Lincoln and York, this was common practice, with posts sometimes driven into the ground as stakes, but more usually placed in post-holes packed with stones. Such posts often do not appear to have been set in pairs, but may sometimes have just acted as stiffeners for substantial cob or clay walls.

Increasingly, however, a continuous trench was dug along the wall lines and the vertical posts or staves set within it, following a technique developed at Middle Saxon sites such as Chalton and Maxey. During the Viking Age this 'post-in-trench' technique was utilized for major buildings at Cheddar, Goltho, Middle Harling (Norfolk), Portchester and North Elmham. At Catholme side walls were set in trenches, whilst the gable ends were supported by individual posts. Alternatively, individual post pits could be excavated to hold massive vertical timbers, each up to 0.6 m (2 ft) across, for substantial structures such as the West Hall at Cheddar.

During the Viking Age a foundation technique of using a 'sill beam' was introduced at urban sites such as Chester, York and London and in rural settings such as Buckden, North

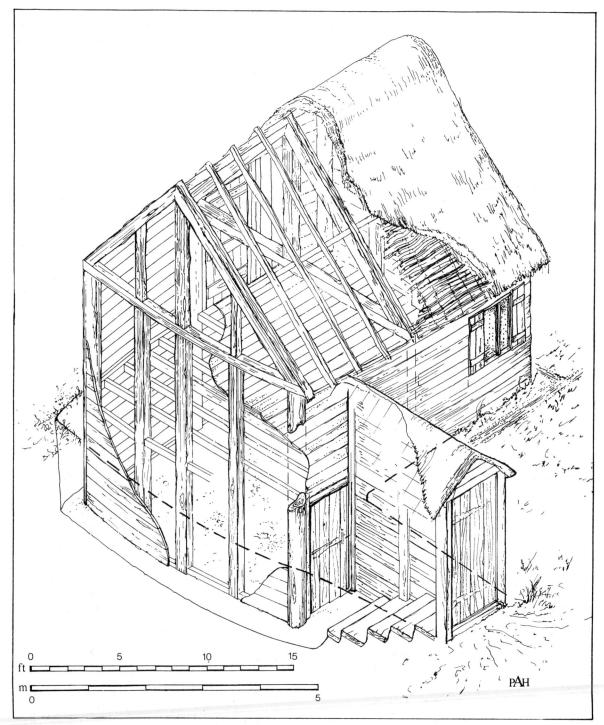

32 *An artist's reconstruction of a sunken building in Chester (P.H. Alebon; Chester City Council Archaeological Service).*

Elmham, Northolt (Middlesex), Portchester, St Neots, Sulgrave and Waltham Abbey. A sill beam is a horizontal beam which may be set in a foundation trench or placed directly on the ground surface. The wall posts rest upon it, and may be held in position by a raised timber lip or sill, or they may be set into the beam in rectangular sockets. At Coppergate, York massive oak beams up to 7 m (23 ft) long with raised sills were set in cuts up to 1.5 m (5 ft) deep as the foundations of the planked sunken buildings.

Another new technique, first used in the mid-tenth or early eleventh century in London, was to employ a foundation bed, such as a rubble platform or stone pads, to support the structural timbers. At Flaxengate, Lincoln, one building rested upon a single course of stone footings which may have supported a raised plank floor to lift perishable materials such as grain off the damp ground.

Walls

The most common walling material at the start of the Viking Age was probably wattlework, following a long Anglo-Saxon tradition. In York in the first half of the tenth century post-and-wattle was the standard method of building construction (33). At neither York nor Lincoln, however, has clay daub been found on the walls, and the small quantities present suggest it may only have been used for lining clay ovens. Clay and straw may also have been used to make cob walls. It is likely that fur or textile drapes may have been hung to cut out draughts. In York screens of woven willow twigs may have been used to provide wall insulation, or may have fallen from the loft.

Wattlework was inappropriate, however, as a walling material for the new class of sunken buildings, as it would have collapsed under the pressure of the surrounding earth. At both London and York wall cladding for the sunken buildings was provided by post-and-plank construction. At York the wall posts, carefully squared and regularly spaced at short intervals, supported layers of horizontal oak planks which were laid edge on edge (34). There was no evidence for the use of pegs, nails or joints in the lower 1.75 m ($5\frac{3}{4}$ ft) of the walls; apparently the planks were held in place against the

33 *Post-and-wattle wall, Coppergate, York (York Archaeological Trust).*

34 *Planked wall of a tenth-century sunken building, Coppergate, York (York Archaeological Trust).*

wall posts by the sill beam and the weight of surrounding earth. These posts appear to have been paired across the building and so were presumably held upright by tie-beams spanning the width of the building at the top of the walls. There are also instances of an inner skin of horizontal planks being fastened to the wall posts to provide a cavity wall (**35**).

Staves, or vertically set planks, first appear in London in the eleventh century, but have now been found earlier at other sites such as Goltho, where half sections of trees about 0.46 m (1½ ft) wide were set in a trench with their curving face outwards. The method is well known from Norwegian stave churches, and was adopted at St Andrew's, Greenstead-juxta-Ongar (Essex), although there is no evidence that its employment in England was due to Viking influence. At Goltho the two structural traditions of stave and post construction persisted side by side until after the Norman Conquest.

Any available wood seems to have been used for wall construction, with a clear preponderance of hazel for wattlework and oak for wall posts and planks, and then willow, alder and birch in descending order of importance. Where joints needed to be fixed, wooden pegs were apparently used more often than iron nails

Roofs, floors and internal fittings

For the smaller buildings roofs generally rested directly upon the walls, although for larger halls such as those at Cheddar and North Elmham their weight appears to have been borne by internal posts. Straw and hay may have been used for thatching, or in some areas turves may have been used. There is little evidence for wooden shingles although most of the hogbacks have shingled roofs.

Floors were most commonly of beaten earth or clay, but sand, gravel and mortar are also known. At Lincoln there was evidence of rushes and other grasses, and at Durham sedges, rushes, heather, bracken, meadowsweet and crowfoot were laid over the sand floor as a sweet-smelling covering which could be replaced before it became unpleasant. At Thetford the floor of one of the sunken buildings had been mortared; another was surfaced with closely packed cobbles. In York several buildings had plank floors resting on joists. At Coppergate the floorboards had been carefully cut to fit flush around the internal wall posts so as to lap against the wall (**36**).

Ground-level buildings generally had at least two entrances, sometimes protected by a

35 *(Above, right) A building with a cavity wall, Coppergate, York (York Archaeological Trust).*

36 *(Below, right) Planked floor, Coppergate, York (York Archaeological Trust).*

wooden porch, as at Portchester. The basements of sunken buildings could have been entered by an internal ladder, but many were entered directly from outside. In Ipswich, London and at the Clarendon Hotel site, Oxford earthen steps have been identified in shallow extensions. At Thetford the cellar of Building J was approached down a 5-m (16-ft)-long ramp revetted with posts. At Coppergate the sunken buildings were entered from the rear along rather grand sunken passageways revetted with stone (37), but may also have had a second entrance at the street front. At Chester each of the sunken buildings had a ramped extension some 2.5 m (8 ft) long cut into the solid rock. These would have been dangerously steep unless provided with a flight of wooden steps, and were probably covered by a porch to keep out the rain.

All buildings must have been provided with wooden doors, although they are rarely found.

37 *Stone-revetted entrance passage leading to a tenth-century sunken building, Coppergate, York (York Archaeological Trust).*

In London one was found lying in demolition debris. It comprised four vertical oak boards secured by diagonal battens on the inner face and fastened together with iron nails. The remains of iron hinges were also found. Various Viking Age lock mechanisms have been excavated, but may have originated from chests.

There is evidence for window glass from two London sunken buildings; but glass is otherwise rare outside of monastic sites, with no traces even on aristocratic sites such as Goltho: it may normally have been robbed as a precious commodity. From Coppergate the remains of a possible window shutter have been recovered. Internal lighting would have been provided by the hearth fire, and by small oil lamps. In the tenth and early eleventh centuries these are stone and pottery lamps with bases splayed to sit on the floor or in a niche on the wall.

All buildings normally had a central hearth, usually consisting of baked clay over a bed of stone. Pottery cooking vessels would be set in the embers. In York a number of industrial hearths, up to 1.2 × 1.8 m (4 × 6 ft) were found

positioned in the centre of the floor, and built one upon the other as the floor level rose (**38**). They had a clay base, of which only a small part was normally burnt, surrounded by a kerb of limestone blocks, reused Roman tile or wooden beams. Specialist kitchen buildings such as that at Goltho were often provided with ovens built of baked clay and wattle on a stone rubble base; in one London example the clay walls were supported by 33 angled stakes. At Portchester one even had a clay dome set on a base of reused Roman tile and lumps of limestone set in clay.

Many buildings presumably had internal timber fittings such as wall benches and beds, although remains are more common in stone buildings, where they survive incorporated in the stone structures. At Coppergate one building had rows of stakes running parallel to both side walls and 0.6 m (2 ft) from the walls for two thirds of the excavated length of the building; these probably represent wattlework revetting for earth-packed wall benches. Substantial pits were dug inside some of the York buildings; these were presumably used for storage, and were originally covered by planks. Storage of valuables would have been undertaken in sturdy wooden chests, with perishable goods

38 *Post-and-wattle buildings with central hearths, c.940, Coppergate, York (York Archaeological Trust).*

stored in pottery vessels. At Pudding Lane, London, two abandoned buildings had smashed fragments of large spouted storage jars lying on the floor.

The life expectancy of timber buildings generally appears to have been fairly short. From Cheddar, Lincoln, London and York there are consistent estimates for a life span of between 5 and 25 years, although one London example was still in use after 40. Floors could be resurfaced every 5–10 years, but wall posts set in earth may have quickly rotted. Fire seems to have been the major cause of destruction in towns, sweeping along rows of thatched houses and resulting in simultaneous redevelopment across a whole site. At Coppergate the positions of structures remained static for some 50 years, even though individual buildings were gutted by fire and totally rebuilt on several occasions. Developments in construction techniques appear to have occurred contemporaneously from tenement to tenement, suggesting that all four Coppergate tenements were under the control of one landlord, or that professional builders were hired to replace the street. At Durham and other sites the primitive nature of wattle construction has suggested that these buildings were DIY affairs. At aristocratic sites, however, where sophisticated stave and other techniques were used we can assume that skilled carpenters were employed.

Stone buildings

In the upland zone of England, in the south-west and in the Isle of Man stone was generally used as the basic building material, with wood reserved for the structural timbers and roof beams. In some areas this may have been determined by the shortage of suitable building timber compared with the availability of building stone, but this is not a full answer, and the reasons for the preference for stone may have been culturally as much as environmentally determined. Norse Vikings generally built their residences in stone; but the use of stone cannot be seen as a Viking trait in itself, as the native population in each of these areas also preferred stone.

The principal building at Ribblehead is in many respects a typical Norse dwelling, although in the absence of comparable sites it is impossible to determine if it is distinguishable in any way from pre-Viking buildings in the area. The hall is some 19 m (62 ft) long by 4 m (13 ft) wide, with walls 1.5–1.8 m (5–6 ft) thick (see **21**). The outer wall faces were marked with a line of boulders and the inner ones constructed of coursed limestone slabs, with limestone rubble and earth used to provide the wall filling and insulation against draughts. A wicker lining could have been used to provide extra protection. Sandstone was used for the hearth and oven. There was a low bench against the west wall in the lower half of the building. The roof timbers apparently came all the way down to the ground at the outer edges of the wall. The roofs may have been thatched or covered with turves, and extended down to the ground. The gable ends were provided with central paved doorways, and the buildings were linked by stone pathways. A walled porch gave the kitchen building extra protection against the wind.

Similar foundations of low stone walls were excavated at Simy Folds, although it was suggested that the walls may have been heightened with turf. Within the hall central paving would have provided footings for vertical posts which supported the ridge post for the rafters. The longhouses were the dwellings, with the smaller subrectangular buildings used for storage, as dairies or as workshops.

In the south-west a number of turf-walled houses have been excavated on Dartmoor. At Hound Tor and Hutholes small houses with turf walls and sunken floors were found beneath later longhouse settlements. The walls were up to 1.5 m (5 ft) thick and had been faced with wattles. The roofs were turf beneath wattle and thatch. The houses had opposed doorways and central hearths, but there was no indication of stalling for animals. They may have been occupied by herdsmen or women who grazed their stock on the open moorland pastures during the summer. Such structures would probably have a life span of 25–30 years on Dartmoor.

At Mawgan Porth the houses were built by stripping the hillside of its turf (which could then be used for roofing) and then terracing the house platforms into the hill to provide level foundations. On the uphill side of the site some of the rock was left upstanding to provide a base for the walls, which were on average 0.75 m (2½ ft) thick. The walls were built of facing stone with a rubble core, without mortar, although clay may have been used as a bonding material. The roofs were supported by timber uprights set in post-holes. The buildings were arranged round four sides of an open courtyard, with their doors opening off it. The principal buildings were of a shortened longhouse type, with both byre and living quarters under the same roof separated by a timber partition (**39**). The byre section had a drain in the floor. The living area was furnished with box beds set in the corners either side of the door, with further beds or benches along the walls. There was a hearth pit with four small stake-holes, possibly for an iron pot-support. The courtyard also had a roofed recess, possibly a dog kennel.

Similar buildings have been excavated on the Isle of Man, where they are assumed to be Viking. Indeed, the assignment of the turf-walled longhouse at Doarlish Cashen to the Viking Age rests on the fact that it is a longhouse with wall benches. Similar structures with wall benches, central hearths and opposed entrances have been recognized in the Norse promontory forts at Cronk ny Merriu and Cass ny Hawin.

A unique combination of bow-sided, rectangular and round stone buildings has been

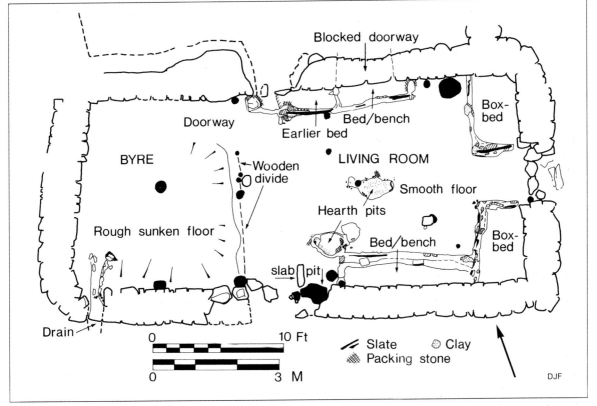

39 *Plan of a building at Mawgan Porth (Cornwall) (after Bruce-Mitford 1956).*

excavated at the Braaid, Isle of Man (**colour plate 4**). The bow-sided hall was a massive structure, 22 × 10 m (72 × 33 ft), whose stone-faced side walls have an earth core. There was little trace of gable walls, however, and these must have been of timber. The rectangular building was interpreted as a stable or byre, although the discovery of internal hearths makes this unlikely. The round stone structure, 15 m (49 ft) in diameter, had originally been interpreted as a stone circle, but the excavation of hearths and wall infill demonstrates that it was a roundhouse. The excavator believed that since it was circular it must be a native Celtic structure, and was forced to assume that it had been abandoned before the Viking settlement, as it was unthinkable that Vikings and Manx should have lived as neighbours. If this were so, however, one would expect it to have been robbed as a convenient source of stone, yet today it survives as well as the other two buildings. Moreover, if the roundhouse site had been deserted, it seems a coincidence that the

later buildings should be placed adjacent to it. It seems more likely, therefore, that all three buildings were occupied at the same time. It is probably simplistic to assume that round buildings must be native whilst rectangular ones are Viking. Medieval roundhouses excavated by Bersu in County Antrim produced Scandinavian-style objects, and there seems no reason why the round building at the Braaid could not have provided some particular function for Norse settlers, even if its construction was influenced by native practice.

In conclusion, it is difficult to recognize anything specifically Viking about the Viking Age buildings of England and the Isle of Man. In general the Scandinavian incomers appear to have adopted native building styles, as there was no reason for them to import their own, although the peculiar class of bow-sided halls might have been a result of Scandinavian influence. Certainly the social and economic changes of the Viking Age led to rapid developments in building technology, with the introduction of new foundation methods such as sill beams, and new types of structure such as cellared buildings.

6
Agriculture

It has been estimated that the population of England may have doubled between the time of Ælfred and the Domesday Book, increasing from less than one million to almost two million. At the same time a larger proportion of people became less self-sufficient, with increasing numbers living and working in towns. Substantial agricultural expansion would have been necessary to support these changes.

Evidence from throughout England shows that during the Viking Age there was a massive increase in the area farmed, with marginal land being taken under cultivation. These changes were aided by improved climatic conditions in the late ninth and tenth centuries, with shorter and milder winters, and longer and warmer summers. The Cambridgeshire Fens were first farmed in the tenth and eleventh centuries, and in Warwickshire there was clearance of woodland from marginal land which in many cases had lain deserted since the Roman period. Both the Peak District and the Yorkshire Dales were recolonized with upland farms such as Ribblehead (see Chapter 3), and there is pollen evidence for vigorous clearance on Fellend Moss and Steng Moss in the mid and late tenth century. On Dartmoor Viking Age farming was being undertaken at sites such as Holne Moor. On the Isle of Man there were new Norse upland settlements such as Doarlish Cashen, and ploughing of new land, as preserved under the burial mound at Cronk Mooar (see **66**). In places such as Gwithian a heavy plough capable of turning a furrow was in use by the tenth century.

The lowland zone continued to be intensively farmed. The area around York, for instance, was already extensively deforested and had become largely agricultural by the start of the Viking Age, with a mixture of arable and pastureland and areas of woodland, some exploited for timber or as coppice for wattle hurdles and fences. Areas of woodland and marsh, some quite close to the town, may have been used primarily for hunting.

The degree to which new farming practices were introduced by Viking settlers remains uncertain. The origins of the open field system of agriculture is a complex question, and one to which there may be no single answer for the whole country. It was certainly in use by the twelfth century, but may have been introduced in the Anglo-Saxon or Viking Age, or after the Norman Conquest. It has been argued that the medieval open field system was introduced in parts of eastern England in the ninth and tenth centuries. As we have seen (see Chapter 3), this was the period in which great estates were being broken up over much of the country, new settlements were being formed, and village tenements were being laid out, although the Vikings were just part of this process.

Plants and cereals

The four main cereals grown over much of Viking Age England appear to have been wheat, barley, oats and rye. Wheat was grown for flour for bread, barley for brewing, and oats may have been used for animal fodder, as well as for porridge. There were some changes from the Roman period in species grown, with the more primitive spelt wheat being less popular. Various legumes and flax and hemp were also cultivated. Apples, sloes, plums, bilberries, blackberries and raspberries were the main fruits consumed; a ninth-century pit from Gloucester full of a residue of apple pips from cider making suggests that apples were not only eaten. Hazelnuts and walnuts were also eaten; linseed and helpseed were probably used for oil. In London figs and grapes were imported in small quantities, although hops, which were presumably brought in for brewing, were relatively abundant.

Most houses, even in towns, seem to have had a quernstone with which to grind their own grain to make bread. The degree of tooth wear common in the period suggests that this was fairly coarse! There is no evidence for windmills before the twelfth century, but a number of earlier water-mills have been excavated, including an eighth- or ninth-century example at Tamworth. Such mills would have been used to process the rents of royal and manorial estates. At Old Windsor (Berkshire) there was a large and sophisticated water-mill with three vertical wheels. Traces of a stone building with glazed windows and a tiled roof nearby may represent the remains of the royal manor. The mill was totally destroyed by fire in either the late ninth or early tenth century, possibly during a Viking raid. The site was devastated and the mill leat filled in; a second mill with a smaller leat and a Norse-style horizontal wheel was constructed later in the tenth century, and continued in use until the early eleventh.

It is unlikely that the Vikings had much effect upon animal husbandry. There is nothing particularly Scandinavian about the bone assemblage at Coppergate, for example, and nothing to suggest the introduction of Scandinavian stock. Nevertheless, there were developments in animal husbandry during the Viking Age in response to general economic trends, and changes, in particular, in the relative importance of various farm animals (40).

Cattle

Cattle bones are predominant on all Viking Age sites, within and outside the Danelaw, and beef and dairy products would have been the dietary mainstays throughout England. A particularly high proportion of cattle bones has been observed in excavated Viking settlements, namely York, Dublin and Lincoln. We know that the keeping of cattle was culturally important to Viking settlers, and Viking immigrants in Greenland and Iceland stubbornly hung on to their cattle herds despite the climatic and environmental difficulties. Neverthe-

less, variations in stock-breeding strategies in England are more likely to have been dictated by local agricultural and economic circumstances than by ethnic affiliations.

Cattle provided most meat in the diet at sites as far apart as Mawgan Porth, Portchester, Cheddar, North Elmham and York. At Flaxengate it has been calculated that cattle provided over 75 per cent of the meat diet. At Coppergate cattle appear to have been brought in on the hoof as required and slaughtered on site, whereas in Durham and Cheddar meat was obtained ready-butchered.

In York the cattle were killed by a blow to the head and butchered in a clumsy and unsystematic fashion which is inconsistent with specialist butchers, in contrast to the Roman period. Evidence from Lincoln suggests that the carcasses were butchered on the floor; they were only hung from timber beams from the eleventh century onwards. There was no careful selection of cattle of a particular age; most were youngish adults, suggesting that cattle had a multipurpose role as milk producers and draught animals as well as sources of meat. On rural sites oxen would also have been important for pulling the heavy plough.

Sheep and goats

Sheep farming was England's major industry during the Viking Age, but sheep were kept mainly as a source of wool and only secondarily for their meat. Woollen cloth had been a major export from early times. A famous letter of complaint from Charlemagne to Offa of 796 mentions the import of woollen cloaks to France: 'Our people make a demand about the size of the cloaks, that you may order them to be such as used to come to us in former times.'

At North Elmham more sheep bones were found than anything else, but most were from mature animals, indicating that they were being kept for their wool. At Portchester there was a steady increase in the importance of sheep throughout the Saxon period, with animals also being kept until they were older. During the tenth century sheep coming to slaughter at Flaxengate were drawn from stock being kept for their milk and wool, but during the eleventh century younger animals bred for their meat were slaughtered.

In York sheep were mainly selected for slaughter between the ages of 18 months and 4 years. In other words, some were being killed

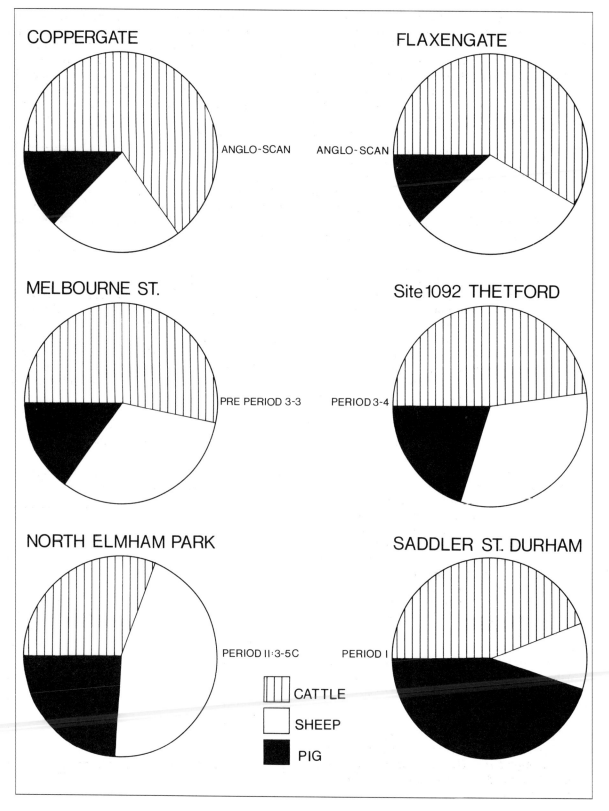

COPPERGATE

ANGLO-SCAN

FLAXENGATE

ANGLO-SCAN

MELBOURNE ST.

PRE PERIOD 3-3

Site 1092 THETFORD

PERIOD 3-4

NORTH ELMHAM PARK

PERIOD II·3-5C

SADDLER ST. DURHAM

PERIOD I

CATTLE

SHEEP

PIG

after one year's woolclip whilst others were kept for breeding. There is a similar range of fleeces from London and York. Most are from sheep of fairly primitive character with 'hairy' or 'hairy medium' fleeces. There is a higher proportion of hairy sheep in the Viking Age than in Roman Britain and earlier Anglo-Saxon England, but it is not clear that these were introduced by the Vikings, as they are not limited to the Scandinavian area of influence. Nevertheless, in London there was a lower percentage of hairy sheep in the tenth and eleventh centuries than in York, where the proportion was closer to that observed on Norse sites in Scotland. Viking Age sheep mainly had white fleeces, although the wool was frequently dyed.

In Lincoln there was a marked increase in the proportion of sheep after the mid-tenth century, and a corresponding decline in the number of cattle. This change was not observed in York, where the percentage of sheep is generally lower. The Vale of York is a flat, low-lying area subject to flooding, whereas Lincoln is on a limestone escarpment, with rolling chalk hills a few miles to the east. Thus the Vale would have been good cattle country in the Viking Age, with sheep being important on the thinner and drier chalk and limestone soils of the Wolds, 20 km (12 miles) from the city. Sheep would have been important in the more immediate hinterland of Lincoln, and the development of settlements in the Wolds in the Viking Age (see Chapter 3) may reflect the growing significance of sheep farming.

Small numbers of goats were also kept in the York area, but formed a minor part of the diet and were principally bred for dairying. The lack of goat bones at Coppergate implies that dairy production was not carried out on a house-by-house basis, but rather that a few suppliers traded milk and cheese in quantity.

Pigs

Viking Age pigs were small dark-skinned hairy beasts with relatively long legs. They were the only animals which could be kept in towns, and so played a significant part in the urban diet.

40 *(Left) Relative proportions of animal bones at urban sites: Coppergate, York; Flaxengate, Lincoln; Melbourne Street, Southampton; Site 1092, Thetford; North Elmham Park; Saddler Street, Durham.*

They were well suited to being fattened and bred in wattle pens in the backyards of urban tenements, although households often probably obtained a pregnant sow from rural farmers. At Coppergate there was a relative increase in the number of pig bones through the Viking Age, and a corresponding decline in cattle bones. At Flaxengate the proportion of pig is fairly constant throughout, unlike cattle and sheep which fluctuate in the tenth century. In Durham it has been suggested that the town residents allowed their pigs to forage in nearby woodland. In the countryside huge herds of pigs may have roamed free-range. In a ninth-century will Ealdorman Ælfred of Surrey bequeathed 2000 pigs to his wife. At Portchester, pigs provided 20 per cent of the diet.

Horses and other animals

Horses were considered to be particularly valuable animals during the Viking Age (**41**). They provided only an occasional minor part of diet (at Portchester less than 2 per cent), but were a high-status means of transport and warfare, as attested by the number of spurs and harness fittings from graves and other ritual deposits (see Chapter 10).

Deer may have been more important as a source of antler than as potential meat and in York most was collected as shed antler over

41 *London compensation rates for the death of animals in the reign of King Æthelstan.*

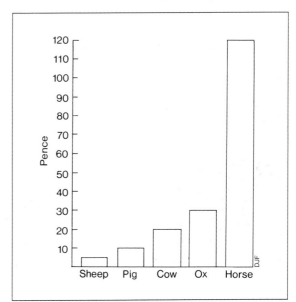

the winter months. At aristocratic sites with access to hunting forests, such as Cheddar and Portchester, or isolated sites with local wild herds, such as Ribblehead, venison provided an occasional part of the diet.

Cats appear to have been tolerated, but were not looked after as pets. Cat skins were routinely collected. At Thetford the remains of some 18 cats and kittens were found in one pit. Dogs were more abundant and better looked after; at Coppergate, Flaxengate and Thetford there was little evidence for disease or injury on any dog bones. In Lincoln and York they ranged in size from those smaller than a fox to those as big as a wolf, and may have been kept as pets, as guard dogs or for hunting. British hunting dogs were famous, and frequently presented as diplomatic gifts in the Viking Age. William of Malmesbury's description of the Welsh tribute to Æthelstan included as many dogs as the king chose 'which could discover with their keen scent the dens and lurking places of wild beasts'. At Thetford all the dogs were of the hound type with relatively long muzzles, and most were the size of a present-day retriever. Some may also have been used as shepherd dogs. At Portchester the absence of dog bones in the domestic refuse has led to the suggestion that the dogs were so highly regarded that they were buried separately.

In towns game animals were relatively rare, but on rural sites such as Ribblehead foxes and hares may have provided a significant supplement to the diet. Certainly the workshops and domestic buildings of the urban centres provided homes for house mice, whilst rats exploited the fringes of the settlements.

Birds

Geese, ducks and chicken were important in both town and country, and were kept around the houses for both meat and eggs. At Portchester the remains of over 80 chickens and 30 geese were excavated, but the chickens appear to have been kept largely for their eggs.

Game birds are also found in rural and urban deposits, although in York wild birds were never a significant component of the diet, except in so far as they contributed variety. From the late tenth to the early eleventh centuries an increasing diversity of birds was brought to Coppergate. They were mainly wetland species, with some woodland birds such as wood pigeon and woodcock, moorland birds including golden plover and black grouse, and cliff-nesting coastal birds such as guillemot and razor-bill. The latter must have been brought from at least 50 km (31 miles) away.

At Portchester the remains of numerous wading birds, including golden plover, dunlin, redshank, curlew and woodcock must represent extensive exploitation of the mud-flats. Game birds were considered part of the lordly diet; the remains of 11 curlews in one pit may indicate the leftovers from just one feast. The proportion of birds, particularly ducks, in the York Minster assemblage may reflect the higher status of the site compared to Coppergate.

Marine resources

Clearly seafood was particularly important at coastal settlements such as Mawgan Porth, Green Shiel and Sandtun (Kent). On Lindisfarne finds included whale and seal; they may have been hunted, but are more likely to represent the exploitation of chance strandings on a nearby beach.

Freshwater fish were also exploited. At Colwick near Nottingham traces of a Viking Age fishing weir have been discovered. In York the freshwater species included pike, roach, rudd, bream and perch, and especially eels, which could be obtained within or near the town. Fish-hooks from Coppergate and Billingsgate suggest that the inhabitants caught many of their own fish, using a long line. In both London and York, however, there is a common pattern in the early eleventh century, with a shift away from the local river resources in favour of the sea. This may be linked to the increased pollution of the rivers as the urban centres expanded. In York there is a decrease in the proportion of salmon and an increase in cod, with herring, haddock, flat-fish, ling and mackerel also being caught. In Lincoln cod, haddock and flat-fish were being brought in from the coast. In Northampton, herring were imported from the coast.

Shellfish were also widely eaten. In York oysters were eaten in substantial quantities, and cockles, mussels and winkles were gathered in smaller proportions. At Thetford mussels, cockles, winkles and whelks were eaten, and oysters, winkles and mussels at Lindisfarne. The inhabitants of Mawgan Porth ate mussels and snails, keeping them unopened in water tanks constructed of slate slabs.

In summary, the inhabitants of Viking Age England enjoyed a reasonably varied diet, with differences in emphasis according to what was available locally. As might be expected, there was more variety on rural sites, but 'exotic' foods were also brought to the Viking towns from some distance. The Viking settlement led to no major changes in the animals kept or crops grown, but as the population expanded so agriculture was forced to intensify.

7

Craft and industry

During the Viking Age the manufacture of basic items such as pottery and iron tools underwent such dramatic changes that it is possible to talk of a 'first Industrial Revolution'. Industrial production on any scale had disappeared in England before the end of the Roman occupation although specialized rural crafts survived under the patronage of kings and later of the Church. Items of fine jewellery circulated as gifts and tribute, rather than being bought and sold in the market-place. Palace sites such as Cheddar also served as centres for craft specialists working in precious metals. Manorial sites often maintained control of rural resources, with weaving at Goltho, gold and silver working at Faccombe, and mass-produced bone tools at Portchester. As urban markets developed, however, they drew craft-workers to them, and acted as centres for the exchange not only of products, but also of ideas. From the early ninth century there were experiments in methods of manufacture, and a trend towards greater standardization which allowed increased productivity. From the late ninth to early tenth century industrial production was revived across a wide range of crafts.

Pottery

Pottery is a very durable artefact and will always survive wherever it is used. The development of the pottery industry during the Viking Age provides a useful index to the process of industrialization.

In the early ninth century no pottery was used over much of the West Midlands and south-west England. In other areas, including Lincoln, York and London, crude pottery was manufactured locally by hand, without the use of a fast wheel, and fired on a bonfire. Only at Ipswich in East Anglia was kiln-fired pottery produced on an industrial scale and traded both overland and along the coast from Yorkshire to Kent.

From the middle decades of the ninth century changes began to occur at a number of centres. These developments cannot be attributed to Viking settlers as they were under way before their arrival. They may be associated with increased marketing opportunities developing in the ninth century. In York we see the first steps towards a specialized industry with handmade wares now produced in standardized forms and fabrics. In the East Midlands potters introduced a new technique using a mould to produce vessels in order to increase their production. In East Anglia the Ipswich potters began to use a wheel to make cooking pots in a sandy fabric on a large scale in what is known as the Thetford tradition.

By 900 wheel-thrown pottery was manufactured over much of eastern England. The manufacture of Thetford-type wares soon spread to other East Anglian towns, and tenth-century kilns have been excavated in Pottergate, Norwich and in Thetford itself. York was producing wheel-thrown pottery by the beginning of the tenth century, and Lincoln by the mid-tenth century. In York wheel-thrown pottery fired at a high temperature developed from the local handmade types. The simple York ware cooking pots could be produced easily by local potters unfamiliar with the wheel, and are the principal domestic ware found at Coppergate throughout the late ninth and early tenth centuries. In the East Midlands the handmade shelly wares at sites such as Eaton Socon develop into the wheel-thrown St Neots ware. In Wessex

42 *Late Saxon Shelly ware vessels, London (Museum of London).*

over 30 centres. This new pottery production was notably town-based: Northampton, Stamford, Stafford, Thetford and Winchester are all examples of new wares which take their names from the towns in which kilns have been discovered. Kilns have been excavated in four of the five Scandinavian boroughs; and their absence at Derby is probably due to the lack of excavation. Stafford ware, or Chester-type ware, as it is sometimes known, was produced at the Tipping Street kilns in Stafford in a Thetford ware tradition from the mid-tenth century, and soon spread throughout the Mercian burhs (see **54**).

Urban potters may have had difficulty acquiring enough fuel, and for this reason, and because of the risk of fire, many kilns may still have been situated on the edges of towns. The St Neots ware potters still fired their vessels to a fairly low temperature on an open bonfire; elsewhere the single-flue kiln was now widely used. Production normally involved the use of local clays. The reputation of Stamford ware was based upon local estuarine clays found on the fen margins which did not require additives. At Torksey the fabric was rougher because of the presence of sandy quartz crystals in the local clay. For St Neots ware the clay was tempered with crushed shells.

industrial pottery production also evolved out of the local handmade tradition. The first results were fairly crude and often finished by hand, but by the mid-tenth century respectable wheel-thrown pots were being fired in single-flue kilns. The range of forms also increased, with bowls, dishes, lamps and pitchers all being thrown.

South of the Thames and in the north-west production continued on a small scale with handmade pots fired on a bonfire continuing as the main products well into the tenth century, alongside wheel-thrown forms. Crude handmade pottery reached Cornwall in the ninth century, and continued in use well into the eleventh. Squat cooking vessels with flat grass-marked bases and distinctive bar-lug handles form most of the assemblage at Gwithian and Mawgan Porth. The style is also found throughout the western Baltic and north Germany, and was once thought to be Viking; it has since been suggested that it was introduced by Frisian traders.

By 950 industrial-scale wheel-thrown production had supplanted handmade wares at

43 *Torksey-type ware storage vessel from Coppergate, York (York Archaeological Trust).*

Decoration might be added to vessels by thumbing, incising, combing, stabbing or rouletting, or by the addition of strips or stamped motifs. Glazing was relatively uncommon and was probably restricted to high-quality luxury items; a number of production sites have now been identified, but the similarities between them suggest that the potters had a common source for their techniques. It may be significant that many of the early glazed-ware production centres are also known for glass manufacture. The potters generally selected white-firing clays, enabling them to achieve a clear yellow or olive-green colour. Experiments in glazing dark reduced wares, such as at Lincoln, tended to be short-lived. Glazed pottery was generally produced according to a restricted range of forms, including spouted pitchers, lamps and sprinklers.

The most famous pre-Conquest glazed pottery form in England is the spouted pitcher with a pale yellow, orange or green glaze produced from a fine off-white clay at Stamford, and traded throughout England. The start of pottery production in Stamford coincides with the Scandinavian occupation in the mid-ninth century. As the settlement developed into a town so pottery production and trade grew. The Stamford potters specialized in four main types of pottery: cooking vessels (small pots and bowls), table wares (for food and drink), lamps and crucibles. The distribution of their kilns suggests that there were several individual workshops lying outside the town walls.

The crucibles and fine tableware, pitchers and jugs were exported far afield, but the bulk of Stamford production was of cooking pots which were distributed locally in south Lincolnshire. The Stamford industry may be characterized as a basic industry sustained by a local market which was growing at a rapid enough rate to support an upsurge in production and a shift to an industrial base. Glaze and red paint were used in Stamford from the beginning, in the late ninth century. Their sudden appearance suggests that they may have been introduced by foreign potters working in Stamford. These are unlikely to have been Danes, as the idea originated in northern France or the Low Countries. Nevertheless, its origin should be seen in the context of Viking disruption in north-west Europe, and the potters may have arrived 'in the Viking baggage train'.

Experiments with glazing local Lincoln wares in the late ninth century may also be seen as Viking-influenced, but the pottery was unsuitable and the attempts were short-lived. In York there is little evidence for experimentation in glazes on local wares. The Early Glazed wares, which have now been identified in tenth-century levels, are all well produced and hard-fired. They are all of a very small size and may possibly have served some specialist function such as containers for oils or perfumes. The similar development of tenth-century glazed wares at Northampton, Winchester, Portchester and Michelmersh can all be seen as inspired by Stamford, or derived from the same continental origin.

Carpentry

The relative abundance of pottery on most sites can lead archaeologists to exaggerate its importance. Other materials which are not found as often may have been just as common at the time. Wood, for example, may have been preferred for bowls which were not to be used for cooking; and wooden barrels may have been used for storage and transport. Wooden objects may have been lavishly decorated, but examples, such as a saddle-bow from Coppergate, rarely survive.

Where wood survives it is often abundant; at the Saddler Street site, Durham, six wooden vessels were recovered compared with 30 pottery ones. At Coppergate, York, bowls made from yew and ash were found (44). Lathe turning was being carried out nearby, as large numbers of waste cores were found; many had been dumped in an abandoned building. In towns there may have been specialist turners and coopers; indeed, the derivation of the name Coppergate is thought to be 'the street of the coopers'. Specialist woodworking tools, including adzes, axes, augers and boring bits, chisels and draw knives have been found on both rural and urban sites and in metalworker's hoards of scrap iron.

44 (Above, right) Wooden cups, bowls and waste turning cores from a wood-turner's workshop, York (York Archaeological Trust).

45 (Below, right) Bone and antler combs, spindlewhorls, needles and textile fragments, York (York Archaeological Trust).

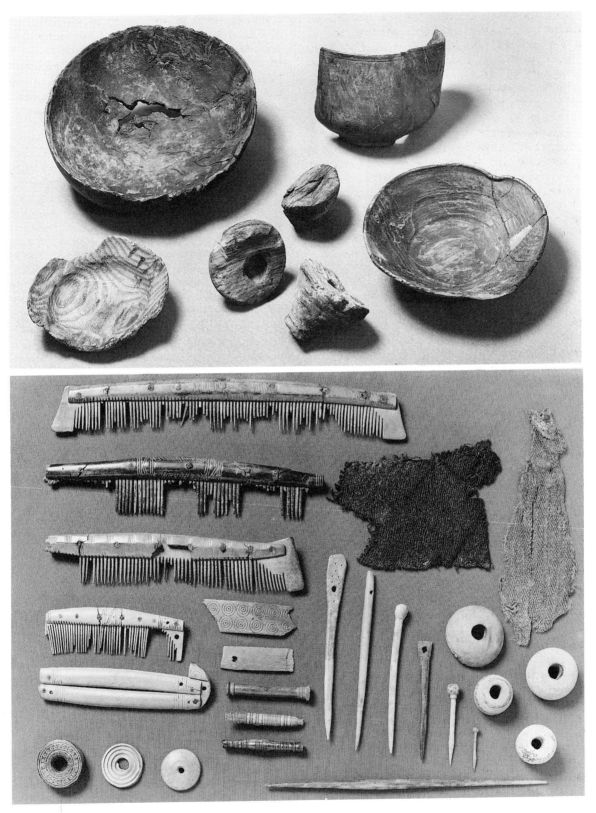

Bone, antler, ivory and horn working

Large-scale antler and bone working, and to a lesser extent horn working, seems to be characteristic of Viking Age towns, although it is unclear whether it should be regarded as a craft or an industry. Many of the simple types of object could have been made by anyone, although the more sophisticated combs were probably made by specialists (45). Analysis of the evidence from Sweden has led to the conclusion that combs were made exclusively by itinerant workers who travelled from one market to another. Antler and bone working certainly seems to have been widespread, and evidence has been recovered from Chester, Ipswich, Lincoln, Northampton, Oxford and several York sites, including Coppergate and York Minster. Animal bones were readily available as domestic waste, although particular bones were deliberately selected for each product. Bone was used occasionally for combs, but also for pins, textile equipment, playing pieces, toggles and skates. Antler was favoured for comb making, but was also used for knife handles. In both Lincoln and York the antler was mostly from shed antlers which must have been collected in the surrounding forests, although there is rather more evidence for the hunting of deer from Lincoln. Walrus ivory was also worked to produce fine mounts and fittings; elephant ivory is rare in Viking Age England, although two fragments are known from York.

Stone

Before the tenth century the development of stone quarrying and building, and stone sculpture was largely in response to demand from the Church. At Raunds the site of a Viking Age quarry has been identified as the source of materials for the new stone church. Good building stone was also quarried at sites such as Portland and the Isle of Wight and transported over distances of more than 80 km (50 miles) for the construction of the new stone churches. Particular types of stone were sometimes selected for certain features, such as Barnack limestone for the alternate long and short ashlar blocks at the corners of church towers.

In the tenth century the Scandinavian aristocracy took over the patronage of the stonemasons and sculptors. Large quantities of crosses and tombstones were produced for this new market (see Chapter 11). Sculptural workshops were established in towns such as Chester and York or around rural sites such as Gosforth (Cumbria). Crosses and grave slabs were generally made from a single piece of local stone which was rarely transported more than 16 km (10 miles). The sculptor's first task would be to give the monument its basic shape. Analysis demonstrates that templates were regularly used, for instance to produce the shape of a cross-head. The decoration would then be laid out in panels; templates and stencils were again used to produce elements of the design. Different workshops produced monuments with distinctive styles and designs. Similarities between groups of sculpture show that itinerant masons travelled between villages. The same template was used to provide the outline of a warrior's helmet on a cross at Sockburn (Durham) as at Brompton (North Yorkshire), some 11 km (7 miles) away. Chisels and punches would be used to carve the stone, which would then be decorated with bright colours. The scrubbed aspect of stone sculpture today makes it difficult to envisage the original intended appearance, which to a modern eye would have been exceptionally gaudy. Gesso, a form of plaster, was sometimes used as a base, and then black, blue, red, brown, orange, yellow

46 *Tenth-century grave-cover fragment, Coppergate, York: the carving shows no sign of weathering and various details appear to be unfinished, suggesting that it was rejected before completion (York Archaeological Trust).*

and white paints would be used to highlight the design. Finally, the sculptor may have added decorative metalwork, jewellery or paste.

Glass

Glass was used for tableware and occasionally for glazing windows. Fragments of window glass have been found in cellared buildings in Thetford and London, at monastic sites, and at the royal mill at Old Windsor. Glass was made with soda lime until the tenth century, when the increased demand for window glass was met by the use of potash. Large-scale Viking Age glass working is mainly known from monastic sites such as Jarrow, Glastonbury and Barking Abbey. Glass beads and other jewellery were manufactured in towns, and glass-smelting crucibles have been found in Gloucester and Lincoln.

Non-ferrous metalworking

The working of copper alloys and precious metals was restricted to aristocratic sites for much of the post-Roman period, and appears to have been carried out under lordly or ecclesiastical patronage. A mould fragment from Whitby Abbey is more likely to represent monastic metalworking than Viking raiders pausing from pillage to melt down church plate. At Cheddar gold, copper, silver, tin and lead were worked in the ninth century. Jewellery was the main product, possibly for gifts from the king to his retinue. At Faccombe, on a site adjacent to an aisled hall, copper alloys and gold were cast in the tenth century. Such communities of craftworkers must have been established at many rural manorial sites.

During the Viking Age non-ferrous metalworking also became an urban enterprise, and evidence has been found in several towns including Chester, Exeter, Lincoln, Northampton, Thetford and York. At Coppergate two adjacent tenth-century tenements were occupied by metalworkers. Each had a large central hearth which may have been used for heating metals, and some 1000 crucible fragments were found. The smallest, no larger than a thimble, appear to have been used for melting gold, but silver, lead and copper alloys were also being worked. The metalworkers were also separating precious from base metals in small ceramic dishes. Their main trade appears to have been jewellery production, and several unfinished objects were excavated. Any

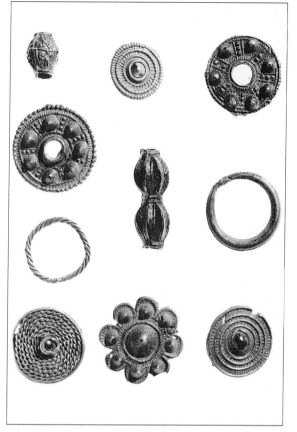

47 *Pewter rings and brooches, found in Cheapside, London, the unfinished stock of a London jeweller. A fragment of a brooch found in Dublin was manufactured from the same mould (Museum of London).*

suitable material might be utilized as a mould; a Roman tile had shapes cut into it for casting blanks for brooches and pendants. Both stone and clay moulds were used for casting ingots, but soapstone moulds were selected for silver casting. Ingots would be used as the raw material for further casting, or might be hammered into arm rings.

During the ninth and tenth centuries the demand for brooches decorated in a Scandinavian style spread beyond those who could afford precious metals. Iron alloys and pewter became particularly popular for mass-produced jewellery (47). A large number of lead-alloy disc brooches appear to have been manufactured at Coppergate. They were decorated with stylized animals and plants and geometric motifs.

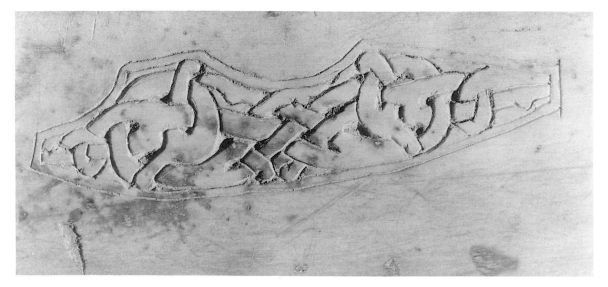

48 Artist's trial-piece, Coppergate, York. This fragment of a cow's rib has been used to practice an intricate interlaced pattern, before execution in metal (York Archaeological Trust).

Designs might first be tested on 'trial-' or 'motif-pieces' of waste bone (**48**).

At Flaxengate, Lincoln, a similar range of metals was worked in the same buildings as glass beads were being made, although silver and copper alloys decline in importance in the late tenth century, to be replaced by iron working. Over 500 crucible fragments have been excavated from ninth–eleventh-century levels. The crucibles were manufactured from local clays or, if they were to be used for melting silver, crucibles imported from Stamford were preferred.

Iron working

Iron was probably the most important raw material during the Viking Age, being essential for both tools and weapons. The blacksmith enjoyed particular prestige, and appears in Scandinavian mythological scenes depicted on stone monuments as a heroic figure, such as Weland the Smith who was lamed by the king to prevent him from escaping with his skills, or Regin who forged the magical sword used by Sigurd the dragon-slayer. A tenth-century cross from Halton (Lancashire), for example, appears to show Regin working at a raised hearth. The role of the smith was also celebrated in death, and smith's tools were some-times placed as grave offerings, such as in the Knoc-y-Doonee burial on the Isle of Man (see Chapter 10).

In Middle Saxon England there was a relatively restricted range of iron products. There were weaponsmiths at a few permanent centres but most smiths were itinerant or village craftsmen manufacturing and mending tools on a small scale for local consumption. In Viking Age England iron smithing became a town industry, and urban excavations invariably provide evidence for iron working. Village communities such as St Neots and more isolated rural sites such as Ribblehead and Simy Folds still undertook production for their own needs, and at higher-status rural sites such as Cheddar most of the iron objects required would also have been made on site. The key developments, however, took place in towns such as Bedford, Northampton, Stamford, Lincoln and York, where smiths experimented with new artefacts and new techniques.

Iron working is a two-stage process. First the ore must be smelted to extract the iron, and then the iron must be worked by the smith to make finished artefacts. Smelting is a very hot and unpleasant process which requires great quantities of fuel. It is likely that most smelting was still undertaken in the country close to the iron ore deposits and abundant supplies of wood, at sites like West Runton, Great Casterton and Ashdown Forest (Sussex). Cast iron bars or scrap iron for recycling would then be traded with the urban centres.

Scrap iron was a precious commodity and

several hoards of broken iron tools and weapons have been found in England, although it is not always possible to distinguish them from ritual river deposits (see Chapter 10). In many cases metalworker's hoards include ancient Roman and Anglo-Saxon objects. At Nazeing (Essex) an eleventh-century hoard found in alluvial gravels on the east side of the river Lea comprised four axes, four spearheads, a gouge, a chisel, a small hammer, a ploughshare, two knives, a fish spear and a copper alloy ring and cup. Similar hoards are known from Hurbuck (Durham), Crayke (North Yorkshire), and Westley Waterless (Cambridgeshire).

Limited smelting was undertaken in a few towns. In Stamford iron was brought from the local ironstone outcrops. In York carbonate ore would have been available from either North Yorkshire or Lincolnshire; analysis suggests that several sources were being exploited. At Coppergate some 21 kg (46 lb) of iron-smelting slag, solidified into the hemispherical shape of the furnace bottom, has been excavated. Nevertheless, the techniques employed were not very efficient and stand out in comparison with the activities of the other Coppergate workers.

Smithing was far more widespread. It has been identified at Flaxengate in Lincoln, and at both the Minster and Coppergate sites in York. In both Lincoln and York there was a close relationship between the ferrous and nonferrous metalworkers; both sets of activities were often carried on in the same buildings, probably by the same workers. Over 180 kg (400 lb) of smithing slag was excavated at Coppergate. Cast iron bars and strips were imported from the smelting sites outside York and large amounts of material were also brought for recycling. It is now believed that even the remarkable Coppergate Anglian helmet probably reached the site as scrap.

The Coppergate smiths displayed a high degree of expertise and were probably permanent craftsmen. A number of classes of object were manufactured on site, including needles, jewellery and Scandinavian-style chest fittings. At the York Minster site the smiths were mass-producing horseshoe nails in a former Roman barrack block. Different grades of iron were selected for different purposes. Some 220 knives were found in Viking Age deposits at Coppergate. Most made use of carbonized steel for the cutting edge. During the ninth century new types of knife were introduced, including a group with long handles, and decoration proliferated, including incised grooves and inlaid designs. Clearly knives and iron dress-fittings were being increasingly used for decoration and display in the Viking Age. Although it is difficult to identify any particular Scandinavian influence, the increased need for status display may be seen as a reflection of the Viking Age circumstances.

Manufacturing techniques were also developing at the same time, and a great variety of methods were in use by the tenth century. There were two principal methods of welding the steel blade to an iron knife. The hardest knives were produced by butt-welding the steel strip along the edge of the iron blade. Another technique was to sandwich-weld a steel blade in between two slices of iron. This second method increased in popularity in York during the tenth century, leading to knives becoming softer. Sandwich-welding was also introduced into Dublin at this time, possibly from York.

Leather working

By the medieval period leather working comprised several specialist tasks such as skinning, tanning, dressing and cobbling, but during the Viking Age these may have been combined under one roof. Leather working developed on a professional basis in towns and was carried out as a commercial activity. In Durham the Saddler Street leather workers obtained uncut oxhide which they made into shoes, boots (**49**) and knife-sheaths. They also acted as cobblers, repairing shoes. In York leather workers made shoes, boots and sword- and knife-sheaths. Hides from cows slaughtered on site would have provided them with a ready supply of leather (see Chapter 6).

Textiles

By the ninth century there was some trade in textiles, but most communities produced cloth for their own needs. Large estates would supply their own wool, flax and dyestuffs, and prepare, spin, weave and dye their own textiles. Some estates were apparently able to employ servants and slaves to work on textile manufacture. At the manorial site at Goltho a weaving house has been identified from the pin-beaters and other textile tools found on the floor of a large outbuilding.

49 *(Above, left) Leather shoes and boots, Coppergate, York. Viking Age shoes and boots had a single-piece flat sole; when this wore out it was taken off, thrown away and replaced (York Archaeological Trust).*

50 *(Below, left) Polished stone spindlewhorls and honestones, Bryant's Gill (Cumbria) (Board of Trustees of the National Museums and Galleries on Merseyside; reproduced by courtesy of SEARCH Archaeology Group).*

Urban communities may also have produced homespun textiles for local demand from raw materials brought in from the countryside. The Coppergate and Flaxengate sites were littered with textile implements, including shears, wool combs, and spindlewhorls (**50**). The wool was then woven into lengths of cloth using a hand loom. In York the warp threads were suspended from the top of the loom and weighted by loomweights made of circles of fired clay. In Lincoln the comparative rarity of loomweights has led to the suggestion that the two-beam vertical loom, in which the warp threads are attached to a wooden beam, was introduced from the Continent in the ninth century. It has been proposed that the treadle-operated horizontal loom was in use in Gloucester by the tenth century, although elsewhere it is not known until the eleventh century.

The people of York probably dyed their own textiles as well, and a variety of dye plants such as madder and woad are characteristic of Viking Age deposits. Viking clothing was probably a mass of colour, with evidence for reds, greens, blues, yellows and blacks. White linen, woven from vegetable fibres, was probably preferred for undergarments and bedlinen. Smooth glass 'linen-smoothers' used for the finishing of linen cloth have been found in both Lincoln and York.

There is very little particularly Scandinavian about the Coppergate textiles, however. The majority of textiles have more in common with those of Anglo-Saxon England and Carolingian Europe than with Scandinavia. Most are local products, although there are some fine broken-chevron twills, probably imported from Frisia, one of which had been dyed purple with lichen. A group of patterned linens, including a honeycomb weave, may have originated in the Rhineland, and may have been brought to York by

51 *Tenth-century sock, from Coppergate, York, made in a technique known as nålebinding, or needle binding, using a coarse needle and a length of plied yarn. This is the only clear Viking textile found in York (York Archaeological Trust).*

Frisian merchants following the wine trade-route. The only indisputably Viking textile is a tenth-century woollen sock made in a technique known as nålebinding, or needle-binding which looks like close-textured crochet work (51). A similar example is known from a textile fragment from a Viking burial at Ingleby (Derbyshire).

Imported silks are known from a number of Viking Age towns, including York, Lincoln, Dublin and London. At Coppergate tabby-weave silks appear to have been cut up and sewn on site, probably for silk head-dresses, possibly in a Scandinavian fashion.

In summary, the origins of industrial production can be observed in many crafts during the Viking Age. The thriving towns of lowland England represented a tremendous commercial opportunity, with a concentration of demand for cheaply-produced metalwork, trinkets and other consumer goods. Within their walls groups of craftworkers and merchants would act together, or in sequence, on certain materials, forming chains of interlinked crafts.

The potential for increased sales provided the incentive for experimentation in new methods which enabled mass production. The significance of the introduction of the kick wheel, and other innovations such as single-flue kilns and glazing, is that they required capital investment and a full-time commitment to pottery production. This was only worthwhile if there was a large demand and a marketing infrastructure, including markets, a transport system and a means of exchange.

The role of Scandinavian settlers and traders in this upsurge in industrial production is not straightforward. The development of the pottery industry, for instance, was already under way in eastern England before the Viking arrival. Glazing is not restricted to Danelaw sites, and is not found at all of them. Nevertheless, wheel-thrown pottery was introduced into most parts of England during the Viking Age. Similarly, Scandinavian-style animal ornament may have become popular throughout England during the Viking Age, but it was executed on Anglo-Saxon disc brooches; Viking tortoise brooches were not made in York. Urban demand and marketing opportunities increased throughout the late ninth and tenth centuries. In the countryside prosperous farmers celebrated their wealth by purchasing Scandinavian-style consumer goods. Although the Vikings may not have started the tenth-century 'Industrial Revolution', they did provide both the stimulus and the mechanism for it to happen.

8

Trade and exchange

In recent years the role of the Vikings in stimulating international trade and peaceful commerce has been emphasized, and their war-like activities played down. Analysis of the foreign goods imported into England, however, suggests that their role as peaceful traders, at least initially, may have been exaggerated. Although the variety of exotic goods does reflect a wide range of long-distance contacts (52), the proportion of imported goods in ninth- and tenth-century England is relatively small.

We have already seen that the Vikings disrupted the Saxon trading sites (see Chapter 4). In contrast to the large number of imports from the sixth to ninth centuries, imported goods are equally rare in tenth-century Ipswich, Norwich, London, Southampton, Winchester and York. Only 500 of the 15,000 objects found at Coppergate were imported, and virtually the only tenth-century imported finds are a silk cap, a brooch from the Low Countries and a Badorf-type amphora. Significantly, there was not a single piece of Scandinavian pottery in some 55,000 pottery sherds found in Viking Age levels at Coppergate. The lifestyle of the inhabitants of York would not have been noticeably affected if trading contacts had ceased.

Traded goods

Traded goods can be difficult to recognize from archaeological evidence. Organic commodities rarely survive, and even where remains of wool, cloth or grain are preserved it is difficult to distinguish imported from local goods. Other items may leave no tangible evidence. The trading of slaves is documented in sixth- and seventh-century Europe, and presumably continued into Viking Age England, as the Vikings were well-attested slavers although there are no archaeological traces. There is an eleventh-century reference to the followers of one Ælfred, son of Æthelred, being captured at Guildford in 1036 and sold as slaves, and another to the selling of slaves at Corbridge. In the Domesday Book slaves are still an important element of the population in some areas, and although the slave trade was outlawed in 1102, slavery was not prohibited.

The principal objects imported to England from Scandinavia for which evidence survives are those of walrus ivory, steatite or soapstone, and schist. In the tenth century a Norwegian ivory trader, Ohthere, visited Ælfred's court, and described his journey from his home in northern Norway to the market-places of southern Scandinavia at Hedeby and Kaupang, where he sold or exchanged the Arctic products he had collected. Walrus ivory is known from York and Lincoln, and an implement from Bramham (West Yorkshire) may have been imported through York before being carried into its hinterland. The quantities, however, are very small, and may have been personal possessions of Viking settlers. Similarly, the soapstone bowls from Flaxengate and Coppergate are so worn that they look more like prized personal heirlooms rather than imported goods (53). Soapstone was also quarried on Shetland and may have been imported from there in preference to Norway. Amber is more likely to have been collected on the east coast than imported from Denmark. Schist honestones, which must have come from southern Norway, are known from several sites with Danelaw links, including York, Lincoln, Northampton, Thetford and London. Even so, the trade may have been directed through the Low Countries in the

Walrus, ivory, furs

Walrus, ivory,
fish, hides

Furs

NORWEGIAN
SEA

FINLAND

Leningrad

Iron

GULF
OF
BOTHNIA

Timber

NORWAY

Iron, soapstone,
whetstones

Sigtuna
Birka

Riga

Shetland Isles
Soapstone

Bergen

Oslo

Helgö

Grobin

Kaupang

Paviken

SWEDEN

SCOTLAND

NORTH
SEA

DENMARK

Lund

Ribe

Truso

Wollin

IRELAND

ENGLAND

Hedeby

Amber

Vistula

Dublin

York

Elba

Oder

POLAND

Limerick
Cork

Chester

Wheat, woollens,
tin, honey, silver

FRISIA

GERMANY

London

BELGIUM

Bristol

Southampton

Quentowic

Mainz

Quernstones, wines, pottery
glass, cloth, weapons

Jewellery, gold, silver

Paris

Rhine

Orléans

52 *Map of Viking Age trade routes in north-*
west Europe (after Graham-Campbell 1990).

Angers

Loire

BAY
OF
BISCAY

Salt, wine

FRANCE

5cm

53 *Fragment of a soapstone bowl, Coppergate, York (York Archaeological Trust).*

hands of Frisian traders from Dorestad, rather than being imported direct from Scandinavia.

In fact, England's Viking Age imported goods demonstrate little change from her Middle Saxon trading partners, and continue links with Germany and northern France, although there is apparently a reduction in volume. The most visible items are quernstones and pottery, although it is assumed that the latter was being imported in association with the Rhenish wine trade. The wine was transported in amphorae as well as narrow barrels like those depicted in the Bayeux Tapestry and found reused as well linings in Milk Street, London, but decorated pitchers and beakers were bought for table use, so that Rhenish wine might be served from Pingsdorf spouted pitchers and drunk from Pingsdorf beakers. Pingsdorf and Badorf ware have been recognized on some 20 sites, but are rarely found in large quantities. Fewer than 15 imported vessels were discarded at Coppergate in 150 years, in contrast to Anglian York where imported pottery was far more common. The distribution of Rhenish wares is not limited to the Danelaw, although there are a few sherds from Lincoln and Thetford, as well as those from York. Outside the Danelaw, in the south

and east, French Red-painted wares are more common than Rhenish products. There are also occasional examples of exotic pottery, such as Islamic wares in early ninth-century levels from Flaxengate, but nothing to link them particularly to Viking traders.

Imported German Mayen-Niedermendig lava millstones may have followed the same route as the wine trade. Their importation was already well established in Anglo-Saxon England. In the Viking Age they are known from towns such as Lincoln, Thetford and York and rural sites such as St Neots and Springfield, although more isolated farmsteads such as Ribblehead were using the inferior millstone grit.

The only imported item which perhaps reveals Scandinavian traders acting as middlemen is silk, for which the nearest production centre was in the east Mediterranean. Silk has been identified on the Danelaw sites of York and Lincoln, and in a tenth-century pit from Milk Street, London. A silk cap from Coppergate is so remarkably similar to a fragment from Lincoln that it might even have been cut from the same bale of material.

Whilst international trade during the Viking age appears to have been fairly limited, there was still a vigorous home market. Most goods that were traded within England were probably perishable agricultural products, and are

89

almost impossible to identify. The remarkable national trade in pottery, however, gives some indication of the likely scale of trade (**54**). Even rural settlements such as Raunds and Wharram Percy were supplied with a full range of Late Saxon pottery. Some pottery may have been transported as containers, and its spread may reflect the commodity trade; the distribution of Thetford ware within and from East Anglia, for example, may represent the movement of grain. Other pottery, such as lead-glazed Stamford ware (see Chapter 7), appears to have been regarded as a luxury product in its own right.

The trade in Stamford ware may well have started with specialist industrial pottery; glazed crucibles are the first Stamford ware pottery to appear on tenth-century metalworking sites in Lincoln, Thetford and York. Later, with the production of fine table wares in the same fabric, the trade expanded dramatically, and Stamford ware pitchers are found throughout central England. By the eleventh century it accounts for almost 25 per cent of all pottery in Lincoln and York. The proportion of Stamford ware decreases gradually with distance away from the Stamford kilns. There is a central core, a circle with a radius of 24 km (15 miles), within which it is the most common fabric, although local shelly and limestone wares still continue in use alongside it, and an outer area of up to 80 km (50 miles) away where it is consistently present in smaller amounts. The local Stamford ware distribution may reflect local farmers coming to market, but outside its local base the pattern of trade of Stamford ware is a Viking one. Its appearance on virtually every Lincolnshire site implies an organized trade involving middlemen who specialized in the sale of pottery. The trade was maintained along coastal and riverine routes. Transport by water would have been slow, but also safe; the rivers Welland and Ouse were navigable, and Stamford ware finds cluster along the former line of the Wash and up the Lincolnshire coast to Whitby and as far afield as Aberdeen and Perth. The trade was not maintained to the same extent southwards; there is no Stamford ware in London before the Norman Conquest, for example.

The distribution of other Viking Age pottery such as Cheddar, Stafford and Late Saxon Shelly wares is also restricted to certain areas (see **54**), although our understanding of what such distributions mean is still in its infancy. Some patterns, such as the Thames-valley distribution of the Oxford shelly wares, may reflect distribution by river, but in other cases we may be plotting the areas of influence of various Viking and Anglo-Saxon groups. In Oxford, for example, it has been suggested that parts of the town tended to trade with certain areas, or displayed cultural preferences in the types of pottery used.

Ships and shipping

Viking Age trade would have depended upon sea and river transport. Our picture of Viking boats tends to be dominated by the longship but in fact there was a wide variety of craft, each with different functions. A table of harbour dues for Billingsgate c.1000 distinguishes between three classes of vessel: a small ship, which was charged $\frac{1}{2}d$; a larger ship with sails, charged 1d; and a barque or merchantman, charged 4d.

The first group probably included simple logboats, like that excavated at Clapton (Greater London) (**55**). Such boats were fairly workmanlike affairs, normally hollowed out of half a split oak trunk, following a north-European tradition going back to prehistoric dugouts. Indeed, it has often been assumed that such craft were pre-Roman, until scientific dating methods proved otherwise. Tree-ring dating of the Clapton boat showed it was carved from a tree chopped down in the tenth century. The Clapton log-boat was 3.75 m (12 ft) long by 0.65 m (2 ft) wide; a replica could carry up to four people. It was propelled by a paddle, with a bulkhead in the centre acting as a seat for the rower. Four such boats have now been recovered in the London area from the river Lea, plus a curved oak rib from the Thames Exchange site which could have come from a small planked boat, or a light dugout with extended sides. Nine eleventh-century logboats have been recovered from the rivers Mersey and Irwell, indicating the degree of river traffic during the Viking Age. Most may have been used primarily for ferrying, fishing, fowling and reed-gathering, but the range in length, 2.75–4.65 m (9–14$\frac{3}{4}$ ft), suggests that some, such as examples from Warrington and,

54 *Map of Viking Age pottery distributions (after Kilmurry 1980, Mason 1985 and Vince 1990).*

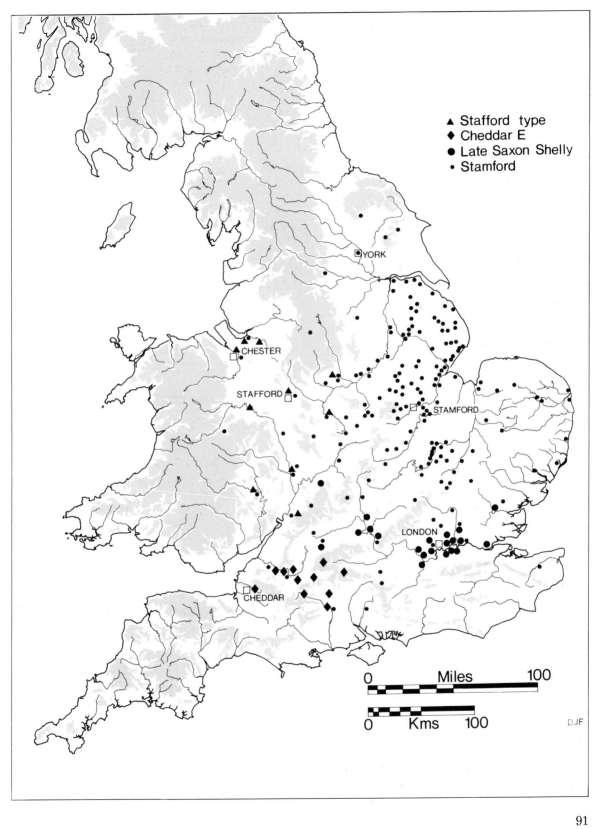

Stafford type
Cheddar E
Late Saxon Shelly
Stamford

YORK

CHESTER

STAFFORD

STAMFORD

LONDON

CHEDDAR

0   Miles   100

0   Kms   100

DJF

91

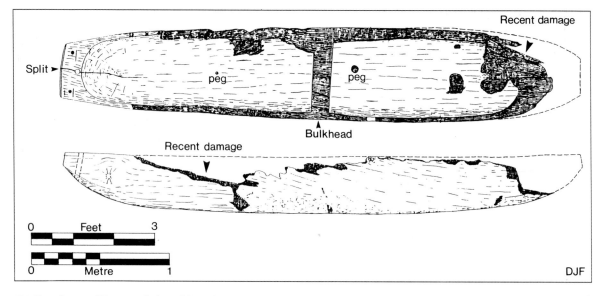

55 *Log-boat, Clapton (after Marsden et al. 1989).*

Irlam may have functioned as bulk-cargo carriers over short distances.

The second group, of small vessels with sails, would have been more suitable for longer river journeys or short sea crossings. The Graveney boat is an example of an excavated boat belonging to this category. She was a clinker-built merchant vessel, constructed c.927, 14 m (46 ft) long and with a beam of 3.9 m (13 ft), which could have carried some 6–7 tonnes of cargo. Residues of hops may represent a cargo from Kent being carried up the Thames Estuary, whilst her ballast of unfinished lava millstones may reflect North Sea crossings. At some point in her career the keel had been repaired after having been badly cracked, perhaps from beaching with a heavy cargo on board. The Graveney boat was finally abandoned c.950 more than 1 km ($\frac{1}{2}$ mile) from the sea in a creek alongside an improvised jetty of upright posts. Fragments of up to four similar ships have been found on the London waterfront; one find, from the Vintry site, suggested the vessel had been rigged for sailing.

The third category, of ocean-going vessels, probably included foreign vessels from northern Europe and Scandinavia. No complete vessels of this period have been recovered from English waters, although finds from the Thames Exchange site, including a carved mast partner which would have supported a mast up to 0.45 m

(1$\frac{1}{2}$ ft) in diameter, show that such large vessels visited Viking Age London.

Coinage
The emergence of commercial trade would have been dependent upon a monetary economy. During the last quarter of the eighth century a regular English coinage based on the silver penny was established by Offa of Mercia. This developed into a proper currency which had a face value far in excess of its silver value.

The coinage of Anglo-Saxon England was not supplied by a central mint issuing to the whole kingdom. Coin production was decentralized and carried out in a number of mints, each based in a burh (**56**). At each mint a number of private individuals, men of substance in the community, acted as moneyers, taking responsibility for the coinage on behalf of royal authority. The number of these moneyers varies according to the importance of the mint, but only in very important towns were there more than ten operating at once. It was established practice that pennies should carry on their obverse the name of the ruler whose authority was recognized at their place of minting, and on the reverse the name of the moneyer.

The role of moneyers and the nature of Viking Age coin production has been greatly illuminated by the Coppergate finds (**57**). An iron coin die of the St Peter's issue, c.921–7,

56 *Map of mints, 957–1016 (after Hill 1981).*

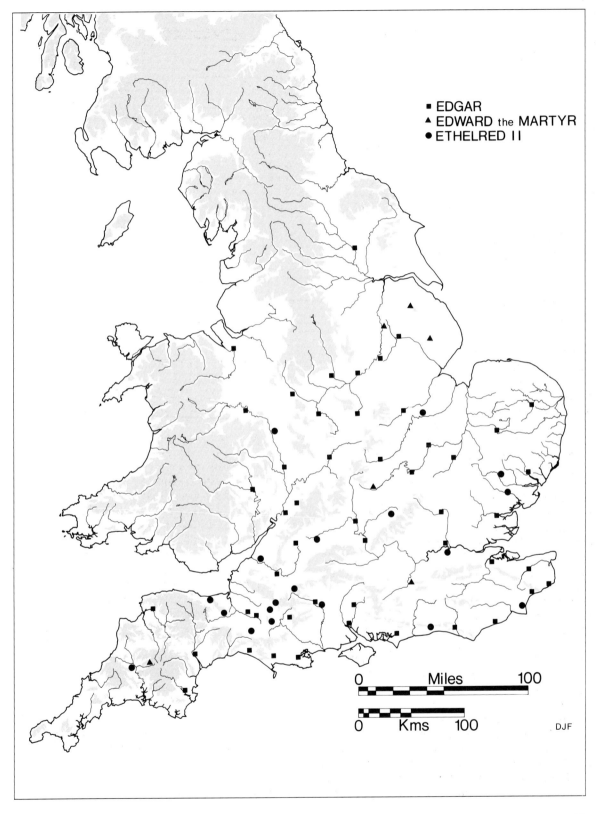

EDGAR
EDWARD the MARTYR
ETHELRED II

0   Miles   100

0   Kms   100

DJF

bearing a sword and hammer and a dedication to St Peter, was found discarded amongst the rubbish in the metalworking shops. The die was cylindrical in shape, flaring outwards at the base, where a tang protruded which could be fixed into a bench or anvil. The head had been specially hardened. Nearby there were also two lead trial-pieces, or test strikings, the cap of a die for a penny of Æthelstan (927–39) and a further lead trial-piece for a penny of Eadwig (955–9), made by the Chester moneyer Frothric. Unless the records for all northern coins were being maintained in York, it appears that dies for Chester issues must also have been manufactured in York. It is possible that the Coppergate excavations accidentally stumbled upon the site of a mint, although the insubstantial nature of the timber workshops is not what anyone might imagine a tenth-century mint would look like. It seems more plausible that only the die production and engraving were carried out here. The remains were found in

57 Coin-manufacturing evidence, Coppergate, York (York Archaeological Trust).

two adjacent tenements, occupied by craftsmen with wide experience in metalworking. The finds must cover a 20–30 year time span, indicating some continuity of production. The lead trial-pieces were presumably tests; the damaged dies may have been returned for recasting. Nevertheless, one assumes that the workshops must have operated under the authority of the moneyers, as the dies could not be allowed to fall into the wrong hands.

From the death of Offa in 796 to Burgred's defeat by the Vikings in 874 the bulk of coinage was produced at, and circulated from, three cities: London, Canterbury and Rochester. During this period there was a rapid expansion in the number of moneyers, reflecting the growing need for coinage resulting from increased economic activity.

As Viking leaders took political control, they started to mint coins for propaganda purposes. By the 880s silver pennies were being struck in East Anglia and the south-east Danelaw area by Viking leaders; they bore the legend 'St Edmund', although the Danes had killed the East Anglian King Edmund in 870. Knutr and

Sihtric had coins struck in York from *c*.890 following Carolingian designs; some bore the legend 'St Peter', others carried religious motifs. From *c*.920 Lincoln also started to mint coins, in the name of St Martin. Nevertheless, the population did not have full confidence in the new coins, which in many areas were only accepted for their silver content and not their face value, as demonstrated by the surface pecking to test their silver content. Finds of silver ingots, such as those recently discovered by metal detector near Easingwold (North Yorkshire), suggest that even within the immediate hinterland of York a bullion economy may have been operating in the late ninth and early tenth centuries.

The Danelaw was originally poorly served by mints, but by the early tenth century mints were operating at Bedford, Chester, Derby, Leicester and Nottingham, as well as York and Lincoln. By the second quarter of the tenth century York was issuing more recognizably 'Viking' coins with Norse legends and pagan motifs such as the raven, swords and Thor's hammer. After the expulsion of Erik Bloodaxe in 954, however, York was absorbed into mainstream English minting practice.

In 973 Edgar reformed the coinage, giving coins a six-year period of use, after which they were no longer legal tender. The king took a profit each time the currency was reminted; therefore Edgar's reforms served to maximize royal profits. He also prohibited the circulation of foreign coins; all silver entering the kingdom was to be reminted, and had to bear the king's head. By the late tenth century the production of coin took place at 50–60 mints operating up and down the country. Æthelstan further regulated the minting of coins by stipulating that 'there shall be one coinage throughout the king's realm, and no man shall mint money except in a town.'

During the eleventh century the continuous heavy wastage from the currency through the export of coin was counterbalanced by the inflow of silver in payment for exports. Despite the continued threat of Viking raids, mints continued to operate at a large number of locations, although sometimes, as at the hillfort at South Cadbury, they were taken inside strongly fortified sites. Even the Isle of Man began producing its own distinctive Hiberno-Manx coinage, not from an urban centre, but more likely from the seat of political power, perhaps on St Patrick's Isle, Peel.

By the eleventh century coinage was in general use, but it is difficult to quantify its importance for the general populace. It has been suggested that finds of pennies cut into half- and quarter-pennies in deposits in London and York shows that coins were being used for small change in everyday transactions. However, whilst a penny might sound like small change we have to remember that during the Viking Age it was worth quite a lot (see **41**).

The number of coins recovered from archaeological excavations is also fairly small. It has been noted that there are 32 burhs in which post-1960 excavations have produced Viking Age deposits but no coins; there are 23 burhs where coins have been found, but only four with more than ten: York, Lincoln, Northampton and Winchester. There was a mint in Bedford from the mid-tenth century at least, but no coin finds until the twelfth century, despite substantial excavation. In Northampton the tenth- and eleventh-century levels at Chalk Lane yielded *c*.9000 potsherds, *c*.5000 animal bones and 4 coins; at St Peter's Street there were *c*.1500 potsherds, *c*.2500 animal bones and 6 coins. Of course, both pottery and animals (apart from a few hens and pigs) also had to be acquired by trade. Both commodities can be as much a record of transactions as coins, but could have been exchanged by barter with no coins changing hands.

The payment of rent was the other major mechanism whereby wealth changed hands. In Middle Saxon England rent was normally paid in kind. One of the earliest records of rent being paid to a royal estate is to Offa of Mercia by the church at Worcester, dated 793–6: 'two tuns full of pure ale and a coomb full of mild ale and a coomb full of Welsh ale, and seven oxen six wethers and 40 cheeses and six long *theru* [untrans.] and 30 ambers of unground corn and four ambers of meal.' The payment of rent in perishable goods was fairly inconvenient, as the king had to travel around his estate in order to eat up his rents. Paying in coin was simpler, and by the time of the Domesday Book most rents had been at least partly commuted to money.

It is perhaps significant that as many coins have been recovered from rural sites as from the urban markets. Viking Age levels at Portchester yielded *c*.11,000 animal bones and 2 coins; those at Cheddar *c*.1000 bones and 5

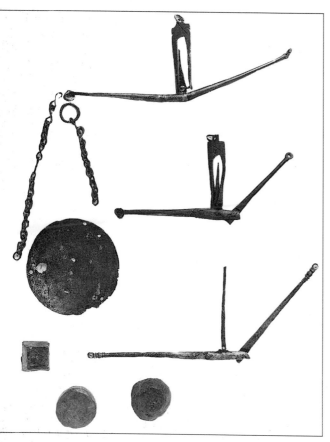

58 *Balances and weights, Coppergate, York: the upper balance, still with a pan, has fixed arms; the other two have folding arms. Three lead weights are at bottom left (York Archaeological Trust).*

coins. Folding scales identical to those from Chester and York (**58**) have been found at Goltho and North Elmham. Coins have even been recovered from isolated farmsteads such as Green Shiel, Mawgan Porth and Ribblehead, although one should be wary of assuming that such sites were integrated within a monetary economy. Isolated coin finds are perhaps more likely to represent silver hoards than exchange losses.

In conclusion, we should perhaps be careful about attributing twentieth-century capitalist motives to Viking settlers. The Viking Age economy would have been far more embedded, or interlinked, with the social system than a modern market economy is. Later literary sources testify to the importance of gift exchange and the giving of silver rings as a means of rewarding followers and winning their continued allegiance. Indeed, the trading of goods simply for monetary reward is frequently scorned. During the Viking Age land and property may have changed hands more often as gifts than as traded items.

1 The 'Edda', a full-scale replica of the Oseberg ship, during one of her earliest trials under sail in 1988. The Oseberg ship had been used as a burial ship for a Norwegian princess, and was excavated in 1904. Measuring 21.75m (71ft) long by 5.1m (17ft) wide, with 15 pairs of oars, it was possibly built in c.800 (M.O.H. Carver and D. Lee).

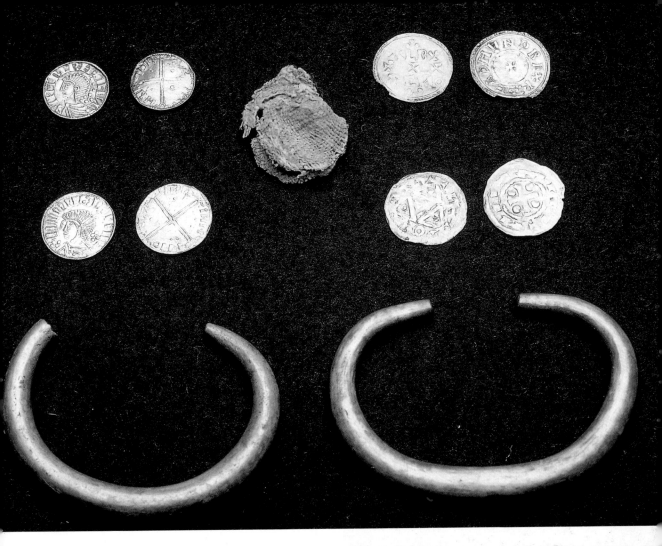

2 The Cuerdale Hoard (Lancashire) was discovered in 1840. Buried *c*.905 in a lead-lined chest it is the largest Viking Age hoard ever found in the British Isles, totalling some 40kg (88lbs) of silver coins, bullion and arm rings (by courtesy of the Trustees of the British Museum).

3 Part of the Kirk Michael hoard, Isle of Man, including two of the silver armlets, a selection of the 79 coins and part of the original cloth bag (Manx Museum and National Trust).

4 Aerial view of the Norse homestead at the Braaid, Isle of Man, including the bow-shaped hall and what is assumed to be an earlier roundhouse (Manx Museum and National Trust).

5 Aerial view of the promontory fort of Cronk ny Merriu, Isle of Man, guarding the entrance to Port Grenaugh (Manx Museum and National Trust).

6 Chester in the tenth century as it might have appeared from the south-west. The defences of the Roman fortress remain substantially intact but are believed to have been extended after the establishment of the Æthelflaedan burh (David Astley, Andrew Beckett and Carl Flint; Chester City Council).

7 Artist's reconstruction of a York quayside scene (Yorkshire Museum).

8 Viking ship burial at Balladoole, Isle of Man. Although no wood survived the stone cairn marks the outline of a boat and some 300 clench nails also attest to its former existence (Manx Museum and National Trust).

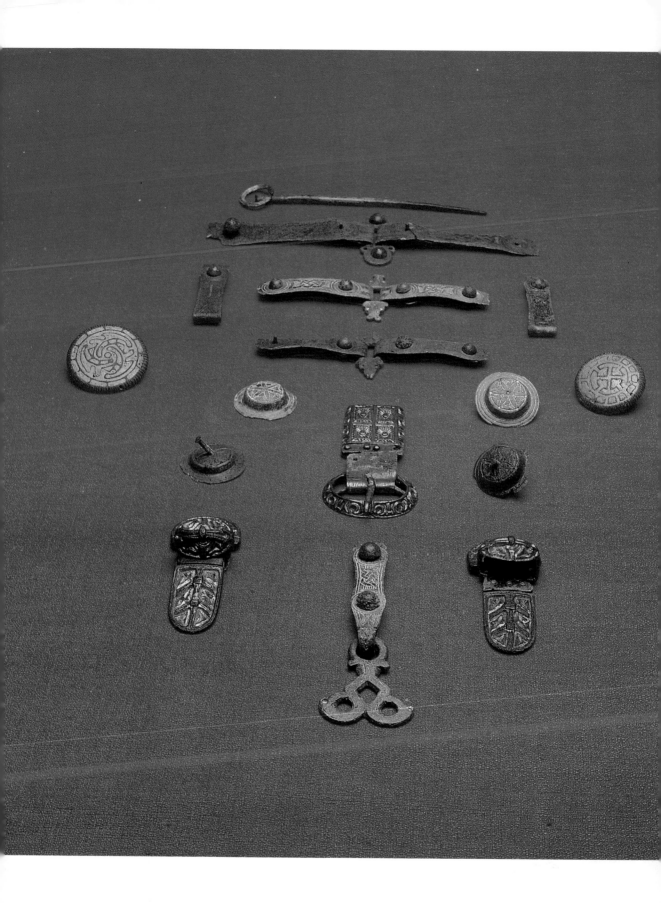

10 A watercolour of Viking grave-goods, Claughton Hall (Lancashire). The Viking Age finds included a pair of gilt-copper alloy tortoise brooches, a Carolingian silver mount, and various iron objects. This may have been a double burial of a male and female, but it is more likely that the burial was male and the brooches formed a ritual deposit of various amulets (Society of Antiquaries).

9 A selection of the finds from the Balladoole ship burial, including incised bronze mounts, elaborate silvered and gilded bronze buckles and strap ends (Manx Museum and National Trust).

11 Kirk Andreas Cross 128, Isle of Man:
Thorwald's Cross. One face is decorated with
a scene from *Ragnarok,* the last great battle
of Norse mythology. This is counterbalanced
by a Christian scene of the triumph of Christ
over Satan on the other face. (C.M. Dixon.)

9

Churches and monasteries

When the Vikings arrived in the British Isles they found a region which had long since been converted to Christianity. In England a network of minster churches is thought to have grown up during the seventh and eighth centuries and now covered the country. These included major town buildings such as Edwin's minster in York, or the church discovered by excavation in Cirencester, and smaller churches attached to rural aristocratic sites. In Atlantic Britain – the south-west peninsula, Wales, the Lake District and south-west Scotland – Christian roots were deeper still, reaching back at least to the fifth or sixth centuries, and probably to the Christianity of Late Roman Britain. On the Isle of Man it is believed that the system of keeils, or small Christian chapels, was already in place. Similar small chapels were also being built in the south-west from the eighth century onwards.

In all areas monasteries – the settlements of religious communities – provided a focus for Christian worship. But to the Vikings they were little more than unprotected storehouses of treasure. Although there are instances of English Christian leaders attacking religious sites, notably King Eadred who destroyed Ripon in 948, the Church had generally been able to depend upon spiritual sanctions for its safety. Viking raiders had no respect for such conventions. Yet there is no evidence that the plundering of churches by Vikings stemmed from any pagan hatred of Christianity; it was simply that they were regarded as available sources of loot.

Monasteries

Monastic sites were particularly vulnerable to attack. Anglo-Saxon monasteries frequently were major landowners and by the eighth century had also amassed considerable portable wealth of their own, as well as often being entrusted with treasure by Anglo-Saxon kings. The eremitic origins of monastic life meant that some early monasteries were sited on isolated coastal sites, with no hope of defence against attack from the sea.

In Northumbria the exposed coastal sites at Tynemouth, Hartlepool, Whitby, Monkwearmouth, Jarrow and Lindisfarne all appear to have been largely abandoned in the ninth century. Historical sources recount how the community of St Cuthbert, displaced from Lindisfarne, wandered for several years before finding a new home at Chester-le-Street. Hexham and Whithorn ceased to function as bishoprics, and even York was reduced to relative poverty. Further south the bishoprics of Dunwich, Elmham and Lindsey came to an effective end, the bishop's throne at North Elmham dramatically blackened by smoke. Exposed Kentish monasteries also disappear from the record, including Reculver, Dover and Folkestone. In the London area Woking and Bermondsey did not survive into the tenth century, and Barking Abbey was burnt down.

However, it is difficult to establish both how far such decline was the direct result of Viking attack, and also how far religious life may still have continued at some of these sites. Some communities certainly collapsed because Vikings seized their estates; others disappeared because of the replacement of the local aristocracy by Vikings who did not share their religious enthusiasms. Along the border between Wessex and the Danelaw, Ælfred seized monastic lands to act as a buffer zone against the Vikings. In short, the Viking Age brought

97

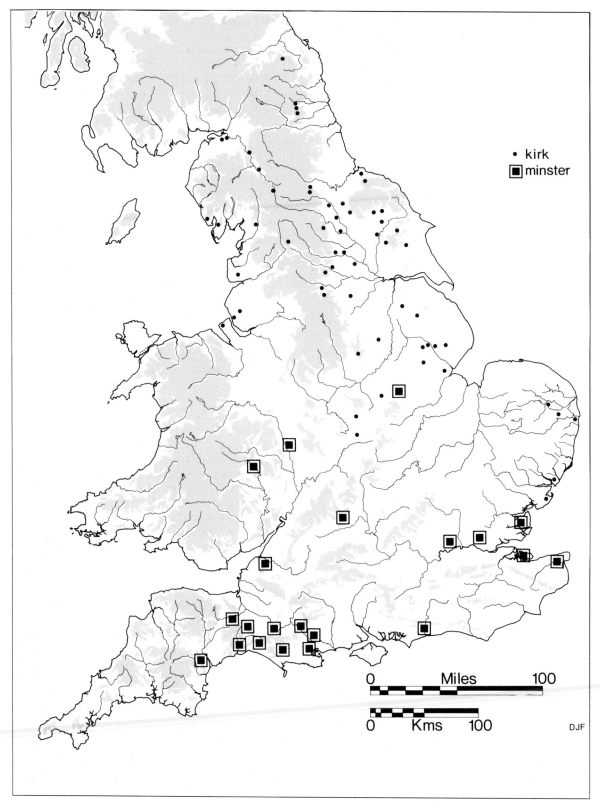

kirk
minster

about a redistribution of monastic land comparable to the Dissolution in the sixteenth century. Nevertheless, it would be a mistake to attribute the ninth-century monastic decline entirely to the Vikings; there was general concern for falling standards and even Ælfred did not blame the Vikings for the poor state of learning in England's monastic houses. Rather, he saw them as a punishment for earlier backsliding. Hartlepool ceased to function before the Viking raids, and although Jarrow and Monkwearmouth were apparently destroyed by fire this could have been at the hands of the Scots, and there appears to have been some religious presence into the Late Anglo-Saxon period.

After the disruption of the Viking raids and settlements, there was growing enthusiasm in the tenth century for a reform of monasticism based on the Benedictine rule. This was encouraged first by Edmund and then by Edgar, both believing that the spiritual support of the Church would be valuable to them. Old communities, including Glastonbury, Winchester and Worcester, were reformed and new ones founded. In the second half of the tenth century the foundation and endowment of monasteries underwent rapid growth throughout East Anglia and the south.

Minster churches

Minster churches frequently originated as part of monastic communities; the Old English *mynster* is derived from the Latin *monasterium*. By the Viking Age their function may have evolved into that of a church serving a congregation, with a community of clergy responsible for the pastoral care of a large area. Priests may have been sent out to preach to local communities, and the laity would come for baptism and burial. Minster churches may also have been founded by the aristocracy in the middle of their estates. Early royal minsters were often set within precinct enclosures, a little way from the royal palace. At Cheddar, for example, the ninth-century minster and palace were placed c.200 m (650 ft) apart, while at Bampton (Oxfordshire) traces of a large enclosure have been

59 *Place-names with the elements* kirk *and* minster *(after Morris 1989). Names with* -minster *occur chiefly in the south-west. Within the Danelaw many place-names include the Old Norse* kirk*, possibly coined by Scandinavians for villages with churches.*

recognized. This was not always the case; St Peter's, Gloucester, was sited within the town with the royal palace at Kingsholm outside the walls. In fact, as we have already seen (see Chapter 4), a high proportion of the new Anglo-Saxon towns grew around minster churches. The developing road system funnelled traffic towards them, and markets were established at their gates.

The wealth of minster churches depended on their monopoly as recipients of fees for burial and a variety of other dues. Many retained, or claimed, exclusive burial rights until well after the Norman Conquest. St Oswald's, Gloucester, for example, continued in importance, probably competing with only three or four other parish churches. At Winchester, the main cemetery was confined within the walls of the Old Minster until the fourteenth century. Nevertheless, the minsters were threatened by the rise of parish churches in the tenth century and gradually lost their special position.

Parish churches

The creation of rural parishes and parish churches went hand in hand with the fragmentation of the great estates during the Viking Age (see Chapter 3). The foundation of new local churches had been taking place spasmodically from the eighth century, but the great age of church building took place in the tenth and eleventh centuries. In fact, the construction of most new churches is thought by some to have taken place within the space of a few decades of 1000. By the time of the Domesday Book it can be demonstrated that there were over 2600 local churches, and arguably several thousands more. Probably almost 500 of these survive to the present day in some form or other.

This boom in the construction of churches was a by-product of the new landowners' quest for status. The possession of a church was an important status symbol, as well as a source of income. Noblemen also attempted to acquire burial rights for their churches, reserved until then by the old minster churches, so that their families could be buried on their estates, in the same way that pagan cemeteries had developed around ancestral graves. The new churches were therefore normally attached to the manorial residence, as at Raunds, where the church was built adjacent to the manorial enclosure. A survey within the archdeaconry of Colchester has revealed that out of a total of 29 churches of definite Saxon origin, 19 are alongside manorial halls.

Church foundations therefore frequently predate the development of the village, although as the manorial churches acquired burial and baptismal rights they also acquired the functions of a parish church. In many areas the modern parish boundaries may preserve the pre-Conquest manorial boundaries. On the Isle of Man a correspondence has been demonstrated between the 'treenland' farms and the existence of keeils, suggesting that each farmer may have erected his own chapel.

The ecclesiastical dues derived from the performance of burial and baptism would frequently have supported a parish priest; this in turn brought about significant changes in the organization of Christianity, as the priests were now brought into daily face-to-face contact with the parishioners.

Most of the manorial churches were new buildings, although some were adapted from existing minster or monastic sites. Many probably began as wooden buildings, but from the eleventh century most were soon transformed into impressive stone edifices. The new churches generally started as simple small rectangular boxes providing a nave only, although chancels were often added later. At Wharram Percy there is some evidence to suggest that an eighth- or ninth-century minster or monastery may have fallen into disuse as a result of Viking disruption. A small timber church was established on a new site in the tenth century (60), perhaps as a private church of an Anglo-Scandinavian lord. This was enlarged in the eleventh century by a small two-celled church consisting of a nave and chancel. The church became a focus for burials of the early lords of the Percy manor, and later of the parish. At Raunds a small rectangular late ninth- or tenth-century church was erected on a stone foundation adjacent to the manorial enclosure. In the eleventh century this building was replaced by a larger church, 15 m (50 ft) long, which by this time must have been serving the residents of the surrounding settlements, who were buried in the graveyard.

Many of the new churches were founded by Scandinavian lords. The sequestration of monastic estates in the Danelaw may even have facilitated the creation of local churches as some minsters lost control of their territories.

60 *View of the excavations inside St Martins, Wharram Percy, a deserted medieval village. The timber church is represented only by postholes, whilst the outline of the two-celled stone structure is shown by the wide foundation trenches (Wharram Research Project).*

At several Yorkshire sites the lords chose to record their benefactions in a prominent position on the church sundial, for all to read. At Kirkdale (North Yorkshire) the Old English inscription of 1055–65 commemorates that a lord with a Norse name, Orm, bought the redundant minster and erected a new church on its site (61). At Aldborough (North Yorkshire) a similar sundial records that 'Ulf ordered the church to be put up for himself and for Gunwaru's soul.'

Urban churches

There was a similar boom in church building in the towns. These new churches were linked to the wealth of towns and the presence of an urban aristocracy. Many were simple single-cell structures, functioning as private house-

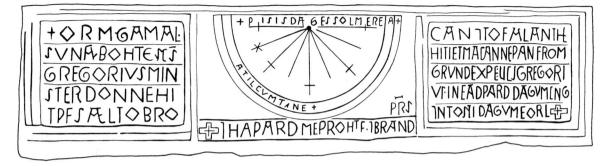

61 *Sundial, St Gregory's Minster, Kirkdale. The inscription records that: 'Orm, son of Gamal, acquired the church of St Gregory when it was tumbled and ruined, and had it rebuilt from the ground in honour of Christ and St Gregory, in the days of Edward the King and Tosti the Earl'.*

hold chapels; others may have been founded by groups of citizens. They were sometimes slow to acquire burial and other parochial rights, which were preserved by the urban minsters. Churches proliferated in towns such as Lincoln, London, York, Norwich and Winchester, although their number may be linked to the number of estates and the wealth of local lords rather than the size of population. In London there were 30 churches by the Norman Conquest; in Norwich there were 24. Most were sited on former domestic tenements in prominent positions on street frontages and particularly at the junctions of major streets. Recorded property disputes reveal that urban churches were treated as private property which could be inherited or bought and sold. Simple rectangular stone structures representing urban churches of the eleventh century have been excavated at the site of St Mark's, Lincoln; St Nicholas Shambles, London; and, perhaps of the tenth century, St Helen-on-the-Walls, York.

Many of these churches may also have been founded by Scandinavian settlers. There are churches dedicated to the Norwegian saint, Olaf, in Chester, York, Exeter, Southwark, Chichester, Grimsby and London. The Anglo-Saxon Chronicle records for 1055 that 'In this year passed away Earl Siward at York, and he was buried in Galmanho in the church which he himself had built and consecrated in the name of God and [St] Olaf'. At St Mary Castlegate, York, a late tenth- or early eleventh-century dedication stone reveals that two of the church's patrons had Norse names. In London, the church of St Clement Danes occupied a site that, significantly, was within a market street.

In both town and country, therefore, the Viking Age witnessed church foundation on a massive scale and the crystallization of the parish system. Changes in ecclesiastical structure mirror those in land ownership. The monopoly of the monasteries and minsters was broken as the old estates were fragmented. New secular landowners sought to demonstrate their power and wealth by the construction of private churches. Later they would tend to endow a chapel within an existing church, but for the present each manor had its own chapel, which would be used for burial. Such displays were not confined to Saxon lords, and Viking settlers competed to demonstrate their authority. Indeed, the changes in land ownership which led to this spate of church building may have been a direct consequence of the Scandinavian settlement.

10

Death and burial

It is one of the most remarkable aspects of Viking Age England that despite several centuries of Scandinavian settlement we have recognized very few graves of the settlers. As testament of the earlier invasion of Anglo-Saxon immigrants there are several thousand cremation and inhumation burials with grave-goods of the fifth to seventh centuries. Yet for the ninth and tenth centuries there are less than 25 pagan burial sites in the Danelaw.

Many Viking Age burials have been excavated in Scandinavia where it appears that there was a revival of pagan burial rites c.900 as paganism began to come into conflict with Christianity. The dead were either inhumed or cremated with their possessions; and either placed in coffins, or in a burial chamber or ship, or on a bier of some sort. Warriors were often buried with their horse and weapons (although not their armour, as once dead they could be killed any number of times without further harm!). Well-to-do females would be laid out with their jewellery, and sometimes a wagon to take them to the next world. Sacrificial offerings of food and drink, and even human slaves, have also been found. Provision was clearly being made for a further life after death of feasting and fighting in Valhalla.

We do know that Vikings were buried in England: from Scandinavia the Nävelsjö stone, for example, records that 'Gurnkel set this stone in memory of Gunnar, his father, Rode's son. Helgi laid him, his brother, in a stone coffin in England at Bath'. Why then should the Vikings, who quite literally caused so much ink to be spilt in monastic scriptoria, be almost invisible archaeologically?

Was it that the number of Vikings involved in the settlement was, after all, very small? Or was it that large numbers of first-generation settlers were rapidly converted to Christianity and adopted English burial practices almost immediately, thus blending into the background? Christianity was not adopted as the official religion of Norway until the early eleventh century and accompanied burial continued to be practised. By the late tenth century the Danes, on the other hand, had been converted to Christianity, and the habit of depositing grave-goods disappeared. It is unlikely, therefore, that later Danish immigrants to England would be buried in pagan graves. This may be part of the answer, but we shall need to examine the processes involved, as burial rites are sometimes resistant to change. For this we should compare England with the Isle of Man where, from an island of c.600 sq. km (232 sq. miles), there are over 40 known Viking burials (62). Why were Danish settlers in England so rapidly assimilated, whilst Norse Vikings on Man chose to preserve their pagan identity in death?

The Isle of Man

When the Norse settlers arrived in the Isle of Man they found lintel- or cist-grave cemeteries associated with many of the early Christian centres. Bodies were placed in shallow stone-lined graves, or cists, generally aligned east–west, and were not accompanied by grave-goods. The Viking attitude to these sites is not altogether clear.

In some cases the Norse appear to have utilized existing Christian cemeteries. Over 300 burials have recently been excavated in the Christian cemetery to the north of St German's Cathedral, St Patrick's Isle, Peel. Most of the Christian burials were in cist-graves although

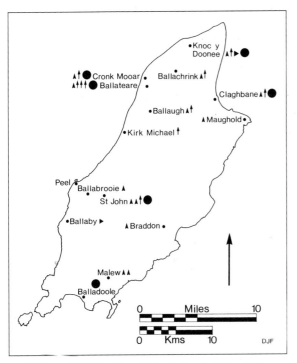

62 *Map of Viking burials, Isle of Man (after Cubbon 1983). For key see* **71**.

symbol. She was also wearing a fine necklace of 71 beads, including glass and amber, from Ireland, England and the Arabic world. An English connection may also be suggested by a pendant of two amber beads and a fossil ammonite trinket. The absence of Scandinavian-style tortoise brooches is curious, and might suggest that this woman was not a Viking at all, but perhaps a local Celt who had married a Viking settler and adopted his burial customs. It is curious that so far it is the only certain pagan female burial from the Isle of Man.

A second adult was buried with a ring-headed pin and a copper alloy buckle. Thirteen silver wire balls, each c.20 mm ($\frac{3}{4}$ in.) in diameter, were found near the knees of the body. These appear to represent the fringes of a cloak that the corpse was shrouded in. A third body had similar small silver balls around both wrists, which must have again fringed a cloak or tunic. A fourth grave contained a copper alloy buckle, a gilt plaque, and a knife in a wooden scabbard. A fifth burial must have been placed in a wooden chest, like some of the Christian burials, as there were the remains of an iron hasp. The body had been buried wearing a cloak, as the grave-goods comprised a ring-headed pin, a strap-end and a buckle. There were also two accompanied child burials. One had a copper alloy bell and a necklace of amber and glass beads; the other had a single multicoloured glass bead. One of the children had an Eadred halfpenny of 946–55 placed in his mouth, apparently respecting the custom of 'paying the ferryman'.

Peel provides the best evidence for continued use of a Christian cemetery, but there are other possibilities at Balladoyne and Cronk ny Howe. There are also a number of Viking weapon finds from Manx churchyards: two swords from Malew; swords from Braddan, Jurby and Maughold; and a spearhead from Kirk Michael. It is likely that the churchyards had been early Christian cemeteries, and the weapons originated from Viking graves disturbed by later gravedigging. Of course, burial in a churchyard does not necessarily imply that the Vikings had been converted to Christianity. There are at least two possible interpretations. The first is that the Vikings had indeed been converted, and chose the churchyards out of respect for the existing burial grounds, although the erection of burial mounds and the presence of weapons does not suggest that they were prac-

these became less well made through time and end up simply as stone slabs which surround and protect the head. The cemetery continued in use into the Norse period with a series of unaccompanied burials in wooden coffins, but there were also at least seven accompanied burials of the tenth century. These are distributed throughout the cemetery, the individual graves being up to 20 m (65 ft) apart, and share the same style of grave construction and alignment as the Christian burials. In short, there is nothing to suggest a break in continuity.

The richest burial was of a female, who had been buried in a well-made cist-grave in the same style as the Christian graves except that it did not have stones at the head and foot. The woman, who suffered from rickets, had been laid with a cushion or pillow to support her head. She was accompanied by various objects, including a cooking spit lying on top of four layers of cloth; two knives, one prestigious with an elaborate handle, the other a plain domestic type; a decorated bone comb, not of Scandinavian form; a work box or bag with two needles; a pair of small domestic shears, suspended from a belt; and a curious 'mortar and pestle' amulet, which may have been a sexual or fertility

63 *Unexcavated Viking Age burial mound, Jurby, Isle of Man: a weapon found in the graveyard may have been disturbed from the grave (L.A.S. Butler).*

tising a Christian burial rite (**63**). The second possibility is that they recognized that the communal cemeteries were important places to the local population, perhaps representing their claim to the land, and chose to bury their dead in these places to assert their dominance, regardless of the wishes of the Christian community.

Some illumination of the relationship between the Manx inhabitants and the first Norse settlers is perhaps to be found at the site of Chapel Hill, Balladoole (**colour plate 8**). Here a Viking ship burial seems to have been deliberately placed so as to destroy Christian cist-graves. Within an Iron Age enclosure a number of cist-graves were dug into the Iron Age occupation layers. In the Viking Age these were overlain by a stone boat-shaped cairn forming the outline of a ship. Although no wood has survived it is clear that an actual vessel had been buried. The distribution of some 300 clench nails marked the outline of a boat some 11 m (36 ft) in length by 3 m (10 ft) broad amidships (**64**). It appears that two corpses were buried in the boat. A male was laid out on his back on the bottom of the boat, and there may have been a female nearby. Parts of two further skulls were found mixed together, although at least one of these may have been disturbed from the earlier graves.

The burial was accompanied by many grave-goods (**colour plate 9**), although their original position had been disturbed by rabbits. These included various personal items comprising a cloak pin, a knife, a honestone, a flint strike-a-light and a silver Carolingian belt buckle and strap-end. There was also an iron cauldron, Continental-style spurs, a horse bit and bridle mounts and a shield which had been placed over the knees. There were no offensive weapons, however, neither sword nor spear. The burial cairn was covered by a layer of cremated bones of a selection of the dead man's livestock, including horse, ox, pig, sheep or goat, dog and cat. A substantial wooden post was erected to the north of the south-west end of the boat. It is impossible to know whether this bore some standard or wooden carving or other marker; perhaps it was the ship's mast, bearing an ornate weather-vane. It must certainly have increased the prominence of the burial in the landscape.

Before the Balladoole boat had been placed in position the old ground surface had been scooped away to make room for it. This had involved removing the cist covers, thereby

64 *Outline plan of a Viking ship burial, Balladoole, Isle of Man. The iron clench nails indicate the position of the boat, which disturbed earlier Christian burials. The dots indicate the position of the skulls of the Christian burials, where known (after Bersu and Wilson 1966). (See also colour plates 8 and 9).*

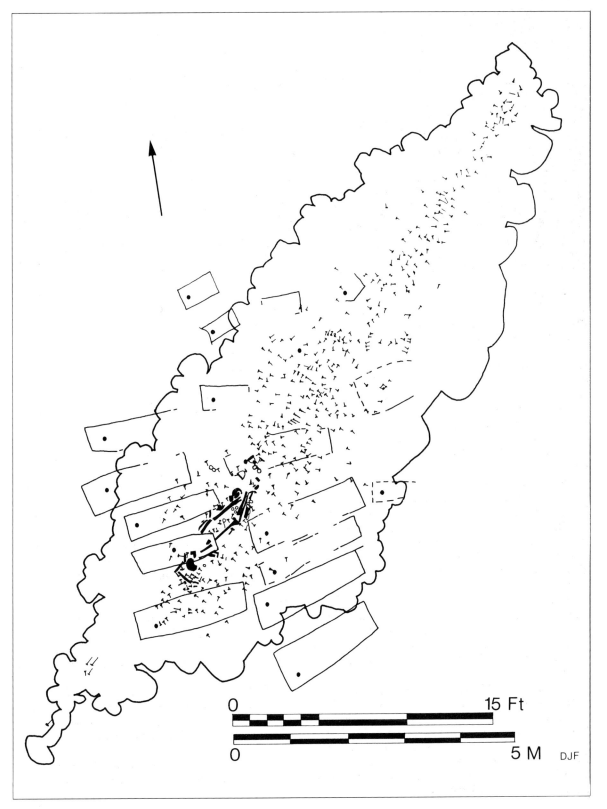

0   15 Ft

0   5 M   DJF

exposing the earlier burials. The bones had frequently been replaced in a disturbed state, or spread out under the boat. Many of the small bones of the hands and feet were still articulated when spread out. Thus they must still have been held together by soft tissue, indicating that very little time can have elapsed before the Vikings disturbed this burial site. There can be little doubt that the Vikings were aware that they were desecrating a recent cemetery; indeed it is difficult not to conclude that at Balladoole, in contrast to Peel, we have the deliberate and symbolic imposition of a pagan burial rite over a Christian cemetery.

Many of the first generation of Viking settlers were buried in prominent mounds sited on low hills overlooking the sea. There is a notable concentration in the parish of Jurby (65), of which two have been excavated. At Ballateare (66) a circular turf mound covered a burial pit 1.2 m (4 ft) in depth and with vertical sides. At the base a rectangular coffin containing the outstretched body of a young male, 20–25 years of age, had been placed. The body was wrapped in a cloak held in place by

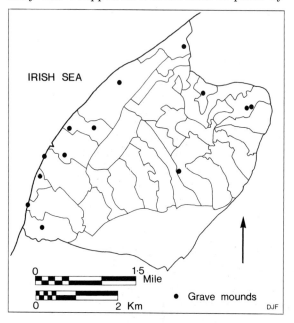

65 *Burial mounds and primary land units, parish of Jurby, Isle of Man. Six out of eight of the quarterland farms on the coastal strip are distinguished by a prominently sited burial mound. Subsequent settlers were forced inland, bringing the total up to 13 mounds in the parish (after Reilly 1988).*

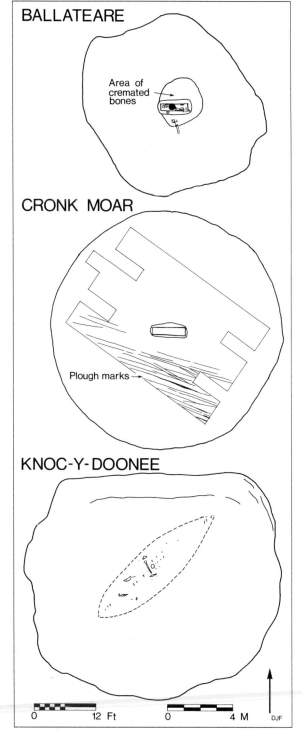

66 *Plans of excavated Viking burial mounds (after Bersu and Wilson 1966 and Kermode 1930).*

a ring-headed pin. Various weapons had been placed outside the coffin, most of which showed evidence of having been deliberately damaged to 'kill' them. The sword had been broken into three pieces and replaced in its scabbard. A shield with traces of painted leather covering wooden board had been placed on the south side. The shield boss had two deep indentations caused by blows of a sword or axe. Two spears had been thrown into the backfill of the burial pit. The spearheads rested 80 cm (32 in.) below the top of the pit, suggesting that they too must have been broken.

A thin layer of cremated animal bone had been spread over the mound, including ox, horse, sheep, and dog; this layer covered and partly included a second skeleton, aligned north–south. The arms were raised upwards, with their upper parts at right angles to the body. This was a young female, aged between 20 and 30; at the top of her skull there was a large hole created by the slashing blow of a heavy implement (**67**). There can be no doubt

67 *Female skull, Ballateare (Manx Museum and National Trust).*

that Ballateare is the grave of a young Viking colonist, buried with the symbols of his power (his weapons) and symbols of his wealth (his possessions, including his animals and a slave-girl). The mound was covered with turves, and the excavator suggests that these also represent a symbolic sacrifice. They were not dug from the immediate vicinity of the mound, and must represent 500 sq. m (5400 sq. ft) of sods brought from the fields of the deceased. Finally, a post was erected in the centre of the mound to draw attention to the burial.

From the burial at Cronk Mooar (see **66**) there is again a wide and commanding view. The mound is of a similar size to that at Ballateare, and the burial shares many similar features. Significantly, at Cronk Mooar the mound was built over plough marks on a previously undisturbed land surface. It is tempting to conclude that this was land which was being taken into arable cultivation for the first time by the Viking farmer whose grave this was. A central rectangular pit was dug into the subsoil, and lined with a planked burial chamber. A dead male was lain in the chamber, wrapped in a cloak and with a knife at his belt. There was

68 *The weapons from the Viking grave at Cronk Mooar, Jurby. Weapons were frequently deliberately damaged or broken before burial (Manx Museum and National Trust).*

a sword in its scabbard in three pieces, although in this case it is not certain if the damage occurred before burial (**68**). The remains of the shaggy woollen cloak contained many fly pupae, indicating that the corpse had been lying in state for some time before burial, and was beginning to rot. Clearly the preparation of the Viking funeral took some time. Traces of burnt bone were again found in the make-up of the burial mound, presumably from various animal offerings.

A fourth Viking mound burial has been excavated at Knoc-y-Doonee (see **66**), in the parish of Andreas. The mound covered a boat represented by some 300 iron clench nails. Neither this nor the Balladoole boat are large enough to have been Viking longships. Both probably had in the region of four pairs of oars and may have been small coastal fishing vessels. The body of a man had been laid in the boat wrapped in his cloak. He was accompanied by a knife, sword, battleaxe, spear and shield and an iron

bowl covered with cloth, possibly a food offering. Various tools, including a smith's hammer and tongs and fishing nets (indicated by a lead weight) had been placed in the stern. A horse with items of harness and possibly a dog were also buried alongside.

There are records of several other Viking mound burials, including Ballachrink, Ballaugh and St John's, but none have been excavated in recent years. Other weapon finds from Ballabrooie and Ballaby may also be regarded as being derived from burials, possibly barrows. At Claghbane, Ramsey, excavation following a chance find revealed a sword, spearhead and shield boss together with a single bead. However, these were undisturbed in a position where they were clearly not part of a burial, and must have been some form of cenotaph memorial or other ritual deposit.

On the Isle of Man, therefore, we have a picture of Norse settlers retaining and initially developing their native pagan burial rites. Their burial mounds assert their power over land, over animals and over people. They did not ignore the Christian burial grounds but, identifying them as important places to the local populace, the Vikings chose to use them as demonstrations of their power. By the time of the second or third generation of settlers, their position now fully secure, they could afford to be assimilated into the local population, and thereafter we can identify no difference between Norse and native burial practices.

Christian burial in England

Viking settlers in England also found a native population who were accustomed to burying their dead in communal cemeteries. In the south-west, as in the Isle of Man, pre-Viking Christian burials were normally placed in cist-grave cemeteries. At Mawgan Porth a cist-grave cemetery of 23 graves has been excavated. The bodies were laid in shallow graves, with their heads to the west. Most were in covered cists built of slate slabs set on edge. None was accompanied by grave-goods. Over much of England, however, by the ninth century, burial was normally undertaken in a churchyard (69), initially around a minster church, but, as the minsters lost their monopoly on burial rites, also around the growing number of manorial churches. It is probable that the majority of English medieval churchyards were in use for burial before the Norman Conquest.

At Raunds 368 burials have been excavated in a tenth- and eleventh-century graveyard clustered around the church within a rectangular ditched enclosure. It has been estimated that the graveyard probably served a community of between 25 and 45 individuals. All the graves were aligned west–east with the head to the west; none were buried with grave-goods. Most of the bodies were simply placed in holes in the ground, although in about 60 per cent of cases slabs of limestone were used as head or foot pillows. There are indications of wooden coffins being used in some cases, and six elite burials were differentiated from the rest by being placed in lidded stone coffins. The cemetery appears to have developed in rows and zones around the church, and post-holes may represent the position of grave markers. It was considered proper to bury infants in the cemetery, unlike in many societies; and these were concentrated to the south and east of the church.

Cemeteries also developed around the Saxon cathedral churches and Viking Age burials have been found during work on many sites, including Carlisle, Exeter, Gloucester, Hereford, London, North Elmham, Oxford, Repton,

69 *Grave slabs, St Martin's, Wharram Percy. The burials of two adults and a child were discovered, marked by limestone slabs, with head- and foot-stones (Wharram Research Project).*

Shrewsbury, Winchester, Worcester and York. Their use as burial places probably followed from their function as shrines and resting places for the bodies or relics of notable saints. Those seeking salvation hoped to gain by being buried in proximity to a holy relic.

At York a wide variety of burial rites has been identified in excavations of Viking Age deposits under the Minster. A cemetery was established on the site of the Roman basilica, beneath the south transept of the present Minster, in the early ninth century. Its limits were apparently defined by the bases of the outer walls of the old Roman headquarters building, and a Roman road which continued in use as a routeway. The Anglo-Saxon church probably lay to the south-west. Over 100 burials have been excavated, with roughly equal numbers of males and females.

Less than 10 per cent of the burials were in coffins. One was in a lidded stone coffin with a recess for the head; up to six may have been in wooden coffins constructed of planks; and four were buried in wooden domestic storage chests, comprising one adult female, two adult males (one with a coin of 841–8), and an adolescent with traces of gold thread from a fine costume. There were also seven cist-type graves, including the use of pillow stones, and one corpse laid on a bed of mortar. Two of the bodies appear to have been placed upon wooden biers, rather than in coffins. The first was an adult male lying between two rows of clench nails which held together the oak planks of a wool-caulked clinker construction. Pillow stones had been positioned to support the head. This grave was also exceptional in that it was aligned east–west, unlike the others which followed the Roman building alignment. The second body laid on a bier was a child, aged 4–6. The rest of the York burials were simply placed in holes in the ground, generally oval-shaped cuts, without coffins or shrouds.

Twelve of the York burials were, however, placed on beds of charcoal. They included both coffined and uncoffined burials. In just one case the charcoal had been laid over the body; otherwise the body was placed on the charcoal. These were not the latest burials and this must be seen as a particular custom reserved for a subset of burials. Charcoal burials are known from other cathedral cemeteries, including Exeter, Hereford, Oxford and Worcester, and appear to range in date from the ninth to the twelfth century. Charcoal may have served the practical function of soaking up fluids from a decaying corpse and avoiding unpleasant smells, but it seems to have been reserved for those of special status; perhaps it was thought to preserve the body from corruption. At Hereford all the burials inside the church were given a charcoal lining.

Twelve of the York Minster burials were marked by recumbent carved stone slabs (**70**). A few had separate head and/or foot stones, including cut-down shafts, or fragments of earlier recumbent slabs. Most had a single recumbent slab decorated on the top only, including two of hogback form (see Chapter 11). One adult male was buried under a reused inscribed Roman memorial to which an Anglo-Saxon inscription had been added. These graves must certainly represent some of the elite of

70 *Grave slabs, York Minster: the slabs and head-stones are decorated with Scandinavian-style ornament (Crown Copyright).*

York who chose to be buried at their minster church. It is impossible to say if they were Vikings or Anglo-Saxons, although it was thought fitting to decorate their memorials with Scandinavian-style ornament. One is reminded that Guthrith, one of the early Viking rulers of York, was buried in York Minster. One can say that at least two of the memorials marked the graves of children, aged 3–5 and 10–12, which is an interesting statement of how high status could be achieved in Viking York: apparently some were born to it.

Burials with Scandinavian-style markers have not been found at other cathedral cemeteries. At North Elmham 194 eleventh-century graves were excavated within a fenced enclosure. All were aligned west–east with their heads in the west. There was no clear evidence of coffins, no trace of grave-markers, and no grave-goods. At the Castle Green (Hereford) 87 burials were excavated from a much larger cemetery dating from the seventh to the twelfth centuries. The burials were initially around a timber church which was replaced by a stone structure in the eleventh century. The method of corpse disposal appears to have been particularly important in the ninth and tenth centuries: of 18 burials, 13 were in charcoal, 12 in coffins and 4 had pillow stones.

Viking burials in England

In contrast to the Isle of Man, it is very difficult to find examples of Viking pagan burials in the Danelaw (71). As on the Isle of Man, a number of Viking Age artefacts, including weapons, have been found in Christian graveyards. One suspects that if it were possible to excavate the depths of the graveyards of many of our early churches this number would be increased. These may be examples of Viking settlers utilizing existing burial grounds, but again we must be wary of assuming that this necessarily means that they were Christians.

In Cumbria a sword, shield boss, iron bar and knife were found in the graveyard at Ormside in 1898. An elaborate silver bowl was found at the same site on a separate occasion, and may represent a second grave. Swords have also been found in the churchyards at Rampside (Cumbria) and West Seaton, Workington (Cumbria). The latter was bent and broken as if it had been ritually 'killed'. There is also a record of a weapon being found in the churchyard at Heysham (Lancashire), and a ring-headed cloak pin was recovered from the churchyard at Brigham (Cumbria). A number of early tenth-century burials with grave-goods were revealed by excavations at Carlisle Cathedral in 1988.

In Yorkshire, when the floor of the church at Kildale was removed in 1867 it is recorded that seven or eight burials were observed, all aligned east–west and all with grave-goods. One burial, possibly in the chancel, had a sword, tweezers, a silver-inlaid knife and a set of scales. There was a burial in the nave with an axe and at least three more with swords and knives. These burials may have been associated with an earlier church, but it is also possible that they pre-date the Christian use of the site. Another male burial was found in Wensley churchyard. This grave was also orientated east–west and contained a sword, spear, knife and an iron sickle. Like those on the Isle of Man, these graves symbolize the sources of Viking power and wealth: through force of arms (the weapons), through trade (the set of scales) and through agriculture (the sickle).

In York, capital of the Viking kingdom, many

years of major excavations have produced less than half-a-dozen pagan Viking burials. Four skeletons were found immediately to the north of the present church of St Mary Bishophill Junior, but the fact that they are on a different alignment to the eleventh-century tower suggests that they may have been buried before the church was built. There were two young males, the first with a silver arm ring on his upper left arm, and the second with a St Peter's penny among his finger bones, a schist honestone and a copper alloy buckle plate. The latter also had a knife blade half way up his back and it has been suggested that it was embedded in it! Two young females were buried with them on the same alignment, but these were unaccompanied by grave-goods. At the neighbouring church of St Mary Bishophill Senior there was a further possible Viking grave with a tenth-century strap-end.

As well as the mass burial (see Chapter 2), a number of Viking burials have been excavated at the east end of the church at Repton. The earliest grave was of a man aged at least 35–40, who had been killed by a massive cut to the top of his left leg. He wore a necklace of two glass beads and a silver Thor's hammer amulet. By his side was a sword in a leather-bound wooden scabbard with a fleece lining, a folding knife and a key. A wild boar's tusk and a jackdaw bone had been carefully placed between his thighs. A substantial post-hole at the eastern end of the grave suggests that it had been marked by a wooden post. Other graves were accompanied by knives and weapons; it is likely that an axe found in the graveyard in 1922 also came from a grave. One burial was accompanied by five silver pennies and a gold finger ring, lying together beside the skull. The coins suggest a burial date in the 870s; it is likely that these were further burials of Viking warriors of the 'Great Army' which wintered at Repton in 873–4.

Finally, in Essex we have two examples of Anglo-Saxon cemeteries that were used for accompanied burials. At Saffron Walden one burial in a row of Late Saxon graves contained a knife and a necklace with silver pendants that had probably been manufactured in Scandinavia in the tenth century. A copper alloy strap-end was also found on the site, and may have been disturbed from a second burial. At Waltham Abbey a Mid-Saxon cemetery with uncoffined burials also continued in use in the

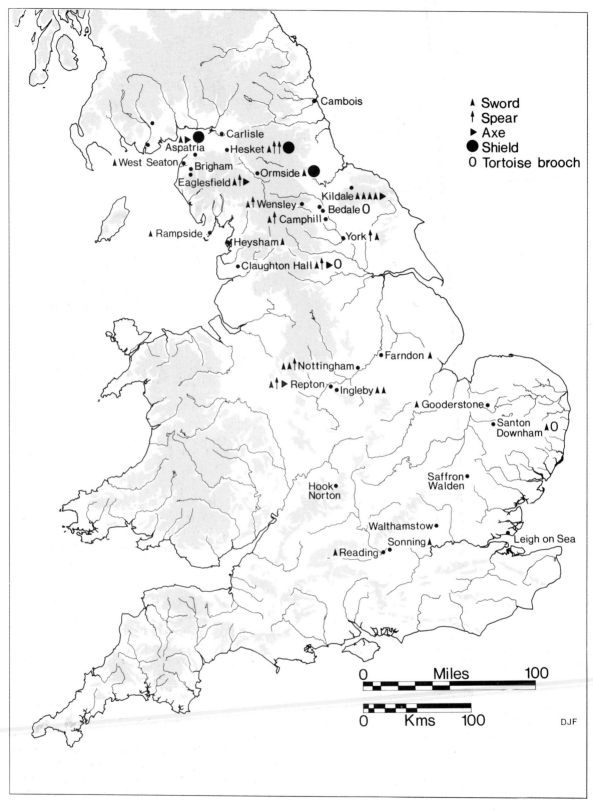

Sword ▲
Spear ↑
Axe ▶
Shield ●
Tortoise brooch 0

Cambois

Carlisle
Aspatria ▲▶
Hesket ▲↑↑ ●
West Seaton ▲
Brigham ●
Ormside ▲
Eaglesfield ▲↑▶
Kildale ▲▲▲▲▶
Wensley ▲↑
Bedale 0
Camphill ▲↑
Rampside ▲
York ↑▲
Heysham ▲
Claughton Hall ▲↑▶ 0

Farndon ▲
Nottingham ▲▲↑
Repton ▲↑▶
Ingleby ▲▲
Gooderstone ▲
Santon Downham ▲0
Saffron Walden
Hook Norton
Walthamstow
Leigh on Sea
Sonning ▲
Reading ▲

0   Miles   100

0   Kms   100

DJF

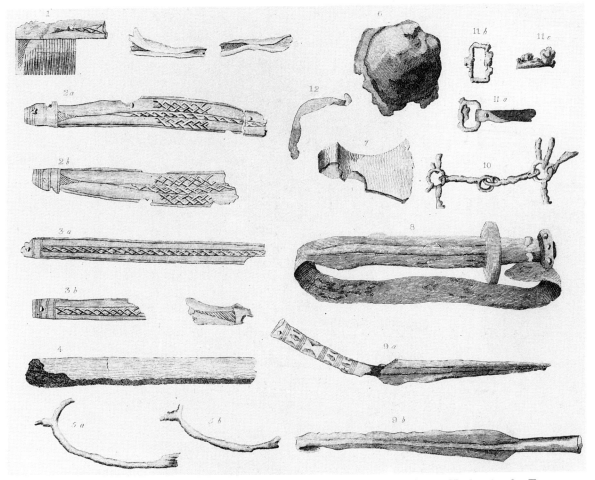

Viking period. One grave contained a copper alloy plate with Viking-style decoration of the late tenth or early eleventh century. Significantly, this burial was some 130 m (426 ft) from the bow-sided hall described in Chapter 5.

Away from the Christian churchyards there are few Viking burials in the Danelaw. One exception is Cumbria, where there is a series of tenth-century accompanied burials of a similar character to those found on the Isle of Man. These may have been Norse immigrants from the Irish Sea area, possibly even from the Isle of Man itself. Many are mound burials and appear to be asserting claims to land.

At Hesket in the Forest a layer of charcoal, bones and ashes with several grave-goods was found in 1822 lying on a bed of sand under a cairn 7 m (23 ft) in diameter (72). All the burnt

72 Viking grave finds, Hesket in the Forest (Cumbria). This nineteenth-century illustration shows: 1–3 antler comb fragments; 4 whetstone; 5 spurs; 6 shield boss; 7 axe; 8 sword 9 spearheads; 10 bridle; 11 buckles; 12 iron fragment (Photo: York Archaeological Trust).

bones were of animals that had been cremated as part of the burial rite; there was no trace of a human skeleton. The weapons had been deliberately damaged. The sword and spears were bent; the shield had been broken in two. The horse and weapons may also have been thrown on the cremation pyre as it was reported that the sword, shield boss and bridle bit were all burnt. A second mound burial was also discovered in 1822 at Claughton Hall, Garstang (Lancashire) when a small sand mound was cut through in the course of road building. There may have been a wooden chamber two or three feet below the surface and the Viking Age finds

71 Map of Viking Age burials in England (after Wilson 1976).

included a Bronze Age axe hammer and a pot containing a cremation, now lost, so this may be a secondary usage of a prehistoric barrow (**colour plate 10**).

At Beacon Hill, Aspatria, a cist burial was found containing a skeleton with a sword and possibly a shield, an axe, a strap-end with a Carolingian-style buckle and an iron bridle bit. Finally, at Eaglesfield six skeletons were found on the limestone crags, although only one was demonstrably Viking, as it was accompanied by a sword, a spear or axe and possibly a ring-headed cloak pin.

Outside Cumbria, Viking mound burials are extremely rare in England. At Cambois, Bedlington (Northumberland) three bodies were found in a cist-grave in a mound. One was female, aged 45–60; the other two were males, the first in his 20s and the second in his 40s. The only grave-goods were an enamelled disc brooch and a bone comb. Lack of weapons perhaps suggests that these may have been relatively peaceful landowners; they are certainly a Viking Age elite in an area with little other evidence for their presence. Further south, a sword and spear buried with a skeleton in a hill at Camphill, Burneston (North Yorkshire) may represent the choice of a natural prominence for a burial to avoid erecting a mound. A spear and sword from Acomb, York, are also thought to have come from a mound burial.

There is an antiquarian record that in 1723 a skeleton, bridle bit and an iron knife with a bone handle were found in the middle of the top of Silbury Hill (Wiltshire), but the finds are now lost and thus impossible to date to the Viking Age. Other possible Viking mound burials have been identified at Hook Norton (Oxfordshire) and Leigh-on-Sea (Essex), where burials were found associated with late ninth-century coin hoards.

The only other mound burials from England come from the unique site at Ingleby, not far from Repton. Here there are about 60 mounds on a commanding site on a natural ridge overlooking the river Trent, 1.2 km ($\frac{3}{4}$ mile) from the river (**73**). Several were excavated in the 1950s, and although some were apparently empty and may have been natural, others did cover burial deposits. The mounds were generally 9 m (30 ft) in diameter and contained cremation hearths, often in stone settings, about 1.8 m (6 ft) in diameter. The hearths contained a layer

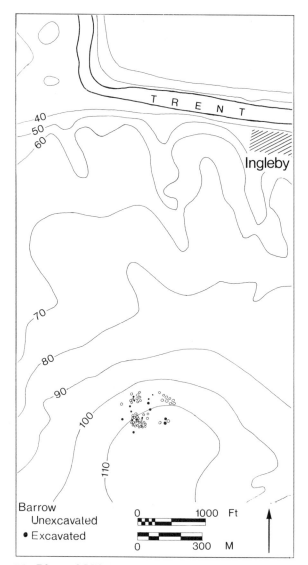

73 *Plan of Viking cemetery, Ingleby (Derbyshire).*

of charcoal and burnt human and animal bone, including both men and women, as well as cattle, sheep, dog, and possibly horse and pig. A number of grave-goods were found mixed in with the burnt remains, including two mutilated swords, iron buckles and a copper alloy strap-end. In one mound there were the remains of an iron spade, three nails and wire embroidery, comparable to finds from ninth- and tenth-century graves at Birka in Sweden.

Ingleby is a curious site, and invites further research. There is no evidence as to where the community which was responsible for the erection of these mounds lived. Apparently the mounds were constructed within a fairly short space of time, but the presence of female graves argues against this being the cemetery of a Viking raiding party or army. Ingleby is particularly interesting because it is the only instance of Viking cremation burial found in England. The small numbers of nails recovered from each mound, although apparently unexciting finds, can also now be seen to be potentially important. They are probably the only remains of the wooden platforms, or biers, on which the dead were cremated. Two of the mounds contained clench nails similar to those interpreted as being from a bier, found at York Minster.

Clench nails may be used to rivet together lapped boards to make crude coffins, but at several other sites clench nails have been interpreted as representing the remains of clinker-built boats. At Sutton Hoo (Suffolk) evidence for a Scandinavian-style royal ship burial has been preserved by an outline of the boat in sand, with lines of clench nails. The Sutton Hoo burial is some 200 years earlier than the Viking Age, although as seen above (p. 104), clench nails preserve the outline of boats in two Viking Age burials from the Isle of Man. There are also some possible instances from England, although none have been properly excavated or recorded.

At Walthamstow (Essex) a clinker-built boat found in 1900 close by a Viking Age sword is now dated as a sixteenth- or seventeenth-century river barge. Another boat was found nearby in 1830, but there is no evidence that there was an associated burial. There is another early report that in 1855 clench nails of a Viking boat were found in a sand pit at Catfield (Norfolk), although no burial was recorded. Where burials with clench nails have been properly excavated it seems more likely that the nails are from wooden biers, although there is the reasonable suggestion that the biers were fashioned from parts of boats which had been broken up for the purpose. The York Minster bier could well have been a reused boat fragment, and the Ingleby burials also contained enough clench nails to represent one or two planks, but certainly not complete ships. Similarly, beneath the former church at Thorpe-by-Norwich (Norfolk) at least two rows of clench nails were discovered with a burial. A Viking Age silver pin was also found, although apparently not with the burial.

At Caister-by-Yarmouth (Norfolk) an extensive cemetery has been excavated containing 12 burials that included clench nails. The cemetery is generally regarded as being Mid-Saxon, but some of the clench-nail burials may be later. Developed Stamford ware was found in two graves, and a silver penny of Ecgbryht of Wessex dated c.830–5 in another. Six of the burials with clench nails were of males; four were of females; one was of an adolescent; the last was of a child aged 3–4 years. At Caister, in almost all cases the nails were spread over the body; only in one case were boat timbers used as a bier. It appears, therefore, that reused lapped planks, probably derived from boats, were being employed as grave covers or coffin lids. At St Peter's Church, Barton-on-Humber there were 16 graves with coffins of wood held together by clench nails; again these are seen as being boats, or parts of boats, used as coffins or covers. Parts of old boats might simply have provided handy materials from which to construct coffins and biers in coastal and riverine regions, but this is really too mundane an explanation. Given the Scandinavian tradition of ship burial it seems reasonable that the symbolism of the boats' timbers was intentional and that even those burials without grave-goods may be Scandinavian settlers who had accepted a Christian-style burials but retained at least one element of their own customs.

Finally, we can complete our catalogue of Viking graves in England with a number of single- or double-inhumation graves discovered with either weapons or jewellery which suggest a Scandinavian link. At Sonning (Berkshire) the skeletons of two young males were discovered in 1966 during gravel quarrying. They were buried with a sword, a ring-headed pin (this perhaps suggesting a northern link), an Anglo-Saxon-style knife and six arrowheads. Not far away, at Reading, a human skeleton had been found with a bent sword and a horse in 1831. At Santon Downham (Suffolk) an iron sword and pair of tortoise brooches were discovered in 1867. They have been interpreted as representing a double burial of the early tenth century, but the brooches may represent an offering, like those at Claughton Hall. A pair of tortoise brooches, wired together, were also found at Bedale (North Yorkshire). The trefoil brooch from Low Dalby (North Yorkshire) may also have originated from a grave, although it was found on its own. And finally, there are

74 *A tenth-century stirrup from the river Witham (Lincolnshire). Most Viking Age stirrups have been recovered from river beds, and may have been ritual offerings (Trustees of the British Museum).*

two swords and a spear from Nottingham, thought to represent two Viking graves, and a seax and knife from Wicken Fen (Cambridgeshire), although the knife is probably Anglo-Saxon.

Ritual deposits
Apart from Viking objects associated with human burials there is also a larger quantity of material, weaponry in particular, discovered in rivers (**74**). In 1965 it was calculated that 34 Viking Age swords had been found in English rivers, as opposed to eight from churchyards and Viking graves. Twenty-four of these were from the Thames or its tributaries. Spears, axes, knives and tools have also been found. Eight axes, six spearheads, a pair of tongs and an anchor have been dredged from under Old London Bridge alone (**75**). Stirrups, shears, a shield boss, a horseshoe and spurs were found in 1884 in the river Cherwell under Magdalen Bridge at Oxford. These finds have often been interpreted as evidence of Viking battle losses, with the corpses of Viking warriors being dumped in the river along with all their armour, weapons and tools. This seems unlikely. A more recent find from Skerne (Humberside) perhaps reveals the true nature of these deposits. Here a number of animal skeletons and Viking metalwork have been found closely associated with the oak piles of a bridge abutment or jetty (**76**). In total there were at least 20 animals, including horses, cattle, sheep and dogs. Only one showed signs of slaughter (a horse had been pole-axed in the forehead); none showed signs of butchery for consumption. Four knives, a spoon-bit, an adze and a Viking sword in a wooden scabbard of willow poplar with fleece lining were also found.

There are similar finds from Scandinavia, continuing an Iron Age tradition of bog offerings of horses and weapons, at sites such as Illerup. These deposits were probably ritual sacrifices, perhaps offered to give thanks for success in a previous battle, or in the hope of good fortune in a forthcoming one.

The Vikings and Christianity
We have seen how the deliberate visibility of Viking burials on the Isle of Man contrasts sharply with their relative invisibility over the rest of England. The catalogue of Viking burials in England is worth enumeration to emphasize how little evidence there is. Apart from a few Norse-style burials from Cumbria (which probably derive from the Irish Sea area anyway) sites like Ingleby stand out as exceptional alien implants. Even on the most minimal estimates, there must have been more Viking settlers than these. Where are the Vikings?

75 *(Above) Viking battle-axes and spears from the river Thames (Museum of London).*

76 *Deposit of animal bones, Skerne (Humberside) (Roger Simpson, Humberside Archaeological Unit).*

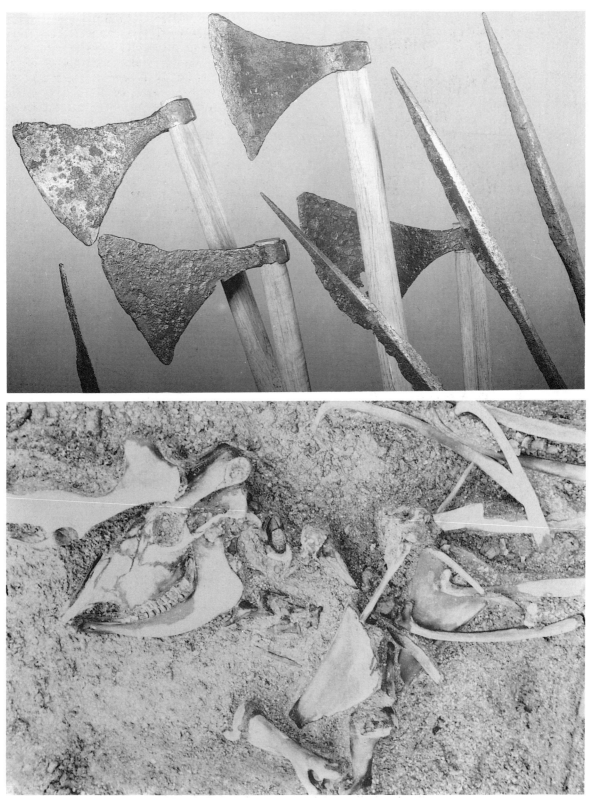

The answer has to be that they were given Christian burial. The graves with Scandinavian-style slabs from York Minster are unlikely to have been the only Vikings in this cemetery. Others were given graves which were indistinguishable from those of the native population. In other areas Scandinavian settlers must also have been buried, without grave-goods, in Anglo-Saxon rural and urban Christian cemeteries. Why did this not happen on the Isle of Man?

Certainly on Man, and in Cumbria, we are dealing with Norse Vikings who may have retained their pagan beliefs longer than their Danish counterparts in eastern and southern England. But the full reason must also depend upon expediency, and whether it suited the Vikings to be assimilated with the native population. Presumably Viking leaders only considered abandoning their pagan views in order to win favour with the native population. Guthrum only agreed to be baptized to be able to make peace with Ælfred after having been defeated by him at the Battle of Eddington. Pagan merchants undertook baptism so that they could do business with their Christian counterparts. Pagan settlers were baptized in order to take Christian English wives. This process was much slower on the Isle of Man, where there was less of a need to integrate with the local population and more of a need to assert dominance over them.

The Scandinavian settlers were particularly adaptable to local circumstances, and so was their religion. Paganism was not an organized religion like Christianity. The pantheon was sufficiently flexible to admit the Christian God, especially since Anglo-Saxon writers endowed Christ with heroic qualities. As we shall see in the next chapter, memorial crosses bearing combinations of pagan and Christian motifs appear in both northern England and the Isle of Man from the mid-tenth century, and in England Scandinavian settlers probably began to build churches at about the same time. Yet the stone sculpture suggests that the conversion was just a little pragmatic and not altogether complete. As late as the reign of Knutr it was felt necessary to condemn the activities of wizards and to forbid the worship of 'idols, heathen gods, the sun or moon, fire or flood, springs and stones or any kind of woodland tree'. Many present-day folk practices still contain fragments of pagan ceremonies.

─── 11 ───
Monuments in stone

One of the most visible surviving forms of evidence of Viking Age England is the Anglo-Scandinavian sculpture that can be found in many of our churches and churchyards, especially in areas of Yorkshire, Lancashire, Cumbria and on the Isle of Man. Yet whilst the stylized animal ornament itself can be seen to be Viking-influenced, the erection of stone crosses was not a Viking tradition.

Viking Age sculpture represents a special blend of Scandinavian, English and Celtic customs. Although some Scandinavians did erect picture-stones and rune-stone memorials, there were no stone carvings in Scandinavia until the end of the tenth century. In England and the Isle of Man, however, there were flourishing Anglo-Saxon and Celtic native traditions of stone sculpture; most early monastic sites had stone crosses. Many may have been grave-markers, but some appear to have been memorials to saints. Recumbent stone slabs were also sometimes used to mark particularly wealthy graves (see **69** and **70**). When the settlers were converted to Christianity they adopted the monastic tradition of erecting stone monuments to the memory of the dead.

The Scandinavian adoption of stone sculpture demonstrates the continuity of a significant aspect of native Christian culture in both England and the Isle of Man. This is most obvious from the distribution of sites that have stone sculpture: where earlier carving is known at a church then it is also likely to have Viking Age sculpture. It has been estimated that there is 60 per cent continuity of site in Yorkshire and south Cleveland; in Cumbria, of 15 sites with Anglo-Saxon sculpture, 12 also have Anglo-Scandinavian crosses.

Continuity is also apparent in the styles of ornament used. Although Viking Age sculpture borrows Scandinavian art styles and motifs that can be found throughout the Viking world, there are also Anglo-Saxon elements in the design. The vine scrolls at Middleton, Brompton and Leeds, for example, are clearly derived from those on the earlier Anglo-Saxon crosses at Ruthwell and Bewcastle. The organization of decoration into distinct panels is also an Anglo-Saxon or Celtic practice rather than a Scandinavian stylistic trait. It is Anglo-Saxon architectural carving that does not survive, except for a few reused fragments such as a decorated stone in the west wall of the tower at Middleton. Apart from the provision of sundials, the enlarged or rebuilt churches of the Viking Age were not generally decorated with sculptured ornament as Anglo-Saxon ones had been.

However, although the practice of erecting stone sculpture was continued and extended by the Vikings, the motives behind it may have changed. The monastic context for stone crosses no longer existed in the Viking Age. With the decline of monasticism, sculptural patronage must have passed into secular control. Although many of the crosses retain religious motifs, others appear to be political statements. We have tended to assume that the crosses normally stood in churchyards as grave-markers, although none has ever been found associated with a burial. Many may be memorial stones erected in public places. The Middleton Cross (North Yorkshire), for example, was once thought to represent a Viking warrior lying in his grave, but is now seen to depict a Viking lord seated on his throne and surrounded by his symbols of power (**77**). Viking lords are also depicted at several other sites,

77 *The Middleton Cross at St Andrew's Church, Middleton (North Yorkshire). It was once thought to represent a Viking warrior lying in his grave, but is now generally interpreted as a warrior lord sitting on his gift-school or throne (Department of Archaeology, University of Durham).*

according to Scandinavian fashion. Certainly those areas where former large estates were being broken up into smaller land units under private ownership often coincide with a high density of sculpture.

In Cumbria there are 115 monuments of the tenth and eleventh centuries from 36 sites. In Yorkshire there are approximately 500 works of pre-Conquest sculpture at over 100 locations, about 80 per cent of which may be dated to the Viking Age. Some are concentrated at known religious centres, but Viking Age sculpture has also been identified at numerous sites where there is no pre-Viking work. These sites represent an expansion in the number of centres commissioning crosses from the tenth century onwards. This increase corresponds with the decline of monastic patronage and the transfer of resources to a new secular aristocracy. These were prosperous landholders, particularly those farming the rich agricultural land of the Vales of York and Pickering.

In pre-Viking times a uniformity of style and ornament can be identified across the whole of Northumbria, maintained by a common monastic tradition and inter-monastic contact. This was broken down in the ninth and tenth centuries after the Viking immigration, and we see the development of identifiable local sculptural traditions and workshops (see Chapter 7).

In the coastal areas of north-west Cumbria there is a concentration of circle-headed crosses, for example. The distribution is centred on the Viking colonies of the western seaboard between Anglesey and northern Cumbria and illustrates the importance of coastal links. An outlier at Gargrave (North Yorkshire) suggests that settlers in the upper river valleys may have originated from the west, rather than the east.

In Yorkshire the grave slabs excavated at York Minster served as a model for many stone monuments, although the motifs were borrowed and modified in Ryedale and other areas. In Ryedale, for instance, the crosses at Kirbymoorside, Middleton and Levisham all share the same peculiar style of cross head, with a raised outer crest on a ring connecting the arms. The sculptors frequently combined new with old elements. In York the tenth-century sculptors promoted original Anglo-Scandinavian-style designs as well as maintaining continuity with Anglian traditions. In the Peak District area of Derbyshire, Anglian origins

including Levisham (North Yorkshire), Weston (North Yorkshire) and Sockburn. In many cases the weapons are given special emphasis in the carving. The distribution is more dispersed, perhaps indicating the presence, if not the centres, of new landholdings. As well as reflecting the presence of suitable stone it also reflects the availability of good agricultural land.

The distribution of Viking sculpture has been used by some as an indication of the distribution of Viking settlement. In fact, there is no reason why the fashion should have been restricted to Scandinavians. Just as Anglo-Saxons may have adopted Scandinavian personal names and place-names, so they may have chosen to represent their power as landowners are again betrayed by the use of round shafts to the crosses, and in the Wharfe Valley of Yorkshire the use of a double-stemmed angular scroll is derived from the Anglian cross at Otley.

Outside the Danelaw there are fewer examples of Viking Age sculpture, although examples from St Oswald's Priory (Gloucester), Ramsbury (Wiltshire) and Bibury (Gloucestershire) do indicate the spread of Scandinavian taste into southern England in the tenth and eleventh centuries. In Cornwall, Scandinavian motifs appear occasionally, such as at Sancreed, Temple Moor, Padstow and Cardynham, displaying links with the Irish Sea area.

The Isle of Man has one of the greatest concentrations of Viking Age sculpture, with 48 crosses produced in a relatively short time span of c.930–1020. On Man there was already a well-developed sculptural school which had produced masterpieces such as the eighth-century Calf of Man Crucifixion. The pre-Viking Manx carvings were often executed on flat slate slabs. The Vikings modified this by borrowing a wheel-headed Celtic form of cross, probably from Scotland, which they superimposed on the flat slab, as in Gautr's Cross (78).

Three aspects, in particular, help to define a Viking or Viking-influenced piece of sculpture: Scandinavian iconography, the hogback form and the use of runic inscriptions.

Iconography

The iconography of the Viking crosses illustrates the close links of the Irish Sea area in the Viking Age. The same motifs and stories are frequently depicted in the Isle of Man and Yorkshire. The ring chain ornament seen on Gautr's cross, for example, is also found in Cumbria, Northumbria and north Wales. Other Manx motifs, such as a distinctive style of knotwork tendril, display links with Yorkshire, particularly Barwick-in-Elmet and Spofforth, and there are further similarities with crosses in Aberford, Collingham and Saxton, all suggesting a great deal of contact and movement between the Isle of Man and Yorkshire. The hart-and-hound motif is found on Man and in Cumbria, Lancashire and Yorkshire. The bound devil depicted at Kirkby Stephen (Cumbria) has parallels in similar figures from Maughold on the Isle of Man. The legend of Sigurd (79) is also a popular scene in both areas, suggesting a shared set of beliefs and traditions.

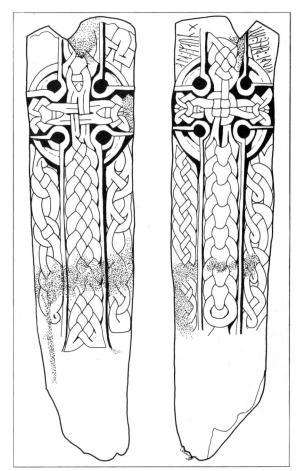

78 *Gautr's Cross, Kirk Michael, Isle of Man. The inscription commemorates the fact that 'Mailbrikti, son of Athakar, Smith, raised this cross for his soul ... Gautr made this, and all in Man'. The first two names in the inscription are Celtic, demonstrating that the patrons for Scandinavian-style crosses were not necessarily Vikings.*

Although most monuments are purely Christian, with the Crucifixion being the most popular scene, Christian, pagan and secular subjects are all depicted. In many cases Christian and pagan stories are combined by the sculptor, giving a Christian twist to a pagan tradition. One of the most startling examples is the Gosforth Cross (80) which has the Crucifixion depicted on one side whilst scenes from *Ragnorok* are shown on the other. At Kirk Andreas, on the Isle of Man, one face of Thorwald's Cross (**colour plate 11**) is also decorated with a scene from *Ragnorok*, whilst the other depicts a Christian figure with serpents. There is no

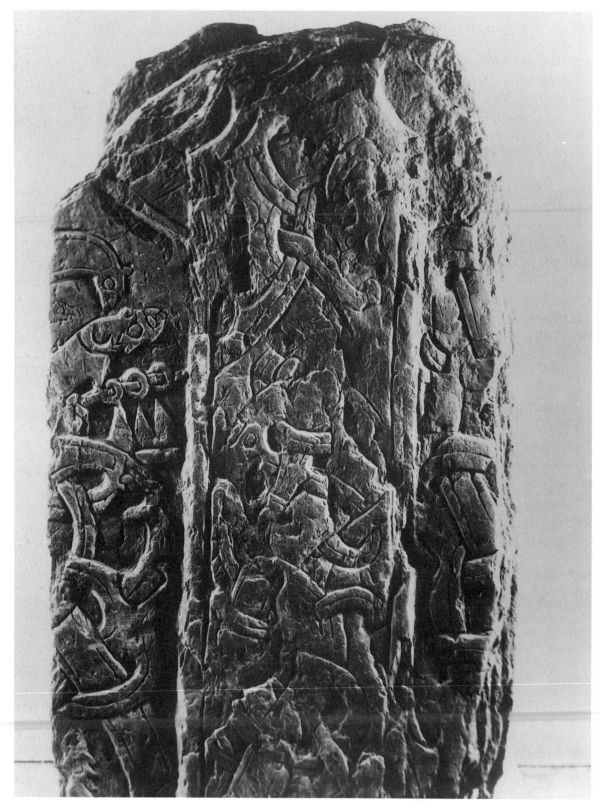

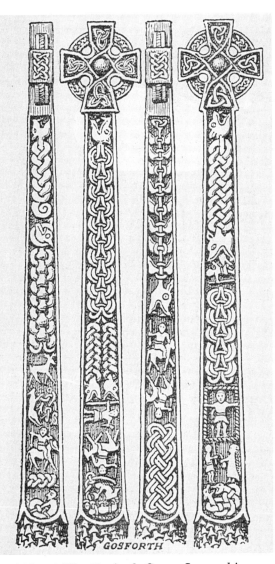

80 *(Above) The Gosforth Cross, Lancashire (after Collingwood): its pictures exploit the links and contrasts between Scandinavian and Christian theology. On one side there is a Crucifixion scene in which Mary Magdalene appears dressed as a Valkyrie, with a trailing dress and long pigtail. On the other sides scenes from Ragnarok are depicted.*

79 *(Left) Kirk Andreas Cross 121, Isle of Man: the Sigurd legend is featured on many crosses in both Yorkshire and the Isle of Man (Manx Museum and National Trust).*

need to read into this scene, as some have chosen to do, the triumph of Christianity over paganism, with the Christian figure trampling on the serpent. At Kirk Andreas the Christian and pagan material are given equal prominence. Clearly the sculptors were aware of the parallels and contrasts between the pagan and Christian theologies, and chose to exploit them. The popularity of Sigurd on many crosses stems from his use to honour the dead by comparison with the Norse hero, but Sigurd's struggle with the dragon also provides a link with Christian themes. It has been suggested that a panel from the cross at Nunburnholme (Humberside) in which Sigurd has been recarved over a Eucharistic scene may be drawing attention to the Sigurd feast as a pagan version of the Eucharist. The heroic figure Weland, the flying smith, is another popular theme with subtle ambiguities. At Leeds (West Yorkshire) he is related to angels and the eagle of St John.

As we have seen (Chapter 10), the Viking settlers in both England and the Isle of Man apparently assimilated Christian ideas quite rapidly. As far as we know, Viking religious beliefs accepted a broad pantheon of gods; perhaps the Christian God was one more to be adopted into the fold. At Gosforth pagan and Christian images may have been seen as of equal value by the craftsmen, rather than as the triumph of the new over the old; perhaps they were even regarded as aspects of the same theme.

Hogbacks

A particularly distinctive form of sculpture associated with the Viking Age is the so-called hogback tomb, named after its arched form. Hogbacks are recumbent stone monuments, generally about 1.5 m (5 ft) in length. They are basically the shape of a bow-sided building with a ridged roof and curved side walls, and are often decorated with architectural features such as shingle roofs and stylized wattle walls. Over 50 hogbacks are also decorated with end-beasts (**81**). These are generally bearlike creatures, although wolves or dogs are also known; sometimes they are shown with two legs, sometimes with four; many are clearly muzzled.

The distribution of hogbacks is mainly restricted to northern England and central Scotland, with a few outliers (**82**). They are especially concentrated in North Yorkshire and Cumbria, with none in the Isle of Man and

123

81 *Hogback tombstones, Brompton (North Yorkshire) with magnificent end beasts; they may well be amongst the earliest in the country (Department of Archaeology, University of Durham).*

only single examples in Wales and Ireland. There are no hogbacks in the Danelaw areas of Lincolnshire and East Anglia, and their distribution appears to be restricted to those areas that also have Hiberno-Norse and Norse place-names. Thus hogbacks appear to have developed in those areas that were settled by Norwegian Vikings, although they have clearly spread east of the Pennines. Their absence from the Isle of Man may be explained simply as a function of the local geology, as the Manx slate would be difficult to cut into substantial three-dimensional forms, being more appropriate to flat slabs. Three Cornish hogbacks from Lanivet, St Tudy and St Buryan demonstrate the long-distance contacts of the Norse. This coastal distribution pattern is also seen around Scotland, emphasizing the coastal structure of much of Norse settlement.

It is likely that hogbacks are a tenth-century phenomenon; it has been suggested that most were carved within the period 920–70. Their origin has been much debated as they have no clear ancestors, either in Britain or Scandinavia. The best parallels are house-shaped shrines. In Anglo-Saxon England stone shrines were used to contain or cover the body of a saint, although no 'shrine-tombs' are known from the area of hogbacks. Recumbent grave slabs were used to mark important Viking burials, but the Viking Age grave slabs excavated from under York Minster have central ridges (see **70**): perhaps hogbacks should be seen as three-dimensional extensions of this idea. Certainly they combine a number of cultural elements, including Viking-style bow-sided halls, Anglo-Saxon shrines and animal ornament. The end-beasts may have originated as animals carved on separate end-stones, as seen at York Minster, which have subsequently

82 *Map of the distribution of hogback tombstones (after Lang 1984).*

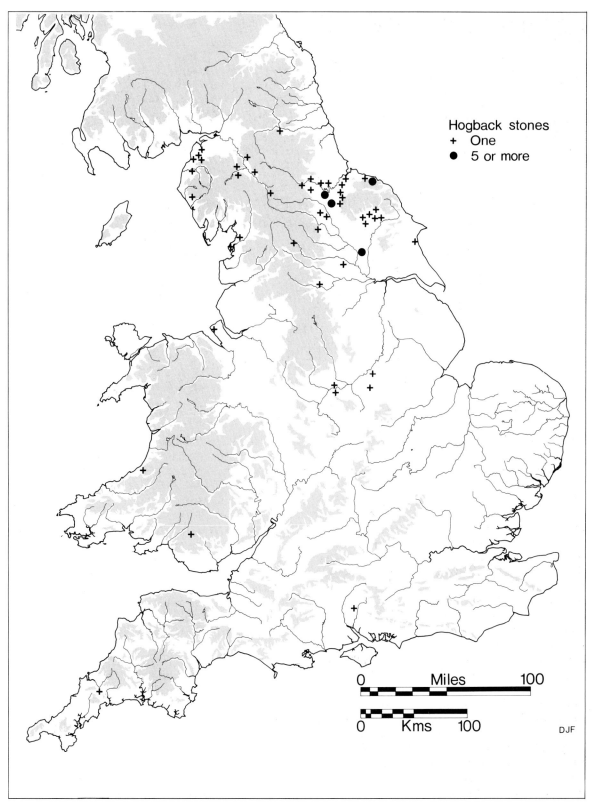

Hogback stones
+ One
● 5 or more

0   Miles   100

0   Kms   100

DJF

been combined in a single three-dimensional monument.

The function of hogbacks is also unclear. They are generally assumed to have been grave markers, although no grave has ever been found in clear association with a hogback stone. There is some evidence that a weapon was found associated with the hogback from Heysham. Some may have formed part of composite monuments with cross shafts at the ends, in the same way that some of the York Minster grave-slabs have end-stones. The so-called Giant's Grave at Penrith combines a hogback stone with cross shafts in this fashion, although the possibility remains that this is a later rearrangement of the stones. Whether or not they actually mark graves or are commemorative memorials, the hogbacks must be seen as further examples of the assertion of a particular Viking colonial identity.

Runes

The use of runic inscriptions is a feature of the Viking Age sculpture of the Isle of Man. Runic alphabets were developed by various Germanic and Scandinavian peoples in northern Europe in the first millennium AD. They continued in use into the medieval period, but always seem to have been reserved for particular functions, such as formal inscriptions. In England Anglo-Saxon crosses such as those at Collingham (West Yorkshire) and Hackness (North Yorkshire) were inscribed with English runes.

Some runes appear to have been endowed with magical properties, and weapons may have been inscribed to give them special powers. The runic script is particularly well suited, however, to being inscribed on wood and stone, the characters being formed of combinations of diagonal and vertical strokes. In some areas of Viking Age Scandinavia it became common practice to erect commemorative rune stones to honour the dead (see 12). They sometimes mark the grave but frequently commemorate the death of someone far from home. Often they were erected at the roadside or at bridging points or meeting-places. In Norway today there are some 40 rune stones; in Denmark less than 200, and in Sweden some 3500. The practice was not, however, always followed in Viking settlements overseas. There are no rune stones from Normandy, none in Iceland, two from the Faroes and only a handful from Ireland. About half a dozen have been found in Scotland, with

83 *Grave slab from St Paul's Cathedral churchyard, London. The rectangular slab shows a dragon-like beast, originally coloured dark blue, with the details picked out in brown and white. (Museum of London).*

similar numbers from Orkney and Shetland.

In Britain the tradition was only developed on the Isle of Man, where the largest collection of runes in the British Isles is to be found inscribed on the stone crosses. The Scandinavians who settled in England did not generally maintain this custom, and Viking runic finds are rare. A fragment of rune stone has been found built into a medieval church tower in Winchester, but the only complete runic memorial in England was discovered in 1852 during excavation for a warehouse on the south side of St Paul's Cathedral (83). It is likely that this eleventh-century stone was in its original position marking a grave, as the remains of a skeleton were found immediately to the north of the slab. Along one edge of the stone was the inscription 'Ginna and Toki had this stone set up' probably to commemorate a Danish or Swedish follower of Knutr. Ginna may have been his widow and Toki his son; the name of the dead man was perhaps on another slab, never found.

The only other Danish runes from England are casual graffiti: inscriptions on animal bones

from eleventh-century butcher's waste from St Albans and a comb case from Lincoln. On the other hand, Norse runes continued in use for some time in the north of England. There are runic graffiti from Carlisle Cathedral, Dearham (Cumbria) and Settle (North Yorkshire), and late eleventh- and twelfth-century inscriptions on a sundial from Skelton-in-Cleveland and on a font from Bridekirk (Cumbria). An inscription from Pennington (Cumbria) records the builder

84 *Cross fragment, Weston church (North Yorkshire). The Weston Cross depicts a warrior and a female figure. It typifies the Viking secular takeover of sculpture as it was carved out of an earlier Anglian cross, preserving the knotwork of the original lower arm, but re-cutting the upper part of the shaft for the figural scene (Photo: York Archaeological Trust).*

and mason of the church in bastardized Norse.

In contrast, there are 31 rune stones from the Isle of Man, not all on stone crosses, which compares favourably with the figure of 40 from the whole of Norway. The Church, rather than banning them for their pagan associations, may have welcomed them as written records; today the inscriptions cluster near the churches, although this may have been the result of collecting the stones together in the more recent past. There are eight examples from Kirk Michael; five each from Kirk Andreas, Braddan and Maughold, two from German and single examples from Ballaugh, Balleigh, Bride, Jurby, Marown and Onchan.

There are two styles of inscription layout: firstly along the edge, generally from the base upwards (as in Norway), or, secondly, on the cross face (which is not found in Scandinavia but may have been copied from Scotland, where examples are known). The earliest surviving runes, from the tenth century, show a clear connection with Norway, particularly the south-western province of Jaeren. The presence of a few examples of Danish runes, however, and one mixed inscription, indicates that there were other incoming groups of Viking settlers. At Maughold there are two Anglo-Saxon incised slabs with English runes.

All the Manx rune stones commemorate the dead, although it is not known whether they originally marked the position of graves. At least sixteen of the inscriptions have a common core in the form 'X erected this cross in memory of Y' which follows the usual Norse wording apart from the substitution of 'cross' for 'stone'. Thus the inscription from Thorleif's Cross at Braddan notes that 'Thorleif erected this cross after Fiac, his son, brother's son of Hafr'. Most commemorate male ancestors, but some were erected for women, such as the cross at Kirk Andreas raised by Sandulrf the Black for his wife Arinbjorg, and that from Maughold: 'Hethin set up this cross after his daughter Hild. Arni carved these runes'. The rune stones should not just be seen as commemorative memorials, however. They also define the relationship between erector and deceased, and may have been used to draw attention to inheritance claims.

The large number of runes from the tiny Isle of Man is perhaps surprising, especially given its links with Norway, which of all the countries of the Viking homeland has the smallest number of rune stones. It is also notable that the Manx runes are used exclusively on stone memorials and that there are no examples inscribed on other artefacts, as found in England. Certainly slabs of easily worked blue slate were readily available to the Manx sculptors, but suitable stone also existed in the Danelaw, where rune stones were not made. Given the existing Manx tradition of erecting stone crosses of various designs and the Norse tradition of erecting rune stones, we may be dealing with a result of the particular mixing of the two cultures. We have seen a similar flowering of stone monuments in areas of the Danelaw, although here the crosses are not inscribed. It has been suggested that perhaps the social classes who were the prime users of runes were not represented in England, but it seems unlikely that they were so differentiated from those on Man. Given the Scandinavian custom of erecting rune stones to those Vikings killed overseas, the particular development of runic memorials on the Isle of Man may reflect the use of the island as a strategic base for raiding in the Irish Sea area and the deaths of several Viking warriors on expeditions abroad.

The stone memorials in the Viking Age must be seen, therefore, as symbols of identity and power. These are secular monuments which took on a Christian practice, and need not be exclusively for Viking patrons. In pre-Viking England and Man the monastic sites were centres of power, and the standing crosses would be recognized by the incoming Vikings as symbols of authority. It was natural, therefore, for the new local elites who came to power as a result of Viking incursions to seek to express their own power through the erection of stone monuments in Scandinavian art styles. The new patrons who commissioned crosses such as that at Gosforth supported craftsmen who drew extensively upon existing English styles, but added motifs from pagan iconography. In Viking Age sculpture we see a true merging of English, Celtic and Scandinavian traditions.

Where to visit

Perhaps the best place to start a study of Viking Age material is the British Museum, where objects from Scandinavia as well as England can be viewed. Other museums also have important collections, notably the Museum of London, the Yorkshire Museum and the Carlisle Museum and Art Gallery. The best-known display is undoubtedly the Jorvik Viking Centre at York, which as well as its reconstruction of the Coppergate buildings and the Viking Dig, also displays the rich range of Viking artefacts recovered from Coppergate. York's Archaeological Resource Centre is also well worth a visit, as are the Viking Age sculptures found in the excavations under York Minster in the 1960s, and now displayed in the Minster Undercroft.

York also provides an ideal base for studying the Viking Age sculpture of the Vales of York and Pickering. There are several crosses, including the famous Middleton warrior, in St Andrew's Church in Middleton, near Pickering. St Gregory's Minster at Kirkdale is also well worth seeing, not just for its sundial but also for the fragments of Viking sculpture, including a Crucifixion and a hogback, built into the walls, and for the carvings in the church. To the west, the best collection of hogback tombs in the country is held in the church at Brompton. More hogbacks can be seen at Lythe (North Yorkshire). Further south, the crosses in the churches at Collingham, Nunburnholme and in Leeds Parish Church may be visited.

Whilst in the area visitors may also like to see the Norman door at Stillingfleet, with its wrought iron depiction of a Viking ship.

On the west coast the most impressive cross is that in the churchyard at Gosforth; there are also two cross heads, two hogbacks and a fragment of a cross shaft in the church. There is also an important hogback in the church at Heysham.

Apart from the crosses, there are few Scandinavian sites in England where there is anything to see. The outline of the farm at Ribblehead can be picked out on the ground with some difficulty. The church which formed part of the Viking Age camp at Repton may be visited, although most of the Viking camp is in grounds of Repton School, where there is nothing to be seen.

For those who wish to study Viking archaeology a visit to the Isle of Man is really essential. The settlement at the Braaid and the promontory forts at Close ny Chollagh and Cronk ny Merriu can each be visited. The outline of the ship burial at Chapel Hill, Balladoole, can also still be seen, as can a number of the burial mounds in the parish of Jurby. The Manx Museum in Douglas has most of the finds from the excavations, as well as a display of casts of the Viking Age sculpture from the island. Notable collections are still to be found in their original sites at Maughold, Kirk Andreas, Kirk Michael and Braddan (old church).

Glossary

Anglo-Saxon Chronicle An annual record of events, compiled in English from the late ninth century, possibly at the instigation of King Ælfred.

Burghal Hidage A tax assessment document of *c*.914–8 which lists those burhs defending the frontiers of Wessex, south of the Thames.

burh A fortified centre; in Mercia and Wessex the burhs developed into towns.

cist-grave or **lintel-grave** A grave lined with stone slabs, known from the Isle of Man.

clench nails Double-headed nails used to join planks, used especially in ship construction.

clinker-built A method of construction, especially of ships, consisting of overlapping planks.

Danegeld Payments of 'protection money' to Viking raiders.

Danelaw The area of England under Scandinavian control, and so following the Danish law.

hack silver Bullion silver, frequently consisting of ingots, cut brooches, ornaments and coins.

hogback A tenth-century recumbent stone monument with an arched back, which may have been used as a Viking grave-marker.

honestone or **whetstone** A sharpening stone.

hundred An administrative division, originally based on taxation unit of 100 hides, each hide being the unit of land required to support one family.

keeil A small Christian chapel on the Isle of Man.

linen-smoother A smooth, rounded glass tool used for the finishing of linen cloth.

loomweight A circular weight of baked clay, about the size of a doughnut, used to provide tension for the vertical threads on a loom.

midden A refuse dump.

pillow stone A stone placed in a burial to prop up the head.

quarterland A basic land unit on the Isle of Man, generally between 50–180 acres (i.e. 20–73 ha). Normally four quarterlands are grouped together into treens.

quernstone or **millstone** A circular block of stone, often of lava, used for milling grain.

reeve The king's representative, responsible for the collection of taxes.

ring-headed pin A form of cloak pin thought to have been introduced into England and the Isle of Man by Scandinavian settlers from Ireland.

seax A heavy single-edged knife or short sword.

shield boss Iron boss mounted in the centre of a shield to protect the hand grip.

shieling Upland grazing.

soapstone A soft stone also known as steatite, quarried in Shetland and Norway and carved into large cooking vessels during the Viking Age.

soke, **sokeland** The central area of an estate, and those areas which owed tribute and services to the lord.

spindlewhorl A small perforated weight made of animal bone, pottery sherds, stone, or occasionally lead, which weighted the hand-held spindle on which woollen thread was spun out.

strap-end A decorated metal tag, usually made of copper alloy, attached to the end of a leather or textile strap to prevent it from fraying.

styca A type of copper coin, minted in ninth-century Northumbria.

toft The land on which a peasant house stood.

tortoise brooch Scandinavian style oval, domed brooch, worn in pairs, one at each shoulder, to fasten clothing.

treenland The smallest administrative unit known on the Isle of Man, normally consisting of four quarterlands.

trefoil brooch A three-cornered brooch, worn centrally on the costume.

trial-piece or **motif-piece** A piece of bone or wood on which a craftsman or woman has tried out an intricate design, or alternatively a fragment of lead on which a coin-die has been tested.

vill Estate centre.

wapentake An administrative division, equivalent of the hundred in some areas, so-called after the brandishing of weapons at an assembly.

wic A town which developed as a major international trading port between the seventh and ninth centuries.

Further reading

1 The Viking Age

There are a number of general books on the Vikings. Amongst the best are Foote and Wilson (1970), Graham-Campbell (1990), Wilson (1970) and Roesdahl (1991). Historical outlines are provided by Loyn (1977) and Sawyer (1971), (1978) and (1982). Scotland and Wales are also outside the scope of this book; for recent surveys of contemporary settlement in these areas see Crawford (1987) and Davies (1982) respectively. For the British Isles also see Hall (1990). For fresh approaches to the evolution of Europe and England see Hodges (1982) and (1989). For contrasting approaches to Denmark see Randsborg (1980) and Roesdahl (1982).

2 Viking raids

For overviews see Wilson (1968) and (1976c); for a useful series of maps see Hill (1981). For English objects in Scandinavia see Bakka (1963) and for the Swedish rune stones see Jansson (1966) and (1990). Fortifications are discussed in Allcroft (1908), Dyer (1972) and Gray (1933); hoards in Blackburn and Pagan (1986), Brooks and Graham-Campbell (1986), Edwards (1985), Graham-Campbell (1983) and Kruse (1986) and (1988).

3 Viking colonization

Gelling (1978b) provides a good general introduction to the study of place-names. Most of the work on Viking place-names in England has been done by Cameron (1958), (1965), (1970) and (1971) or Fellows-Jensen (1972), (1975), (1982) and (1984). For the Isle of Man see Fellows-Jensen (1978) and (1983) and Gelling (1978a). For personal names see Fellows-Jensen (1968) and Smart (1986); for other linguistic evidence see Page (1971).

There is a general description of the archaeological evidence in Rahtz (1976) and a stimulating discussion about the East Midlands which raises wider issues in Stafford (1985). Settlement patterns are discussed in D. Hall (1988), Jones (1965), Unwin (1988), and Winchester (1985). A minimalist view of the density of settlement is propounded in Sawyer (1958) and modified in (1969) and (1979).

There are regional studies in Baldwin and Whyte (1985), Beresford (1979), Drewett et al. (1988), Higham (1985) and (1986), Hughes (1984), Morris (1977), (1981) and (1982), Newman (1984), O'Sullivan (1984), Todd (1987) and Wilson (1976a).

For general discussion of the Manx settlement see Cubbon (1983), Dolley (1981), Megaw and Megaw (1950), Reilly (1988) and Wilson (1974). For settlement sites on the Isle of Man see Bersu (1949) and Gelling (1970).

The following offer discussions of specific English sites. Barton Blount: Beresford (1975); Bryant's Gill: Dickinson (1985); Catholme: Losco-Bradley and Wheeler (1984); Cheddar: Rahtz (1979); Eaton Socon: Addyman (1965); Goltho: Beresford (1987); Lindisfarne: Beavitt et al. (1985) and (1986); Little Paxton: Addyman (1969); Mawgan Porth: Bruce-Mitford (1956); North Elmham: Wade-Martins (1980); Portchester: Cunliffe (1976); Raunds: Boddington and Cadman (1981), Cadman and Foard (1984) and Foard and Pearson (1985); Ribblehead: King (1978); St Neots: Addyman (1972); Simy Folds: Coggins et al. (1983); Springfield: Buckley and Hedges (1987); Sulgrave: Davison (1968); Tresmorn: Beresford (1971); Treworld: Dudley and Minter (1966); Waltham Abbey: Huggins (1976) and (1984); Wharram Percy: Beresford and Hurst (1990) and Hurst (1984).

4 Towns

Carver (1987) considers the aims and methods of the urban archaelogy of Saxon towns. Clarke and Ambrosiani (1991) provide the most recent survey of Viking Age towns. There are general discussions of the Wessex burhs in Biddle (1976), Biddle and Hill (1971), Hill (1978) and (1988) and Radford (1970) and (1978). Mercian burhs are covered in Haslam (1987) and Rahtz (1977). For regional studies see papers in Haslam, ed. (1984), especially Astill, Aston, Haslam and Hinton; see also Atkin (1985) and Tatton-Brown (1988). The most recent survey of the Danelaw is Hall (1989). Urban environments are covered in Hall *et al.* (1983) and Kenward *et al.* (1978).

The following offer discussions of specific English towns. Bath: Cunliffe (1984); Chester: Mason (1985); Derby: Hall (1974); Exeter: Allan *et al.* (1984); Gloucester: Heighway (1984) and (1987); Ipswich: Wade (1988); Lincoln: Perring (1981); London: Clark (1989), Dyson and Schofield (1984), Milne (1989), Milne and Goodburn (1990) and Vince (1990); Norwich: Carter (1978); Northampton: Williams (1979), (1984*a*) and (1984*b*); Oxford: Hassall (1986); South Cadbury: Alcock (1972); Southampton: Holdsworth (1984); Stamford: Mahany *et al.* (1982) and Mahany and Roffe (1983); Tamworth: Gould (1967) and (1968); Thetford: Davison (1967), Dunmore and Carr (1976) and Rogerson and Dallas (1984); York: Hall (1978), (1984*a*), (1988) and ed. (1978), Moulden and Tweddle (1986), Ordnance Survey (1988) and Radley (1971).

5 Buildings

Rahtz (1976) gives a general overview of Anglo-Saxon buildings. The following offer discussions of building technology on particular sites. Chester: Mason (1985); Durham: Carver (1979); London: Horsman *et al.* (1988); York: Hall (1982) and (1984*b*).

6 Agriculture

Anglo-Saxon agriculture is discussed in Fowler (1976) and (1981). Animal resources are covered by Clutton-Brock (1976), and there are two excellent site reports which try to make some generalized conclusions by O'Connor (1982) and (1989).

7 Craft and industry

Viking Age artefacts are catalogued in Graham-Campbell (1980*a*), MacGregor (1978) and

(1982), Mann (1982), Roesdahl *et al.* (1981), Shetelig (1940) and (1954) and Tweddle (1986). Wilson (1976*b*) covers most industries apart from pottery, for which see Gilmour (1988), Hurst (1976), Kilmurry (1980), Mainman (1990), Mellor (1980) and Vince (1985). In addition, for antler and bone see MacGregor (1985); for stone see Jope (1964); for iron see McDonnell (1989) and Ottaway (1990); and for textiles see Pritchard (1984) and Walton (1989).

8 Trade and exchange

There are general discussions of the nature of Viking Age trade in Hodges (1982), Sawyer (1986), and Vince (1989). Numismatic evidence is discussed by various papers in Blackburn (1986) and by Dolley (1976), Hinton (1986) and Pirie (1986). For slave trading see Pelteret (1981). The trading site at Meols is discussed in Bu'lock (1960). For ships see Fenwick, ed. (1978), McGrail (1978), McGrail and Switsur (1979), and Marsden *et al.* (1989).

9 Churches and monasteries

By far the best book on the development of the church is Morris (1989), but see also Morris (1983). Minster churches are covered in Blair (1988) and Radford (1973). The following offer discussions of specific churches. Barton-on-Humber: Rodwell and Rodwell (1982); Raunds: Boddington (1987); St Mark's Lincoln: Gilmour and Stocker (1986); Wharram Percy: Bell *et al.* (1987).

10 Death and burial

For Late Saxon cemeteries see Dawes and Magilton (1980), Phillips and Heywood (forthcoming), White *et al.* (1988), and also Huggins (1988). Manx Viking burials are reported in Bersu and Wilson (1966), Bruce and Cubbon (1930) and Kermode (1930). Viking burials in England are described in Alexander (1987), Biddle and Blair (1987), Clarke and Fraser (1946), Clarke *et al.* (1949), Cowen (1948) and (1967), Edwards (1969), Evison (1969), Fenwick (1978), Posnansky (1956), Sheppard (1939) and Wenham *et al.* (1987). The interpretation of Viking burials has been discussed by Graham-Campbell (1980*b*), Reilly (1988) and Wilson (1967). For ritual deposits see Dent (1984), Seaby and Woodfield (1980) and Wilson (1965).

11 Monuments in stone

The best introductions to Viking Age sculpture

are Bailey (1980) and Lang (1988). For Yorkshire see Lang (1978). For the Isle of Man see
Kermode (1907) and Wilson (1971) and (1983).
Hogbacks are catalogued in Lang (1984). For
runes see Page (1980), (1983) and (1987).

Bibliography

Addyman, P. V. (1965). 'Late Saxon settlements in
the St Neots area: I. The Saxon settlement and
Norman castle at Eaton Socon, Bedfordshire',
Proceedings of the Cambridge Antiquarian Society
58, pp. 38–73.

—— (1969), 'Late Saxon settlements in the St Neots
area: II. The Little Paxton settlement and enclosures', *Proceedings of the Cambridge Antiquarian
Society* 62, pp. 59–93.

—— (1972), 'Late Saxon settlements in the St Neots
area: III. The village or township at St Neots',
Proceedings of the Cambridge Antiquarian Society
64, pp. 45–99.

Alcock, L. (1972), *'By South Cadbury is that Came-
lot...': The excavation of Cadbury Castle, 1966–
1970*, London.

Alexander, M. L. (1987), 'A "Viking-Age" grave from
Cambois, Bedlington, Northumberland', *Medieval
Archaeology* 31, pp. 101–5.

Allan, J., Henderson, C., and Higham, R. (1984),
'Saxon Exeter' in Haslam (ed.), pp. 385–411.

Allcroft, A. H. (1908), *Earthworks of England*, London.

Astill, G. (1984), 'The towns of Berkshire' in Haslam
(ed.), pp. 53–86.

Aston, M. (1984), 'The towns of Somerset', in Haslam
(ed.), pp. 167–201.

Atkin, M. (1985), 'The Anglo-Saxon urban landscape
in East Anglia', *Landscape History* 7, pp. 27–40.

Bailey, R. N. (1980), *Viking Age sculpture in northern
England*, London.

Bakka, E. (1963), 'Some English decorated metal
objects found in Norwegian graves', *Arbok for
Universitetet i Bergen*, humanistisk serie, 1.

Baldwin, J. R., and Whyte, R. D. (eds) (1985), *The
Scandinavians in Cumbria*, Edinburgh.

Beavitt, P., O'Sullivan, D., and Young, R. (1985),
Recent fieldwork on Lindisfarne, University of
Leicester Department of Archaeology Occasional
Papers, No. 1.

—— (1986), *Holy Island: A guide to current archaeological research*, Lindisfarne Excavation Project.

Bell, R. D. *et al.* (1987), *Wharram Percy: The church
of St Martin*, Soc. Med. Arch. Mon. Ser. 11.
London.

Beresford, G. (1971), 'Tresmorn, St Gennys', *Cornish
Archaeology* 10, pp. 55–73.

—— (1975), *The medieval clay-land village: Excavations at Goltho and Barton Blount*, London.

—— (1979), 'Three deserted medieval settlements on

Dartmoor', *Medieval Archaeology* 23, pp. 98–158.

—— (1987), *Goltho: The development of an early
medieval manor c.850–1150*, English Heritage
Archaeological Report 4.

Beresford, M., and Hurst, J. G. (1990), *Wharram
Percy: Deserted medieval village*, London.

Bersu, G. (1949), 'A promontory fort on the shore of
Ramsey Bay', *Antiquaries Journal* 29, pp. 62–79.

—— and Wilson, D. M. (1966), *Three Viking graves
in the Isle of Man*, Soc. Med. Arch. Mon. Ser. 1.
London.

Biddle, M. (1976), 'Towns', in Wilson (ed.), pp. 99–
150.

—— and Blair, J. (1987), 'The Hook Norton hoard of
1848: a Viking burial from Oxfordshire?', *Oxonien-
sia* 52, pp. 186–95.

—— and Hill, D. (1971), 'Late Saxon planned towns',
Antiquaries Journal 51, pp. 70–85.

Blackburn, M. A. S. (ed.) (1986), *Anglo-Saxon monetary history: Essays in memory of Michael Dolley*,
Leicester.

—— and Pagan, H. (1986), 'A revised check-list of
coin hoards from the British Isles, *c*.500–1100' in
Blackburn (ed.), pp. 291–313.

Blair, J. (1988), 'Minster churches in the landscape'
in Hooke (ed.), pp. 35–58.

Boddington, A. (1987), 'Raunds, Northamptonshire:
Analysis of a country churchyard', *World Archaeology* 18, pp. 412–25.

—— and Cadman, G. (1981), 'Raunds: An interim
report on excavations 1977–1980' in *Anglo-Saxon
Studies in Archaeology and History*, British
Archaeological Reports, (British Series), 92, pp.
103–22.

Brooks, N. P., and Graham-Campbell, J. A. (1986),
'Reflections on the Viking-Age silver hoard from
Croydon, Surrey' in Blackburn (ed.), pp. 91–110.

Bruce, J. R., and Cubbon, W. (1930), 'Cronk yn How:
An Early Christian and Viking site, at Lezayre,
Isle of Man', *Archaeologia Cambrensis* 85, pp.
267–308.

Bruce-Mitford, R. L. S. (1956), 'A Dark Age Settlement at Mawgan Porth, Cornwall', in R. Bruce-
Mitford (ed.), *Recent Excavations in Britain*, London, pp. 167–96.

Buckley, D. G., and Hedges, J. D. (1987), *The Bronze
Age and Saxon settlements at Springfield Lyons,
Essex: An interim report*, Chelmsford.

Bu'lock, J. D. (1960), 'Celtic, Saxon and Scandinavian settlement at Meols, Wirral', *Transactions of
the Historical Society of Lancashire and Cheshire*
112, pp. 1–28.

Cadman, G., and Foard, G. (1904), 'Raunds. Manorial
and village origins' in Paull (ed.), pp. 81–100.

Cameron, K. (1958), 'The Scandinavians in Derbyshire: the place-name evidence', *Nottingham Medieval Studies* 2, pp. 86–118.

—— (1965), *Scandinavian settlement in the territory*

of the Five Boroughs: The place-name evidence, Nottingham.

——(1970), 'Scandinavian settlement in the territory of the Five Boroughs: The place-name evidence, part II: Place-names in *Thorp*', *Medieval Scandinavia* 3, pp. 35–49.

——(1971), 'Scandinavian settlement in the territory of the Five Boroughs: The place-name evidence, part III: The Grimston-Hybrids', in P. Clemoes and K. Hughes (eds), *England before the Conquest*, Cambridge, pp. 147–63.

Carter, A. (1978), 'The Anglo-Saxon origins of Norwich: The problems and approaches', *Anglo-Saxon England* 7, pp. 175–204.

Carver, M. O. H. (1979), 'Three Saxo-Norman tenements in Durham city', *Medieval Archaeology* 23, pp. 1–80.

——(1987), *Underneath English towns: Interpreting urban archaeology*, London.

Clark, J. (1989), *Saxon and Norman London*, London.

Clarke, C., and Fraser, W. (1946), 'Excavation of pagan burial mounds: Ingleby, Derbyshire', *Derbyshire Archaeological Journal* 66, pp. 1–23.

——————and Munslow, F. W. (1949), 'Second Report' [Ingleby], *Derbyshire Archaeological Journal* 69, pp. 78–81.

Clarke, H., and Ambrosiani, B. (1991), *Towns in the Viking Age*, Leicester.

Clutton-Brock, J. (1976), 'The animal resources' in Wilson (ed.), pp. 373–92.

Coggins, D., Fairless, K. J., and Batey, C. E. (1983), 'Simy Folds: An early medieval settlement in Upper Teesdale, Co. Durham', *Medieval Archaeology* 27, pp. 1–26.

Cowen, J. D. (1948), 'Viking burials in Cumbria', *Transactions of the Cumberland and Westmorland Antiquarian and Archaeological Society* New Series 48, pp. 73–6.

——(1967), 'Viking burials in Cumbria: A supplement', *Transactions of the Cumberland and Westmorland Antiquarian and Archaeological Society* New Series 67, pp. 31–4.

Crawford, B. E. (1987), *Scandinavian Scotland*, Leicester.

Cubbon, A. M. (1983), 'The archaeology of the Vikings in the Isle of Man' in Fell *et al.* (eds), pp. 13–26.

Cunliffe, B. (1976), *Excavations at Portchester Castle. Volume II: Saxon*, Society of Antiquaries Research Report No. 33.

——(1984), 'Saxon Bath' in Haslam (ed.), pp. 345–58.

Davey, P. (ed.) (1978), *Man and Environment in the Isle of Man*, Brit Archaeol Rep, (Brit Ser), 54.

Davies, W. (1982), *Wales in the Early Middle Ages*, Leicester.

Davison, B. K. (1967), 'The Late Saxon town of Thetford: An interim report on the 1964–6 excava-

tions', *Medieval Archaeology* 11, pp. 189–207.

——(1968), 'Excavations at Sulgrave, Northamptonshire, 1968', *Archaeological Journal* 125, pp. 305–7.

Dawes, J. D., and Magilton, J. R. (1980), *The cemetery of St Helen on the Walls, Aldwark* AY12/1, London.

Dent, J. (1984), 'Skerne', *Current Archaeology* 91, pp. 251–3.

Dickinson, S. (1985), 'Bryant's Gill, Kentmere: Another "Viking-Period" Ribblehead?' in Baldwin and Whyte (eds), pp. 83–8.

Dolley, M. (1976), 'The coins' in Wilson (ed.), pp. 349–72.

——(1981), 'The palimpsest of Viking settlement on Man' in *Proceedings of the Eighth Viking Congress*, Odense, pp. 173–81.

Drewett, P., Rudling, D., and Gardiner, M. (1988), *The South East to AD 1000*, London.

Dudley, D., and Minter, E. M. (1966), 'Excavation of a medieval settlement at Treworld', *Cornish Archaeology* 5, pp. 34–58.

Dunmore, S., and Carr, R. (1976), 'The Late Saxon town of Thetford: An archaeological and historical survey', *East Anglian Archaeology* 4.

Dyer, J. (1972), 'Earthworks of the Danelaw frontier' in P. J. Fowler (ed.), *Archaeology and the landscape*, London, pp. 222–36.

Dyson, T., and Schofield, J. (1984), 'Saxon London' in Haslam (ed.), pp. 285–313.

Edwards, B. J. N. (1969), 'The Claughton Viking burial', *Transactions of the Historical Society of Lancashire and Cheshire* 121, pp. 109–16.

——(1985), 'Viking silver ingots from Bowes Moor, Yorkshire', *Antiquaries Journal* 65, pp. 457–9.

Evison, V. I. (1969), 'A Viking grave at Sonning, Berks', *Antiquaries Journal* 49, pp. 330–45.

Faull, M. L. (ed.) (1984), *Studies in Late Anglo-Saxon settlement*, Oxford.

Fell, C., Foote, P., Graham-Campbell, J., and Thomson, R. (eds) (1983), *The Viking Age in the Isle of Man*, London.

Fellows-Jensen, G. (1968), 'Scandinavian personal names in Lincolnshire and Yorkshire', *Navnestudier* 7.

——(1972), 'Scandinavian settlement names in Yorkshire', *Navnestudier* 11.

——(1975), 'The Vikings in England: A review', *Anglo-Saxon England* 4, pp. 181–206.

——(1978), 'The Manx place-name debate: A view from Copenhagen' in Davey (ed.), pp. 315–8.

——(1982), 'Scandinavian settlement in England: The place-name evidence' in H. Bekker-Nielsen and H. Frede Nielsen (eds), *Nordboer i Danelagen*, Odense, pp. 9–32.

——(1983), 'Scandinavian settlement in the Isle of Man and north-west England: The place-name evidence' in Fell *et al.* (eds), pp. 37–52.

—— (1984), 'Scandinavian settlement in Cumbria and Dumfriesshire: The place-name evidence' in Baldwin and Whyte (eds), pp. 65–82.

Fenwick, V. (1978), 'Was there a body beneath the Walthamstow Boat?', *International Journal of Nautical Archaeology and Underwater Exploration* 7, pp. 187–94.

—— (ed.) (1978), *The Graveney Boat: A tenth-century find from Kent*, British Archaeological Reports, (British Series), 53.

Foard, G., and Pearson, T. (1985), 'The Raunds area project: First interim report', *Northamptonshire Archaeology* 20, pp. 3–21.

Foote, P. G., and Wilson, D. M. (1970), *The Viking Achievement*, London.

Fowler, P. J. (1976), 'Agriculture and rural settlement' in Wilson (ed.), pp. 23–48.

—— (1981), 'Farming in the Anglo-Saxon landscape', *Anglo-Saxon England* 9, pp. 263–80.

Gelling, M. (1978a), 'Norse and Gaelic in Medieval Man: The place-name evidence' in Davey (ed.), pp. 251–61.

—— (1978b), *Signposts to the past*, London.

Gelling, P. S. (1970), 'A Norse homestead near Doarlish Cashen, Kirk Patrick, Isle of Man', *Medieval Archaeology* 14, pp. 74–82.

Gilmour, B. J. J., and Stocker, D. A. (1986), *St Mark's Church and Cemetery* ALXIII-1, London.

Gilmour, L. A. (1988), *Early medieval pottery from Flaxengate, Lincoln* ALXVII-2, London.

Gould, J. (1967), 'First report on excavations at Tamworth, Staffs., 1967: The Saxon defences', *Transactions of the Lichfield and South Staffordshire Archaeology and History Society* 9 pp. 17–29.

—— (1968), 'Third report on excavations at Tamworth, Staffs., 1968: The western entrance to the Saxon borough', *Transactions of the Lichfield and South Staffordshire Archaeology and History Society* 10, pp. 32–43.

Graham-Campbell, J. (1980a), *Viking Artefacts: A select catalogue*, London.

—— (1980b), 'The Scandinavian Viking-Age burials of England: some problems of interpretation', in P. Rahtz, T. Dickinson and L. Watts (eds), *Anglo-Saxon Cemeteries 1979*, British Archaeological Reports, (British Series), 82, pp. 379–82.

—— (1983), 'Viking-Age silver hoards of the Isle of Man' in Fell *et al.* (eds), pp. 53–80.

—— (1990), *The Viking World* (2nd edn), London.

Gray, H. St G. (1933), 'Trial excavations in the so-called "Danish camp" at Warham', *Antiquaries Journal* 13, pp. 399–413.

Hall, A. R., Kenward, H. K., Williams, D., and Greig, J. R. A. (1983), *Environment and living conditions at two Anglo-Scandinavian sites*, AY14/4, London.

Hall, D. (1988), 'The Late Saxon countryside: Villages and their fields' in Hooke (ed.), pp. 99–122.

Hall, R. A. (1974), 'The pre-Conquest burgh of Derby', *Derbyshire Archaeological Journal* 94, pp. 16–23.

—— (1978), 'The topography of Anglo-Scandinavian York' in Hall (ed.), pp. 31–6.

—— (1982), '10th-century woodworking in Coppergate, York' in S. McGrail (ed.), *Woodworking Techniques before AD 1500*, British Archaeological Reports, (International Series), 129, pp. 231–44.

—— (1984a), *The Viking Dig*, London.

—— (1984b), 'A late pre-Conquest urban building tradition' in P. V. Addyman and V. E. Black (eds), *Archaeological Papers from York Presented to M. W. Barley*, York, pp. 71–7.

—— (1988), 'York 700–1050', in Hodges and Hobley (eds), pp. 125–32.

—— (1989), 'The Five Boroughs of the Danelaw: A review of present knowledge', *Anglo-Saxon England* 18, pp. 149–206.

—— (1990), *Viking Age archaeology in Britain and Ireland*, Princes Risborough.

—— (ed.) (1978), *Viking Age York and the North*, CBA Research Report 27, London.

Haslam, J. (1984a), 'The towns of Wiltshire' in Haslam (ed.), pp. 87–147.

—— (1984b), 'The towns of Devon' in Haslam (ed.), pp. 249–83.

—— (1987), 'Market and fortress in England in the reign of Offa', *World Archaeology* 19, pp. 76–93.

—— (ed.) (1984), *Anglo-Saxon Towns in Southern England*, Chichester.

Hassall, T. (1986), 'Archaeology of Oxford City', in G. Briggs, J. Cook and T. Rowley (eds), *The Archaeology of the Oxford Region*, Oxford, pp. 115–34.

Heighway, C. M. (1984), 'Anglo-Saxon Gloucester to AD 1000' in Faull (ed.), pp. 35–53.

—— (1987), *Anglo-Saxon Gloucestershire*, Gloucester.

Higham, N. J. (1985), 'The Scandinavians in north Cumbria: Raids and settlement in the later ninth to mid-tenth centuries' in Baldwin and Whyte (eds), pp. 37–51.

—— (1986), *The Northern Counties to AD 1000*, London.

Hill, D. H. (1978), 'The origins of the Saxon towns' in P. Brandon (ed.), *The South Saxons*, Chichester, pp. 174–89.

—— (1981), *An Atlas of Anglo-Saxon England*, Oxford.

—— (1988), 'Towns as structures and functioning communities through time: The development of central places from 600 to 1066' in Hooke (ed.), pp. 197–212.

Hinton, D. (1984), 'The towns of Hampshire' in Haslam (ed.), pp. 149–65.

—— (1986), 'Coins and commercial centres in Anglo-Saxon England' in Blackburn (ed.), pp. 11–26.

Hodges, R. (1982), *Dark Age economics: The Origins*

of towns and trade AD *600–1000*, London.

—— (1989), *The Anglo-Saxon Achievement*, London.

—— and Hobley, B. (eds) (1988), *The rebirth of towns in the West AD 700–1050*, CBA Res. Rep. 68, London.

Holdsworth, P. (1984), 'Saxon Southampton' in Haslam (ed.), pp. 331–43.

Hooke, D. (ed.) (1988), *Anglo-Saxon settlements*, Oxford.

Horsman, V., and Milne, C. and G. (1988), *Aspects of Saxo-Norman London: 1. Building and street development*, Middx. Arch. Soc. Spec. Pap. 11, London.

Huggins, P. J. (1976), 'The excavation of an 11th-century Viking hall and 14th-century rooms at Waltham Abbey, Essex, 1969–71', *Medieval Archaeology* 20, pp. 75–133.

—— (1984), 'A note on a Viking-style plate from Waltham Abbey, Essex and its implications for a disputed Late-Viking building', *Archaeological Journal* 141, pp. 175–81.

—— (1988), 'Excavation on the north side of Sun Street, Waltham Abbey, Essex, 1974–75: Saxon burials, precinct wall and south-east transept', *Essex Archaeology and History* 19, pp. 117–53.

Hughes, M. (1984). 'Rural settlement and landscape in Late Saxon Hampshire' in Faull (ed.), pp. 65–79.

Hurst, J. G. (1976), 'The pottery' in Wilson (ed.), pp. 283–348.

—— (1984), 'The Wharram Research Project: Results to 1983', *Medieval Archaeology* 28, pp. 77–111.

Jansson, S. B. F. (1966), *Swedish Vikings in England: The evidence of the rune stones*, London.

—— (1990), *Runes in Sweden*, Sweden.

Jones, G. R. J. (1965), 'Early territorial organization in northern England and its bearing on the Scandinavian settlement' in A. Small (ed.), *The Fourth Viking Congress*, Edinburgh, pp. 67–84.

Jope, E. M. (1964), 'The Saxon building-stone industry in southern and Midland England', *Medieval Archaeology* 8, pp. 91–118.

Kenward, H. K. *et al.* (1978), 'The environment of Anglo-Scandinavian York' in Hall (ed.), pp. 58–70.

Kermode, P. M. C. (1907), *Manx crosses*, London.

—— (1930), 'A ship-burial in the Isle of Man', *Antiquaries Journal* 10, pp. 126–33.

Kilmurry, K. (1980), *The pottery industry of Stamford, Lincolnshire, c. AD 850–1250*, British Archaeological Reports, (British Series), 84.

King, A. (1978), 'Gauber high pasture, Ribblehead: An interim report' in Hall (ed.), pp. 21–5.

Kruse, S. (1986), 'The Viking-age silver hoard from Scotby: The non-numismatic element', *Transactions of the Cumberland and Westmorland Antiquarian and Archaeological Society* 86, pp. 79–83.

—— (1988), 'Ingots and weight units in Viking Age silver hoards', *World Archaeology* 20, pp. 285–301.

Lang, J. T. (1978), 'Anglo-Scandinavian sculpture in Yorkshire' in Hall (ed.), pp. 11–20.

—— (1984), 'The Hogback: A Viking colonial monument', *Anglo-Saxon Studies in Archaeology and History* 3, pp. 85–176.

—— (1988), *Anglo-Saxon sculpture*, Princes Risborough.

Losco-Bradley, S., and Wheeler, H. M. (1984), 'Anglo-Saxon settlement in the Trent Valley: Some aspects' in Faull (ed.), pp. 101–14.

Loyn, H. R. (1977), *The Vikings in Britain*, London.

McDonnell, G. (1989), 'Iron and its alloys in the 5th to 11th centuries AD in England', *World Archaeology* 20, pp. 373–82.

McGrail, S. (ed.) (1978), *Logboats of England and Wales*, British Archaeological Reports, (British Series), 51.

—— and Switsur, R. (1979), 'Medieval logboats of the river Mersey: A classificatory survey' in McGrail (ed.), *The archaeology of ships and harbours in Northern Europe*, British Archaeological Reports, (International Series), 66, pp. 93–115.

MacGregor, A. (1978), 'Industry and commerce in Anglo-Scandinavian York' in Hall (ed.), pp. 37–57.

—— (1982), *Anglo-Scandinavian finds from Lloyds Bank, Pavement and other sites*, AY17/3, London.

—— (1985), *Bone, antler, ivory and horn*, London.

Mahany, C. M. *et al.* (1982), *Excavations in Stamford, Lincolnshire 1963–1969*, London.

—— and Roffe, D. (1983), 'Stamford: The development of an Anglo-Scandinavian borough', *Anglo-Norman Studies* 5, pp. 197–219.

Mainman, A. (1990), *Anglo-Scandinavian pottery from 16–22 Coppergate*, AY16/5, London.

Mann, J. E. (1982), *Early medieval finds from Flaxengate, I: Objects of antler, bone, stone, horn, ivory, amber and jet*, ALXIV-1, London.

Marsden, P. *et al.* (1989), 'A late Saxon logboat from Clapton, London Borough of Hackney', *International Journal of Nautical Archaeology and Underwater Exploration* 18, pp. 89–111.

Mason, D. J. P. (1985), *Excavations at Chester: 26–42 Lower Bridge Street 1974–6: The Dark Age and Saxon Periods*, Grosvenor Museum Arch. Excav. and Surrey Reports 3, Chester.

Megaw, B. R. S. and E. M. (1950), 'The Norse heritage in the Isle of Man', in C. Fox and B. Dickins (eds), *The early cultures of north-west Europe*, Cambridge, pp. 143–70.

Mellor, M. (1980), 'Late Saxon pottery from Oxfordshire: Evidence and speculation', *Medieval Ceramics* 4, pp. 17–27.

Milne, G. (1989), 'Lundenwic to London town: From beach market to merchant port', *Arkeologiske Skrifter fra Historisk Museum, Universitetet i Bergen* 5, pp. 160–5.

——and Goodburn, D. (1990), 'The early medieval port of London AD 700–1200', *Antiquity* 64, pp. 629–36.

Morris, C. D. (1977), 'Northumbria and the Viking settlement: The evidence for landholding', *Archaeologiá Aeliana*, Fifth Series 5, pp. 81–103.

——(1981), 'Viking and native in northern England: A case-study' in *Proceedings of the Eighth Viking Congress*, Odense, pp. 223–44.

——(1982), 'The Vikings in the British Isles: Some aspects of their settlement and economy' in R. T. Farrell (ed.), *The Vikings*, Chichester, pp. 70–94.

Morris, R. K. (1983), *The church in British archaeology*, CBA Res. Rep. 47, London.

——(1989), *Churches in the landscape*, London.

Moulden, J., and Tweddle, D. (1986), *Anglo-Scandinavian settlement south-west of the Ouse*, AY8/1, London.

Newman, R. (1984), 'The problems of rural settlement in northern Cumbria in the pre-Conquest period' in Faull (ed.), pp. 155–76.

O'Connor, T. P. (1982), *Animal Bones from Flaxengate*, ALXVIII-1, London.

——(1989), *Bones from Anglo-Scandinavian levels at 16–22 Coppergate*, AY15/3, London.

Ordnance Survey (1988), *Viking and medieval York: Historical map and guide*, RCHME and York Archaeological Trust, Southampton.

O'Sullivan, D. M. (1984), 'Pre-Conquest settlement patterns in Cumbria' in Faull (ed.), pp. 143–54.

Ottaway, P. J. (1990), *Anglo-Scandinavian ironwork from 16–22 Coppergate, York c. 850–1100 AD*, unpublished D.Phil. thesis, University of York.

Page, R. I. (1971), 'How long did the Scandinavian language survive in England? The epigraphical evidence' in P. Clemocs and K. Hughes (eds), *England before the Conquest*, Cambridge, pp. 165–81.

——(1980), 'Some thoughts on Manx runes', *Saga-book* 30, pp. 179–99.

——(1983), 'The Manx rune-stones' in Fell *et al.* (eds), pp. 133–46.

——(1987), *Runes*, London.

Pelteret, D. (1981), 'Slave raiding and slave trading in early England', *Anglo-Saxon England* 9, pp. 99–114.

Perring, D. (1981), *Early Medieval Occupation at Flaxengate, Lincoln*, ALIX-1, London.

Phillips, D., with Heywood, B. (forthcoming), *Excavations at York Minster*, vol. i, London.

Pirie, E. J. E. (1986), *Post-Roman coins from York excavations 1971–81*, AY18/1, London.

Posnansky, M. (1956), 'The pagan-Danish barrow cemetery at Heath Wood, Ingleby', *Derbyshire Archaeological Journal* 76, pp. 40–56.

Price, N. S. (in prep.), *Vikings and Scandinavians: Aspects of cultural contact and identity in Northumbria in the 9th–11th centuries AD*. Unpublished D. Phil thesis, University of York.

Pritchard, F. A. (1984), 'Late Saxon textiles from the City of London', *Medieval Archaeology* 28, pp. 46–76.

Radford, C. A. R. (1970), 'The later pre-Conquest boroughs and their defences', *Medieval Archaeology* 14, pp. 83–103.

——(1973), 'Pre-Conquest minster churches', *Archaeological Journal* 130, pp. 120–40.

——(1978), 'The pre-Conquest boroughs of England, ninth to eleventh centuries', *Proceedings of the British Academy* 64, pp. 131–53.

Radley, J. (1971), 'Economic aspects of Anglo-Danish York', *Medieval Archaeology* 15, pp. 37–58.

Rahtz, P. A. (1976), 'Buildings and rural settlement' in Wilson (ed.), pp. 49–98.

——(1977), 'The archaeology of West Mercian towns' in A. Dornier (ed.), *Mercian Studies*, Leicester, pp. 107–29.

——(1979), *The Saxon and medieval palaces at Cheddar*, BAR, (British Series), 65.

Randsborg, K. (1980), *The Viking Age in Denmark*, London.

Reilly, P. (1988), *Computer analysis of an archaeological landscape: Medieval land divisions in the Isle of Man*, British Archaeological Reports, (British Series), 190.

Rodwell, W. and K. (1982), 'St Peter's church, Barton-upon-Humber: Excavation and structural study, 1978–81', *Antiquaries Journal*, 62, pp. 283–315.

Roesdahl, E. (1982), *Viking Age Denmark*, London.

——(1991), *The Vikings*, London.

——*et al.* (1981), *The Viking in England*, London.

Rogerson, A., and Dallas, C. (1984), 'Excavations at Thetford 1948–59 and 1973–80', *East Anglian Archaeology* 22.

Sawyer, P. H. (1958), 'The density of the Danish settlement in England', *University of Birmingham Historical Journal* 6, pp. 1–17.

——(1969), 'The two Viking Ages of Britain: A discussion, *Medieval Scandinavia* 2, pp. 163–207.

——(1971), *The Age of the Vikings*, London.

——(1978), *From Roman Britain to Norman England*, London.

——(1982), *Kings and Vikings: Scandinavia and Europe, AD 700–1100*, London.

——(1986), 'Anglo-Scandinavian trade in the Viking Age and after' in Blackburn (ed.), pp. 185–99.

Seaby, W. A., and Woodfield, P. (1980), 'Viking stirrups from England and their background', *Medieval Archaeology* 24, pp. 87–122.

Sheppard, T. (1939), 'Viking and other relics at Crayke, Yorkshire', *Yorkshire Archaeological Journal* 34, pp. 273–81.

Shetelig, H. (ed.) (1940), *Viking antiquities in Great Britain and Ireland*, 5 vols, Oslo.

—— (ed.) (1954), *Viking antiquities in Great Britain and Ireland*, Vol. 6, Oslo.

Smart, V. (1986), 'Scandinavians, Celts, and Germans in Anglo-Saxon England: The evidence of moneyers' names' in Blackburn (ed.), pp. 171–84.

Stafford, P. (1985), *The East Midlands in the early Middle Ages*, Leicester.

Tatton-Brown, T. (1988), 'The Anglo-Saxon Towns of Kent' in Hooke (ed.), pp. 213–32.

Todd, M. (1987), *The South-West to AD 1000*, London.

Tweddle, D. (1986), *Finds from Parliament Street and other sites in the city centre*, AY17/4, London.

Unwin, T. (1988), 'Towards a model of Anglo-Scandinavian rural settlement in England' in Hooke (ed.) pp. 77–98.

Vince, A. G. (1985), 'The Saxon and medieval pottery of London: A review', *Medieval Archaeology* 29, pp. 25–93.

—— (1989), 'The urban economy in Mercia in the 9th and 10th centuries', *Arkeologiske Skrifter fra Historisk Museum, Universitetet i Bergen* 5, pp. 136–59.

—— (1990), *Saxon London: An archaeological investigation*, London.

Wade, K. (1988), 'Ipswich' in Hodges and Hobley (eds), pp. 93–100.

Wade-Martins, P. (1980), 'Excavations in North Elmham Park 1967–1972', *East Anglian Archaeology* 9.

Walton, P. (1989), *Textiles, cordage and raw fibre from 16–22 Coppergate*, AY17/5, London.

Wenham, L. P., Hall, R. A., Briden, C. M., and Stocker, D. A. (1987), *St Mary Bishophill Junior and St Mary Castlegate*, AY8/2, London.

White, W. J., *et al.* (1988), *Skeletal remains from the cemetery of St Nicholas Shambles, City of London*, Middx. Arch. Soc. Spec. Paper 9, London.

Williams, J. H. (1979), *St Peter's Street, Northampton: Excavations 1973–1976*, Northampton.

—— (1984a), 'A review of some aspects of Late Saxon urban origins and development' in Faull (ed.), pp. 25–34.

—— (1984b), 'From "palace" to "town": Northampton and urban origins', *Anglo-Saxon England* 13, pp. 113–36.

Wilson, D. M. (1965), 'Some neglected late Anglo-Saxon swords', *Medieval Archaeology* 9, pp. 32–54.

—— (1967), 'The Vikings' relationship with Christianity in northern England', *Journal of the British Archaeological Association*, Third Series 30, pp. 37–46.

—— (1968), 'Archaeological evidence for the Viking settlements and raids in England', *Frühmittellaterliche Studien* 2, pp. 291–304.

—— (1970), *The Vikings and their origins*, London.

—— (1971), 'Manx memorial stones of the Viking period', *Sagabook* 18, pp 1–18.

—— (1974), *The Viking Age in the Isle of Man: The archaeological evidence*, Odense.

—— (1976a), 'Scandinavian settlement in the north and west of the British Isles: An archaeological point-of-view', *Transactions of the Royal Historical Society*, Fifth Series 26, pp. 95–113.

—— (1976b), 'Craft and industry' in Wilson (ed.), pp. 253–81.

—— (1976c), 'The Scandinavians in England' in Wilson (ed.), pp. 393–403.

—— (1983), 'The art of the Manx crosses of the Viking Age' in Fell (ed.), pp. 175–87.

—— (ed.) (1976), *The archaeology of Anglo-Saxon England*, Cambridge.

Winchester, A. J. L. (1985), 'The multiple estate: A framework for the evolution of settlement in Anglo-Saxon and Scandinavian Cumbria' in Baldwin and Whyte (eds), pp. 89–101.

Index

(Page numbers in **bold** refer to illustrations)

INDEX